WHATCHA GONNA LEARN FROM

COMICS?

WHATCHA GONNA LEARN FROM

COMICS?

HOW TO USE COMICS TO TEACH LANGUAGES

Jerry Steinberg

Cartoons by Ambre Hamilton

Pippin Publishing Limited

150 Telson Road
Markham, Ontario
L3R 1E5

Canadian Cataloguing in Publication Data

Steinberg, Jerry

Whatcha gonna learn from comics?: How to use comics to teach languages

ISBN 0-88751-037-X

1. English language — Study and teaching as a second language.*
2. Comic books, strips, etc. in education. I. Title.

PE1128.S74 1992 428'.0071 C91-095774-6

Designed by John Zehethofer
Edited by Dyanne Rivers
Printed and bound by The Alger Press Limited

10 9 8 7 6 5 4 3 2 1

About the Author

Jerry Steinberg attended the University of Toronto and McMaster University and received a degree in linguistics and French from the University of Guelph after graduating from Hamilton Teachers' College, where he had specialized in teaching French as a second language. He has taught English and French as second languages to children and adults in Ontario, Quebec and British Columbia since 1968.

In addition to his duties at Columbia College in Burnaby, B.C., he conducts workshops based on his book, *Games Language People Play*, with language professionals throughout Canada and the United States. He also presents workshops on using comics to teach languages, based on this book, *Whatcha Gonna Learn from Comics?*

He is the volunteer executive director of AIRSPACE Non-Smokers' Rights Society in Vancouver and is also the founder of No Kidding!, a social group for couples and singles who don't have children.

He lives with his wife, cat and three dogs in South Surrey, British Columbia.

Contents

PREFACE

When I started teaching 22 years ago, I decided to do everything I could to make teaching more satisfying for me and learning more enjoyable for students — without sacrificing discipline, efficiency and progress. To this end, in teaching English and French as second languages to children and adults, I've used jokes, songs, games and comics as honey on the bread of more mundane pedagogical activities.

In my very first year of teaching, I used jokes to entice reluctant students to work hard during the lesson and get the assigned work finished in the allotted time. Time left over was designated "joke time," when we shared jokes (as long as they weren't racist, sexist or profane) with the class. The jokes, I should add, rarely had anything to do with the day's learning; they were simply rewards for working well. While you might prefer to call them bribes, no matter what they're called, they worked!

I've always tried to stay familiar with the songs of the day (although, I admit, it becomes harder as I get older!) and incorporate their lyrics into my teaching. I've found that students, especially teenagers, often sing many of the popular songs without really understanding the lyrics. Studying those lyrics from a grammatical, syntactical and sociological perspective can be fascinating for teacher and students alike. I usually tape — or videotape — the songs and transcribe the lyrics. Occasionally, when I get lazy (or can't make out the lyrics, as is more often the case), I buy the song sheets from a music store. From time to time, I challenge small groups of students to decipher various songs and transcribe their lyrics. I give each group an audio (or video) tape of the song and they work together, replaying parts as often as necessary, to write down the lyrics.

The 110 games in my book, *Games Language People Play*, are the more popular ones I've used during my teaching career and have proven very helpful in increasing the students' enjoyment of learning. As I outline in the introduction to this book, the games are suitable for all levels of language learning and all ages of learners, they make use of all four linguistic skills (listening, speaking, reading and writing) and I use them to achieve all the following educational and behavioral goals: reinforce newly acquired information; review material that was taught days, weeks, months and even years ago; reward students for superlative behavior; relax students (and myself); overcome reserve or nervousness; raise attentiveness; and provide motivation and restrain rebellion.

I first started using comics as a technique to determine students' oral facility with the target language. I found a comic strip called *Doug Wright's Family* perfectly suited to this purpose because it was action-oriented and relied on visual humor rather than dialogue. At first, the students made up their own names for the two young brothers in the strip. Once in a while, they would forget these names and the ensuing confusion distracted them from the task. To remedy this, I suggested that we agree on names for the boys and use the same names throughout. The names I offered were Pete for the older brother and, for the younger brother, Re-Pete. The concept was easily understood and the humor of the suggestion was appreciated by everyone. The students enjoyed the situations portrayed and loved telling the stories in their own words. This gave me the opportunity to evaluate each student's ability to use the language and enabled me to note general and individual problems. Nearly any comic strip can be used for this activity, as long as the story is portrayed through action and existing dialogue is removed.

Comics, including comic books, comic strips and cartoons, provide a useful and versatile format for learning because they combine pictures and words. The pictures increase students' interest and comprehension by helping to establish period, setting, physical appearance, emotions, costumes, facial expressions and gestures in each reader's mind.

Through teaching and giving workshops to teachers, I've learned that there are as many levels of understanding as there are people in the room. This became absolutely clear during one of my first workshops stemming from *Games Language People Play*. Moments after I suggested a tic-tac-toe format as an alternative method for teaching a particular construct, one brave soul interrupted to ask, "What is tic-tac-toe?" Assuming that she was familiar with another name for the game, I offered Xs and Os. Nope! Perhaps she had been raised in Britain — how about naughts and crosses? Still nothing! It was then that I realized that it was the *idea* of the game that was new to her. I very quickly drew the grid (two vertical and two horizontal lines) on the board and explained that the object is to place three markers (X or O) in a row, vertically, horizontally or diagonally. She thanked me and we continued the workshop. As a result of this experience, I no longer assume that everyone understands any particular point. At some point while reading this book, one person might be thinking, I knew that! You don't have to be so simplistic! at the same time as another is thinking, So that's what that means! Thanks for explaining it for me.

Whatcha Gonna Learn from Comics? is organized into two sections. The first, titled Activities, contains generic suggestions that can be used in conjunction with commercial comics found in newspapers and comic books. The second, titled Linguistic, Cultural and Social Concepts, contains ideas designed for use with the reproducible comics, drawn by Ambre Hamilton, that appear at the end of the book. They illustrate and help explain specific concepts such as slang, gestures, gambits and so on.

I sincerely hope that the comics and suggestions help you make teaching and learning more fun.

Why John, Jessica, Andy and Katie?

In the section titled Linguistic, Cultural and Social Concepts, I decided to use my own comic characters instead of commercial characters for several reasons. First, different newspapers carry different strips and you and the students might not recognize certain characters. Second, using my own characters gives the activities a certain cohesiveness and, third, comic strips come and go and I didn't want to date this book by choosing a strip that might fade into oblivion in the near future (remember *Pogo*, *Mutt and Jeff*, *Dick Tracy* and *Little Orphan Annie*?). Fourth, I could control the size and complexity of each frame and, fifth, the names I've chosen for my characters are popular

English names, easily remembered and easily pronounced — no interdentals, like /θ/, as in the /th/ in Thelma to cause students to bite off and spit out their tongues, and no /l/ and /r/, as in Larry, to confuse. Finally, and perhaps most important, using copyright material from newspaper comics may have necessitated obtaining expensive permissions and this book might have cost 10 times what you paid for it.

Gender References

To avoid a lot of awkward he or shes, his or hers and so on, I've used the generic feminine throughout. After all, I chose to use the generic masculine in *Games Language People Play* and fair's fair.

Methodology

Every one of the following activities has pedagogical merit. However, you know the students you're teaching and, based on your knowledge of their ages, personalities, language and life experiences, intellectual abilities, rapport with you and one another, and their linguistic, social and behavioral needs, you must decide which activities will provide the greatest benefit and use and adapt them accordingly.

ACTIVITIES

This section of *Whatcha Gonna Learn from Comics?* consists of generic activities designed to help students become comfortable working with comics and to increase their familiarity with the comics. The activities will augment vocabulary and improve reading skills. They're designed to be performed with commercial comics found in newspapers and comic books.

Familiarity Breeds Comfort and Fun

When students are unfamiliar with comics in general or with the particular comics in our local newspaper, I often suggest that they search for specific items in the strips to help them become comfortable and get acquainted with the concept or characters. They can choose to work in pairs or individually.

I ask students to collect newspaper comic sections for a couple of weeks and bring them to class, then give them a list of things to look for within a time limit. The list and time limit depend on the abilities and ages of the students. Some sample items are a strip that has a person's name for its title, two comics with animals in them, a drawing of somebody's home, the names of three comic strip characters (other than leading characters), a sad face, five different punctuation marks, a word you don't know, the drawing of a person that looks the most real, a color word, the names of four cartoonists, a strip dealing with history or the past, five different adjectives, a comic dealing with politics, a past tense verb, a strip that is serial in nature, a number word, a bubble with more than 15 words in it, a strip that teaches us a lesson, two strips drawn by men and two by women, the comic strip you found the funniest and so on.

Vocabulary

To help develop vocabulary, invite individual students to read the comics and make a list of unfamiliar words. They can then work with a partner to find out the meaning of each new word and make up a sentence using the word correctly. As their vocabularies expand, the new words can be entered in a personal (picture) dictionary.

To strengthen their understanding of action words, suggest that they find pictures portraying actions, cut them out and glue them above the appropriate verb. This makes an interesting display for easy and ready reference. Students can perform this activity in reverse, as well, by making a list of action words, then finding a picture to go with each.

Word Study

Remove a word or two of dialogue from a strip and invite students to suggest suitable replacements. Because the context usually makes it clear that only a verb (or noun, etc.) is appropriate to fill in the blank, this is an excellent activity for reinforcing understanding of parts of speech.

Punctuation

To review punctuation, photocopy a comic, then use white-out to remove punctuation marks. Make photocopies of the whited-out version and challenge teams of three or four students to fill in the missing punctuation. Compare the original with what the teams came up with.

Oral Reading

To improve oral reading skills, invite students to recount a comic strip story to the rest of the class, describing not only what is said, but also the action and background in each frame. Encourage them to add realism to the dialogue by trying to speak exactly as they think the characters might. Writing out what they are going to say often makes this easier and more efficient.

Choral Reading

If individual students are inhibited about reading aloud, choral reading, with groups taking various roles, often bolsters their self-confidence.

Finger Puppets

Younger students especially like making finger puppets from cut-out characters and acting out stories from their favorite strips. The cut-outs can simply be taped to students' fingers.

Mime

In groups, students mime a comic strip and challenge the rest of the class (which has the full page of strips) to figure out which strip is being acted. This is another opportunity to encourage participation by students who dislike speaking in front of the group.

Challenges

Use the names of comic strips and characters to make up crossword puzzles, word scrambles (in which the letters of words are mixed up, such as RDIB — bird) and word finds (in which complete words are hidden in a grid of letters and students must find and separate them). The students also enjoy creating these themselves and challenging others to decipher them.

Parts of Speech Collage

In groups of three to five, students choose a part of speech (verb, noun, adjective, etc.) and search the comics to find as many examples of their part of speech as they can. The words are cut out and pasted in a collage, which can be displayed for others to see.

Greeting Cards

Comic characters can be cut out and pasted onto greeting cards students have made themselves for giving to friends and family on special occasions — or for no reason other than to say, "I was thinking of you."

Details

Another enjoyable activity is to invite students to read different strips individually, then take turns answering who, what, when, where, why and how questions from the others about the strip they read.

Main Idea

Challenge individual students to find the main idea of a strip, give it a title and explain why they believe the title is appropriate. Occasionally, I give the same strip to two or three students and encourage them to debate which of their titles is best.

Predicting Outcomes

Remove the words from the final bubble in a strip and invite students to suggest what it should say. This enables them to predict and change outcomes. It's also a lot of fun.

Inference

Students should be able to infer what a character is feeling from the drawing and from what is said. I sometimes suggest that they list the emotions they perceive in various strips and compare their findings with one another.

I may also suggest that they find characters who portray positive and negative social values, such as honesty and dishonesty, modesty and pride, compassion and indifference, and so on.

Invite students to point out a strip that they, as individuals, don't understand or don't find funny. With help from the teacher, if necessary, others can explain or clarify the humor (if it does, indeed, exist).

Direct and Indirect (Reported) Speech

Students write out the story line from a strip, using phrases such as "she said," "he yelled," and "they explained" to quote dialogue. To practice reporting what another has said, students must convert a character's exact words into indirect speech (e.g., "Are you coming to the party?" becomes "She asked him if he was coming to the party.").

Role-Playing

With the class, discuss the personalities of certain comic characters and invite students to assume their roles in certain situations. I might, for example, suggest that a student role-play Archie trying to explain girls to Robot Man, Cathy on a date with Hagar, Dennis the Menace trying to convince his dad to quit smoking, or Snoopy as the King of Id's dog.

Question Exchange

Each student chooses a comic strip and writes three questions about the strip on a piece of paper. Students then exchange strips and questions and try to answer each other's questions.

That's Me!

Each student is challenged to find a character in a comic strip who is like her in some way. She then explains the similarities to the class.

How Old?

Many comics have been with us a long time and some have been drawn by a number of cartoonists over the years. Invite students, individually or in pairs, to research the history of their favorite strip. They can write to the appropriate syndicate for detailed information. Addresses can be obtained from the newspaper office.

Sentence Typing

For this activity, students are divided into four groups of equal size and each is assigned a type of sentence — assertive, interrogative, exclamatory or imperative. Each group is challenged to find, cut out and paste up sentences that fall into its category. The group with the most correct examples wins.

Reports

There are a variety of ways of reporting on comic strips. Students can draw their own version of the strip, write out the story in either direct or indirect speech, tell the class about the strip in an oral presentation or act out the story for the class.

Poetry

Invite students, working alone or in pairs, to write a poem about a strip they have read. These can be free verse, Haiku or any form students are comfortable with.

Arithmetic

Students create equations using comic characters' names and challenge each other to solve their equation. Here are some examples (the letters in square brackets do not appear when the challenges are presented to students):

HERO - O = [HER]
WOMAN - WO = [MAN]
Solution: [HER + MAN = HERMAN]

NOEL - NO =
WOODEN - EN =
Solution: [EL + WOOD = ELWOOD]

JUGGLE - GLE = [JUG]
HE + AD = [HEAD]
Solution: [JUG + HEAD = JUGHEAD]

On Average

Each student chooses a word that is used frequently in the comics and, over the course of a week, counts the number of times the word appears on a page of strips. Then, they calculate the average number of times their word appeared each day. The average daily use of each chosen word might be charted on a graph.

Jigsaw Puzzles

Each student draws a picture of her favorite comic strip character on a piece of construction paper or Bristol board about 8 inches by 10 inches (20 cm X 25 cm). When the drawing is complete and colored, it is cut into 20 to 30 irregularly shaped pieces. Students then challenge one another to piece together each other's puzzle.

Interviews

Each student assumes the character of one of her favorite comic strip characters and is interviewed by another student. If the interview is recorded, the tape can be played for classmates who might offer suggestions for improving both roles.

Interviewers should plan their questions, which can be about topics of interest to the students and to the chosen character. For example, Archie might be asked about dating, sports, cars, studying, girls in general and so on, while Cathy might field questions about dating, dieting, relationships, parents, men, babies, etc. Hagar might like to discuss war, marriage, weapons, wives and ships while Spiderman would certainly know a lot about criminals and crime and Andy Capp could be considered an expert on pubs and avoiding work. Mr. Butts could explain why children should start smoking (for a more mature group of students only!).

Songs

Suggest that students work individually or in small groups to create a song about their favorite comic strip character. The songs can be taped and played for the entire class.

Sounds like . . .

Students work in groups of three to five to record sounds (not words) that portray an emotion (happiness, sadness, disappointment, anger, fear, etc.) exhibited by a certain comic character. When the tape is played back to the entire class, the other students try to guess which emotion is being portrayed.

Advice Column

Each student chooses a comic character and writes — but doesn't send — a letter to Abby, Ann Landers or another advice columnist requesting help with a perceived problem. For example, Andy Capp's wife, Flo, could ask how to get her husband to do things around the house, Cathy might seek advice about how to stop her mother from nagging her about marriage, Beetle Bailey might want some pointers on handling the Sarge, Dennis the Menace could ask how to get his father to stop smoking, Snoopy or Garfield could try to find out how to get fed more often and so on. Students then play the role of advice-giver and make suggestions to the writer, who chooses the best advice.

T-Shirts

Invite students to bring an old T-shirt from home (with parents' permission, where applicable). With pencil, they draw their favorite comic character on the front of the T-shirt, then trace over the design with an indelible marker. If a partner holds the T-shirt stretched out on the floor, it makes the task easier. The more talented, or faster, students may also enjoy drawing a picture of the back of the character on the back of the T-shirt, creating a coming-and-going drawing.

Musical Background

Each student chooses a comic, then selects music — instrumental or vocal — to accompany her selection. She then plays the music while showing the strip to the class and explains why she thinks it is appropriate.

Emotional Collage

Students find pictures of comic characters displaying various emotions and assemble them into a collage. Each picture might be labeled with the name of the emotion displayed.

Function

In groups of two or three, students find comics that persuade, ridicule, exaggerate, entertain, praise, inform, stimulate action and arouse interest. Each group makes a presentation to the class demonstrating the function their selections perform. The editorial cartoons published by most newspapers are excellent examples of satirical cartoons.

Popularity Survey

Invite students to conduct a survey of the school or neighborhood to find out which comic strips are the most popular and why. If the interviews are taped and played back to the class, a graph showing the results can be prepared. The information may be quite sophisticated if the age, occupation and gender of the interview subjects is considered.

Stereotyping

With the class, discuss various kinds of stereotyping (men, women, businesspeople, teenagers, highly educated people, politicians, various ethnic groups, etc.). Then encourage small groups of students to scan the comics to find examples of stereotyping and group them according to category. Each group can present its findings to the class, showing how the cartoonist has demonstrated stereotyping.

Alien Civilizations

Suggest that students pretend they are a group of aliens from another planet whose introduction to life on Earth is a page of comics. What would they likely determine about Earth people? They should take into account institutions, technology, dominant life forms, social, political and family groupings, activities, objects, and ideas that Earth people value, and so on.

Creative Writing

Invite students to write a mock obituary for their favorite — or least favorite — comic character. An appropriate cause of death (for example, Snoopy choking on a bone, Hagar dying in battle or Mr. Butts dying from heart disease, cancer or emphysema caused by smoking) should be mentioned. Students can refer to the newspaper for examples of obituaries.

Classified Ads

With students, examine newspaper classified ads and talk about the abbreviations used. Then invite students, working individually or in pairs, to create a classified ad that they think a chosen comic strip character might place in the newspaper. For example, Archie might be looking for parts for his jalopy, Cathy might be searching for a mate, Garfield might want a new master (one who would feed him more frequently), Elwood might be seeking a new apartment, Dagwood might be looking for a used lawnmower (because Bert has never returned the one he borrowed), Blondie might be trying to find an alarm clock guaranteed to get Dagwood out of bed on time, Dennis the Menace might be looking for a skateboard that is quiet enough not to disturb Mr. Wilson, and Shoe could be looking for someone to help him organize his cluttered desk.

Trivial Pursuit

Students make up question and answer cards for a *Trivial Pursuit* game based on information from the comics. I find this activity works best if students are familiar with the format of the commercial game. They can use its board and markers. If students work alone, it means that only one student will be certain to know the answer to a particular question, because she is the one who created it.

Headlines

In teams of two to four, students create catchy headlines for several comic strips. Like the newspapers, they can use puns, satire, metaphors and alliteration to summarize their strips. A contest could be held to determine which headlines are the best for summarizing the strip, humor, piquing readers' interest and so on.

Serial Stories

Some comic strips, such as *Mary Worth*, *Rex Morgan* and *Doonesbury* tell a continuing story. Challenge groups of two to four students to find a serial strip, follow it for several weeks and analyze it in terms of its fictional elements — setting, protagonists and antagonists, plot and character development, dialogue, conflict (and resolution), climax and *dénouement*.

Editorial Cartoons

Invite groups of three to five students to choose a political figure and search several weeks' of editorial cartoons for those that deal with that person. Based on the portrayal presented in the cartoons, encourage them to draw conclusions about the person's character and the incidents she has had to deal with.

Categorizing Editorial Cartoons

Students collect editorial cartoons for several weeks and, in groups of two to four, categorize them according to scope — municipal, provincial or state, national or international. The political issues covered are then presented to the rest of the class. Another interesting activity that students enjoy is comparing and contrasting editorial cartoons on the same topic.

Editorial Cartoon Analysis

In small groups, students choose and examine an editorial cartoon, analyzing it by considering its use of satire and sarcasm, humor, political bias, caricature, inference and interpretation, the cartoonist's perspective and students' opinions. Students can also compare and contrast written editorials with an editorial cartoon on the same topic.

LINGUISTIC, CULTURAL AND SOCIAL CONCEPTS

Comics can be used to introduce linguistic, cultural and social concepts. Sometimes, I explain the examples to the entire class and we search newspaper comic strips for others that fit into the same category. On other occasions, I divide the class into groups based on their needs and abilities and each group works on a specific concept. Then, the groups make a presentation to the entire class.

Often, students are asked to read the comics on their own and bring problems to the attention of the entire class. Together, we clarify and look for other examples of the same concept to reinforce and expand our understanding. The new information often provides a jumping-off point for comparisons with other cultures, languages and social situations.

To make the book easier to use, the small comics in this section have been numbered to correspond to their full-size counterparts, which follow. These can be photocopied for distribution to individuals and groups.

Slang

Slang is informal and nonstandard, and meanings are unlikely to be found in most dictionaries. Nevertheless, becoming familiar with slang expressions is necessary when learning a new language for they are used frequently by native speakers and can be a source of confusion for those who aren't familiar with them.

Some slang expressions are modifications of blasphemies, transformed so as not to offend. In English, words such as *gosh* and *golly* (for God) and *heck* (for hell) are useful as they allow the speaker to express anger and frustration without offending most listeners. Some Canadian French examples are *colline* (for *calice* — chalice), *tabernouche* or *tabarouette* (for tabernacle) and *crime* (for Christ). Many other languages, I have discovered, also modify blasphemous expressions in the same way.

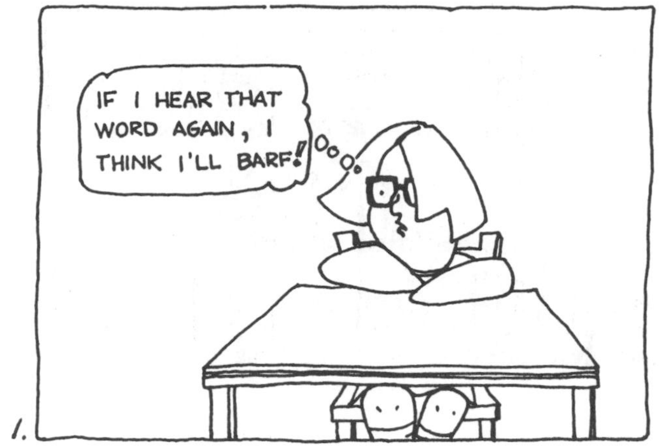
IF I HEAR THAT WORD AGAIN, I THINK I'LL BARF!
1.

Barf is a word not found in most dictionaries, but it is used by many native speakers. I usually talk about other synonyms, such as vomit, regurgitate, retch, spit up, throw up, heave, disgorge, puke, upchuck, hurl, spew, honk and so on, that students can learn and use when needed.

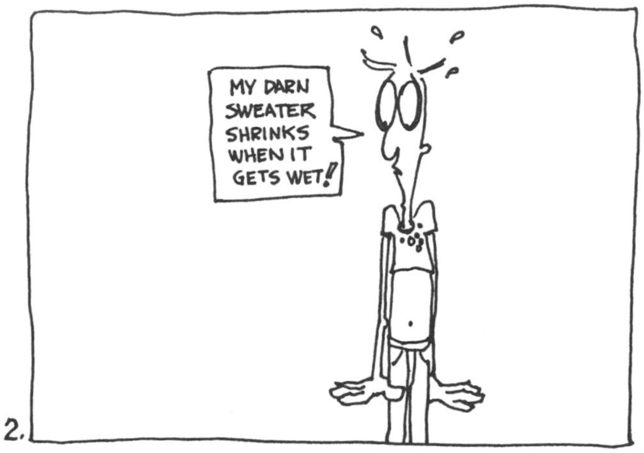
MY DARN SWEATER SHRINKS WHEN IT GETS WET!
2.

Darn is a versatile dilution of *damn* that is used in a variety of expressions. It shows up as an adjective (This darn shoelace!), adverb (She runs darn fast!), or verb in both active and passive voices (Darn this stupid car! and I'll be darned!).

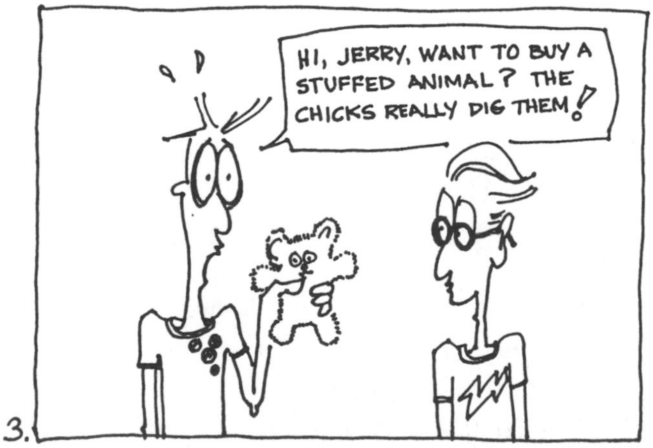
HI, JERRY, WANT TO BUY A STUFFED ANIMAL? THE CHICKS REALLY DIG THEM!
3.

The word *chick* usually means a young chicken or bird but, when used as slang, it means a young woman and is considered, by many, to be derogatory. *To dig* in slang means to like or enjoy, not to gouge a hole in the earth.

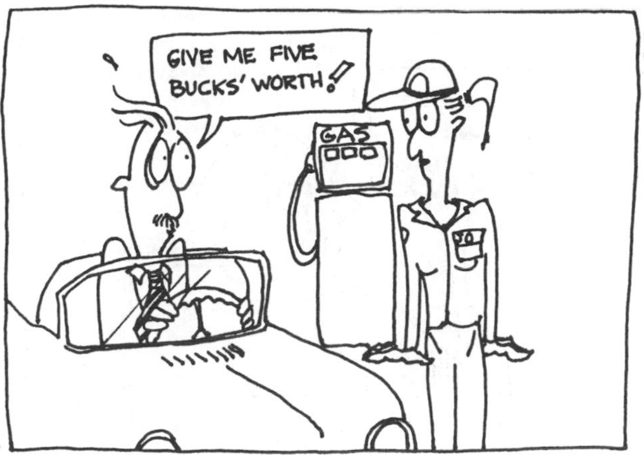
GIVE ME FIVE BUCKS' WORTH!
GAS

4.

Buck, as defined by a dictionary, is a male animal such as a deer or antelope. It's used here to signify *dollar*. Other slang for money includes words such as *greenback* (for a dollar bill), *deuce* (for a two), *fin* (for a five), *10-spot* (for a 10), *C-note* or *C* (for $100) and *G-note*, *G* or *grand* (for $1,000). In Canadian French slang, a dollar is known as *douille*, usually used in the plural.

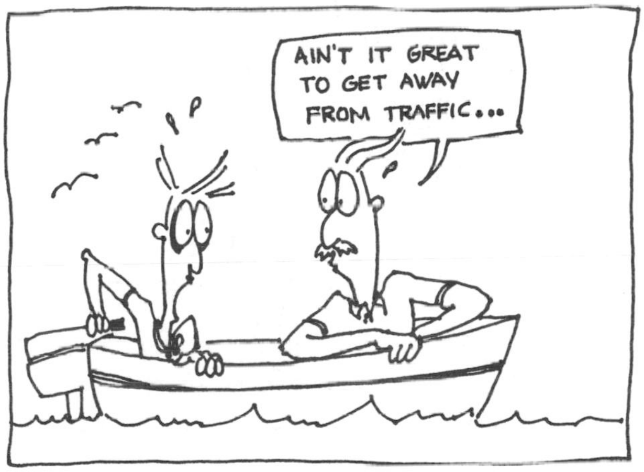
AIN'T IT GREAT TO GET AWAY FROM TRAFFIC...

5.

Most educated speakers still consider *ain't* unacceptable and, therefore, slang. It is used as a contraction of am not, is not and are not and can be used with all persons, singular and plural as well as in tag questions such as, She's smart, ain't she?

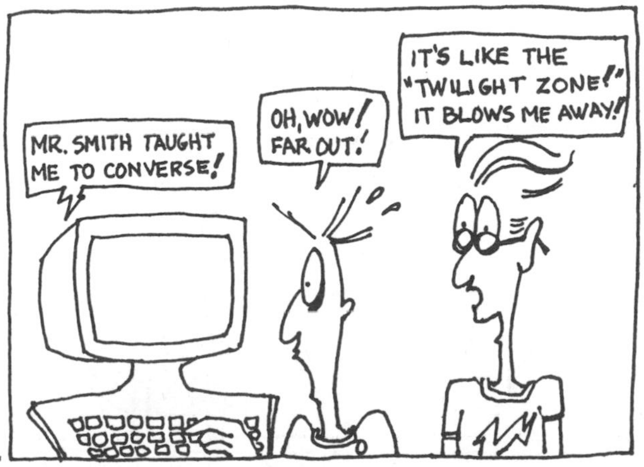
MR. SMITH TAUGHT ME TO CONVERSE!
OH, WOW! FAR OUT!
IT'S LIKE THE "TWILIGHT ZONE!" IT BLOWS ME AWAY!

6.

Far out is a term that originated in the 1960s among young people and is used to mean unconventional, extreme or wonderful. *To blow away*, in slang use, means to impress or overwhelm. When used by gangsters, it can also mean to assassinate.

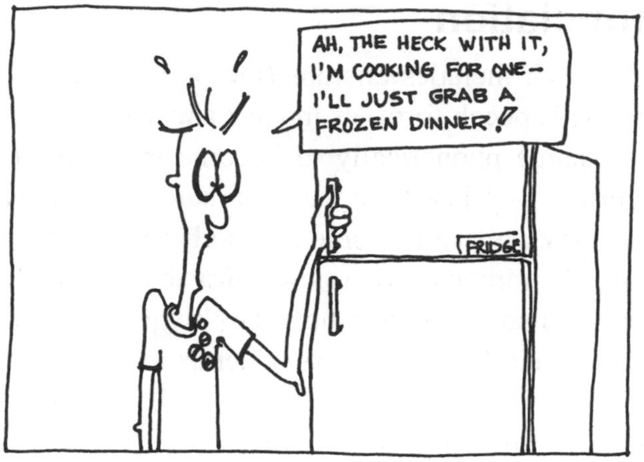
AH, THE HECK WITH IT, I'M COOKING FOR ONE– I'LL JUST GRAB A FROZEN DINNER!
FRIDGE
7.

The heck with it means never mind, forget it or it's not worth the trouble. It is, of course, a dilution of *the hell with it*.

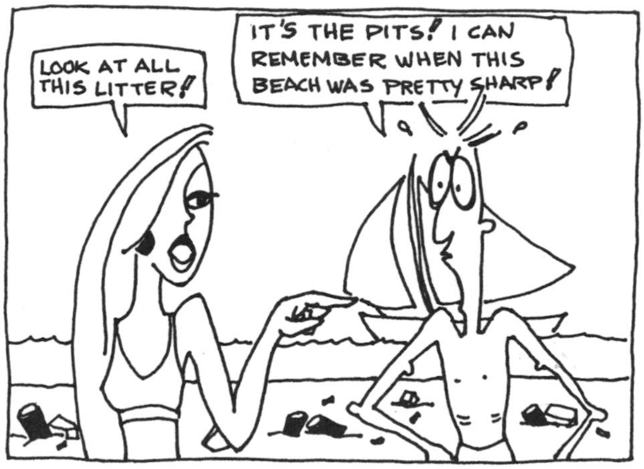
LOOK AT ALL THIS LITTER!
IT'S THE PITS! I CAN REMEMBER WHEN THIS BEACH WAS PRETTY SHARP!
8.

The pits is another expression left over from the '60s. It conveys a negative quality, meaning no good or terrible (e.g., The party last night was the pits! Only three people came and two of them fell asleep.).

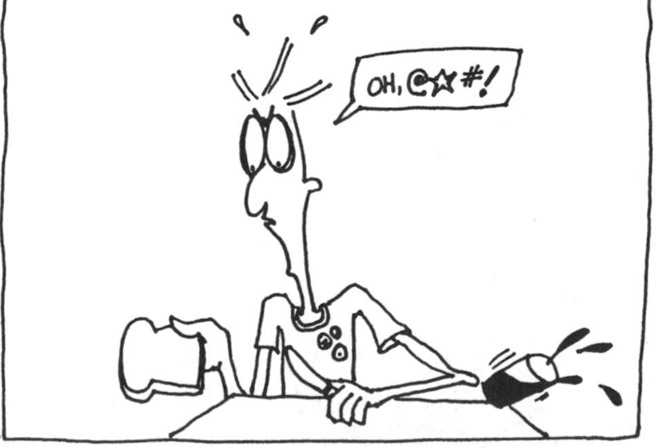
OH, @☆#!
9.

Comics use a series of symbols to represent swearing in English. Discuss how swearing is represented in other languages.

Vernacular Pronunciation

Vernacular pronunciation, which includes elisions (the omission or dropping out of a sound or sounds resulting in a shortened speech form, as in *isn't* and *dogs 'n' cats*) and assimilations (the process by which sounds change phonetically to become more like neighboring sounds as in *gonna*), is one of my favorites — I just love teaching students how native speakers *really* say things. In casual social contexts, very few people are likely to say, "I am going to buy a new pair of shoes." Most would say, "I'm gonna buy a new paira shoes." While I teach my students the precise way of saying things, I also teach them how they're going to hear it from native speakers. This reduces the potential for confusion caused by unexpected or unfamiliar pronunciations. Students have a lot of fun practicing the vernacular. Remember though, vernacular pronunciation works only at normal speaking speed and stress, never at a reduced speed or exaggerated stress. When speech is slowed down, interrupted or emphasis is used, vernacular pronunciation reverts to what I refer to as written or textbook pronunciation. The same is true of contractions. For example, at normal speed and stress, I would say, "You're gonna call 'er." By reducing the speed and increasing the emphasis, however, the same sentence would be pronounced, "You are going to call her!"

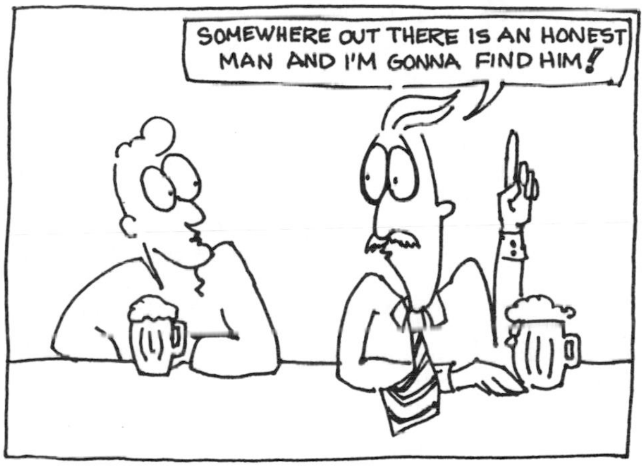
SOMEWHERE OUT THERE IS AN HONEST MAN AND I'M GONNA FIND HIM!
10.

Gonna replaces going to when used to indicate future action or intention. It never replaces going to in expressions where it means to travel or move to as in, "I'm going to Mexico." However, "I'm gonna go to Mexico" is perfectly acceptable where future action or intent is implied.

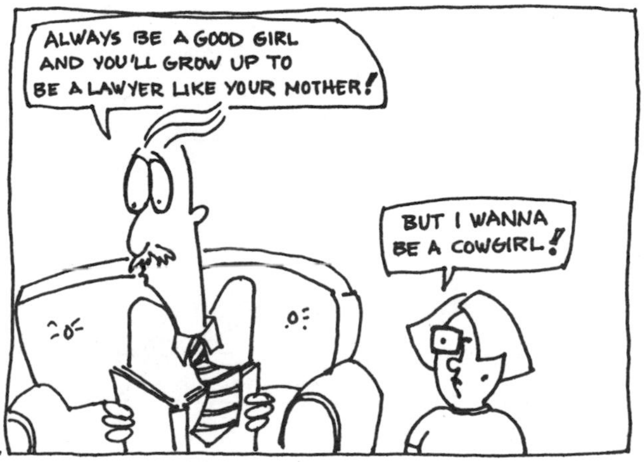
ALWAYS BE A GOOD GIRL AND YOU'LL GROW UP TO BE A LAWYER LIKE YOUR MOTHER!
BUT I WANNA BE A COWGIRL!
11.

Wanna is the vernacular version of want to.

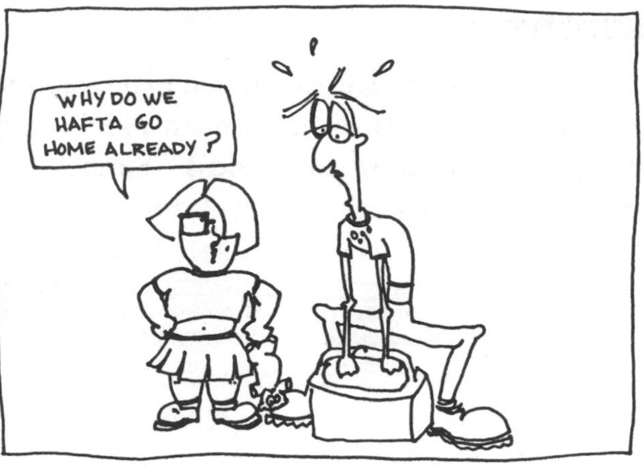
WHY DO WE HAFTA GO HOME ALREADY ?

12.

Hafta is the vernacular pronunciation of have to, meaning must.

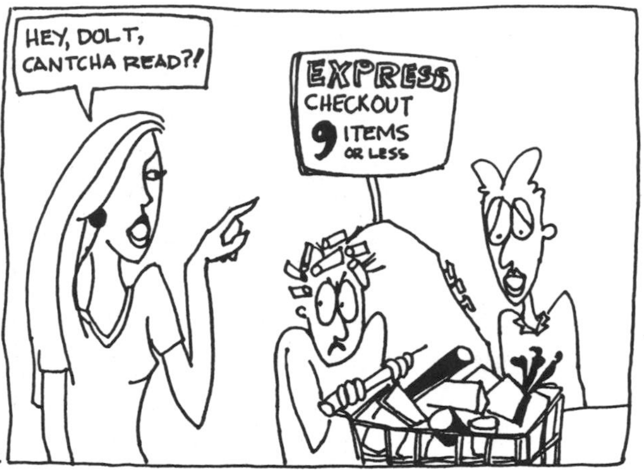
HEY, DOLT, CANTCHA READ?!
EXPRESS CHECKOUT 9 ITEMS OR LESS

13.

Cantcha (or *cancha*) is the vernacular pronunciation of can't you.

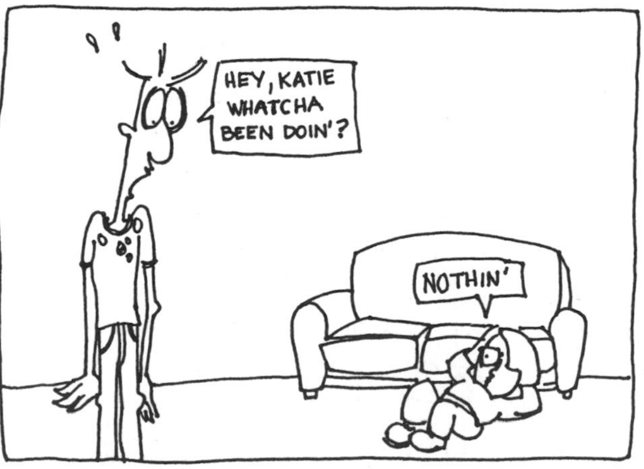
HEY, KATIE WHATCHA BEEN DOIN'?
NOTHIN'

14.

Whatcha (or *wha'cha*, *whatya* or *whatrya*, etc.) is the vernacular pronunciation of what are you when it is followed by a verb as in "Whatcha reading?" *Doin'* is a common vernacular pronunciation of doing. The final *g* of present participles and gerunds is frequently dropped in normal speech as in eatin', sleepin' or drinkin'. The missing *g* is replaced by an apostrophe.

Students want very much to fit in and they don't want their speech pattern to alienate them from others. Learning vernacular pronunciation is one way to ensure that their speech patterns won't make them sound like robots and stand out as "foreigners" (a.k.a. "outsiders").

Idiomatic Expressions

The dictionary definition of an idiomatic expression is "an expression in the usage of a language that is peculiar to itself either grammatically (as in 'it wasn't me') or that cannot be understood from the meanings of its separate words (as in 'take cold')." Simply put, an idiomatic expression has a meaning different from the one that seems apparent from its ingredients.

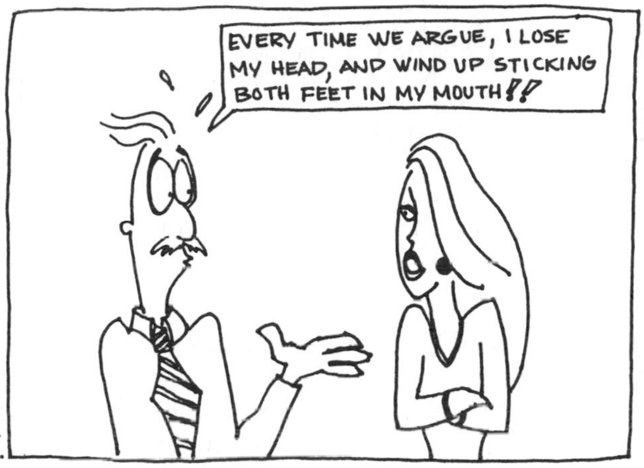
EVERY TIME WE ARGUE, I LOSE MY HEAD, AND WIND UP STICKING BOTH FEET IN MY MOUTH!!
15.

To lose one's head means to become very excited or to lose one's self control. It does not mean, of course, to misplace one's head. Similar expressions are *to lose one's cool* and *to lose one's touch*, the first being similar in meaning to lose one's head and the second meaning to fail at what one used to do well or to cease to interest others. None of the foregoing expressions is in any way related to losing one's hair, which has only a literal meaning. *To stick one's foot* (or *feet*) *in one's mouth* usually suggests that one has said something inappropriate that has caused embarrassment.

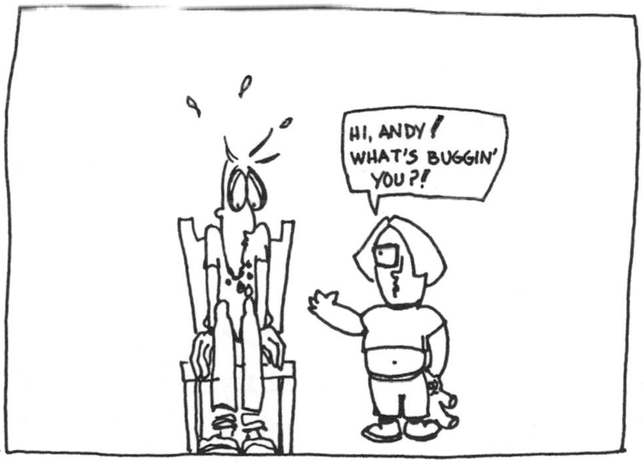
HI, ANDY! WHAT'S BUGGIN' YOU?!
16.

The word *bug* usually means insect, but *to bug someone* has nothing to do with small (usually) winged animals with three pairs of legs. It means to bother, annoy or disturb someone. To bug a place, such as someone's home, means to listen in electronically.

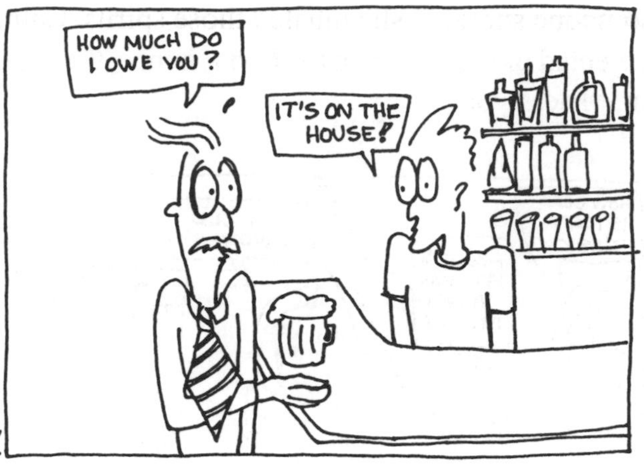
HOW MUCH DO I OWE YOU?
IT'S ON THE HOUSE!

17.

The expression *on the house* means the speaker or the business will pay.

Cultural Concepts

Cultural concepts are ways of behaving or reacting that are peculiar to a particular culture. This is an excellent opportunity to start a class discussion of games and customs around the world.

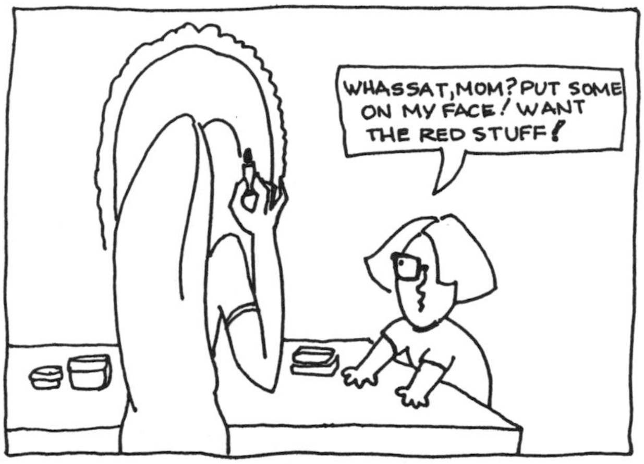
WHASSAT, MOM? PUT SOME ON MY FACE! WANT THE RED STUFF!

18.

For example, women in some cultures wear no makeup, whereas in western cultures, women wearing makeup are quite commonplace.

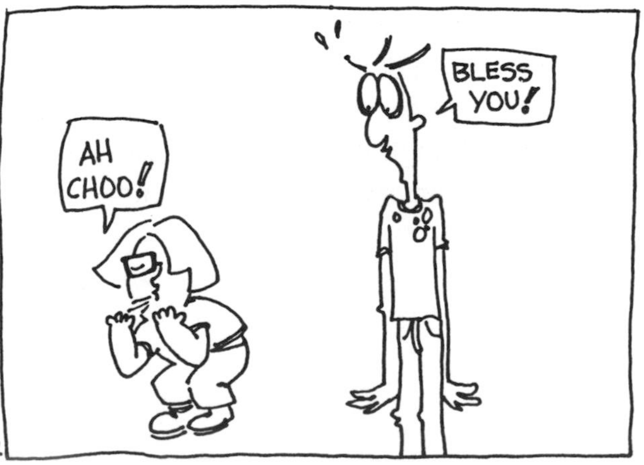
AH CHOO!
BLESS YOU!

19.

When someone sneezes, it is quite common for people nearby, even strangers, to say, "Bless you!" This behavior is thought to originate in a time when people believed that invisible evil spirits inhabited the air. When someone sneezed, she inhaled those spirits. Calling upon God to bless the sneezer protected her and ejected the spirits from her body; hence, the expression, "God bless you!" or the abbreviated version, "Bless you!"

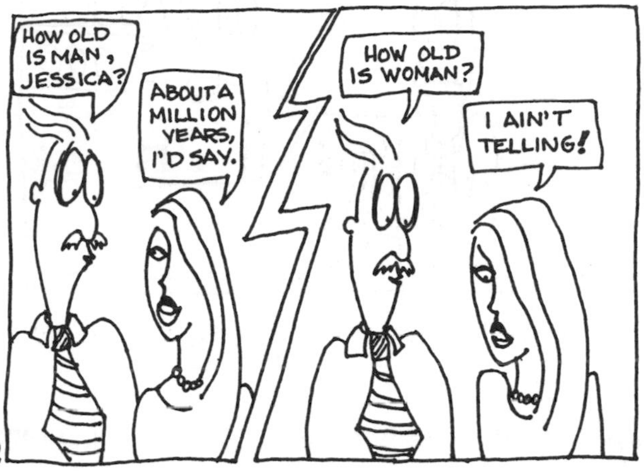
HOW OLD IS MAN, JESSICA?
ABOUT A MILLION YEARS, I'D SAY.
HOW OLD IS WOMAN?
I AIN'T TELLING!

20.

Some women — and men — in western society are reluctant to divulge their age. In other cultures, however, women don't think twice about telling others how old they are, while, in still others, it is impolite to ask either men or women their age.

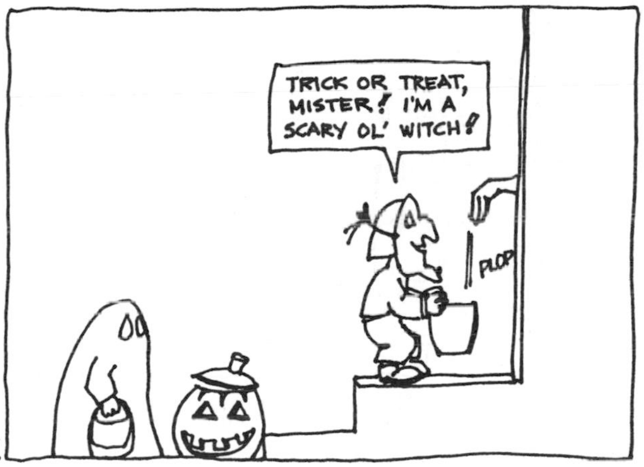
TRICK OR TREAT, MISTER! I'M A SCARY OL' WITCH!
PLOP

21.

The tradition of donning costumes and going from house to house to beg for treats on October 31 is unknown in many parts of the world. Those who live elsewhere in North America are often surprised to discover that fireworks are part of Halloween celebrations in southwestern Canada and the northwestern United States, though the custom is losing favor because large numbers of children are injured every year and firecrackers are now prohibited by law in many places.

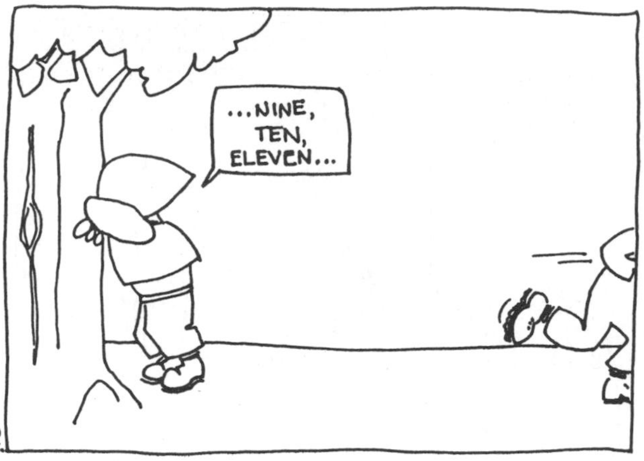
...NINE,
TEN,
ELEVEN...

22.

Though the game of hide and seek is common in many parts of the world, some students are surprised to discover that children in North America play it as well, while others, who have never played it, have the opportunity to add yet another game to their repertoire.

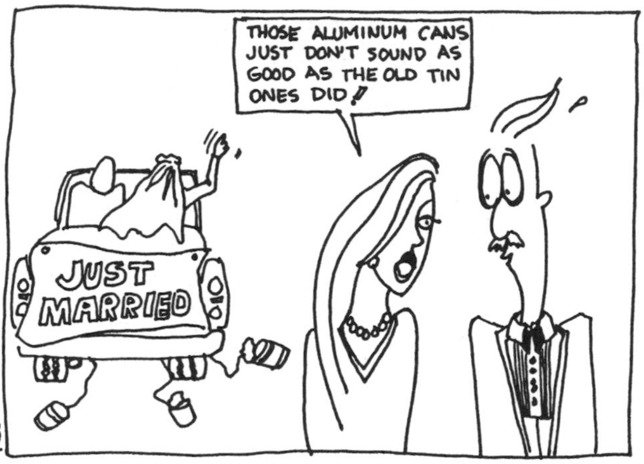
THOSE ALUMINUM CANS JUST DON'T SOUND AS GOOD AS THE OLD TIN ONES DID!
JUST MARRIED

23.

Not many cultures are in the habit of putting signs on, and tying tin cans and old shoes to, the car that newlyweds will drive on their honeymoon.

Accents

People who speak English with a heavy accent are sometimes difficult for native speakers to understand. Imagine the problems that language learners have! Comics give us an opportunity to examine the effect of various background languages on pronunciation and enable students to decode foreign accents more easily.

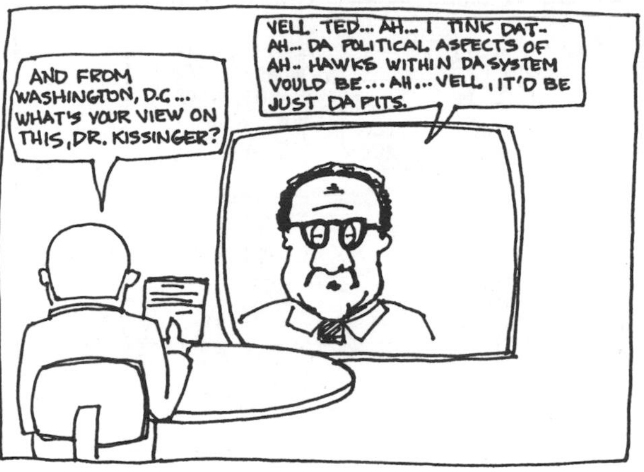
AND FROM WASHINGTON, D.C... WHAT'S YOUR VIEW ON THIS, DR. KISSINGER?
VELL TED... AH... I TINK DAT- AH... DA POLITICAL ASPECTS OF AH.. HAWKS WITHIN DA SYSTEM VOULD BE... AH... VELL, IT'D BE JUST DA PITS.

24.

Dr. Henry Kissinger's German accent is certainly discernible.

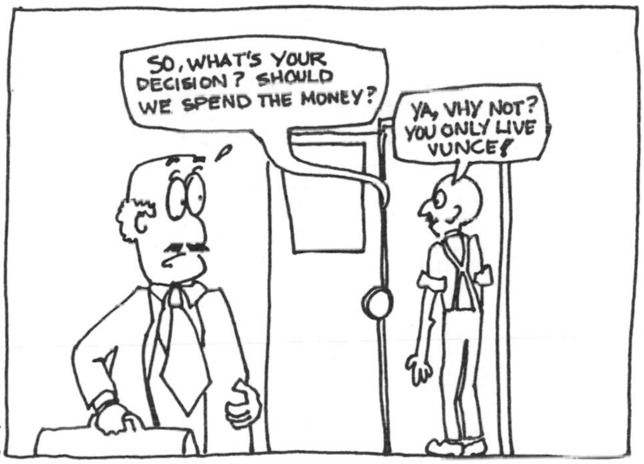
SO, WHAT'S YOUR DECISION? SHOULD WE SPEND THE MONEY?
YA, VHY NOT? YOU ONLY LIVE VUNCE!

25.

A Scandinavian accent substitutes /v/ for /w/.

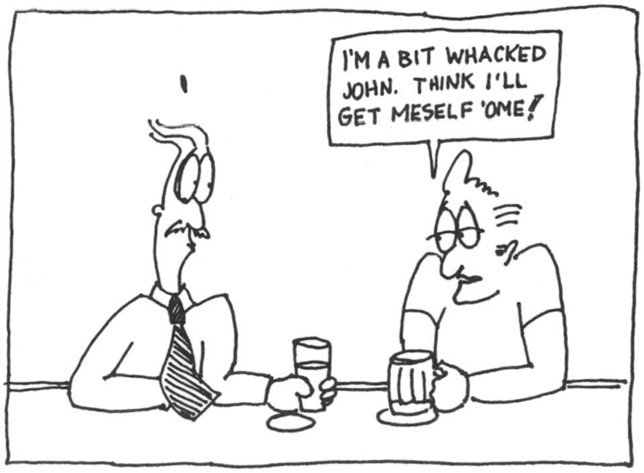
I'M A BIT WHACKED JOHN. THINK I'LL GET MESELF 'OME!

26.

The British frequently drop /r/ and aspirated /h/.

27.

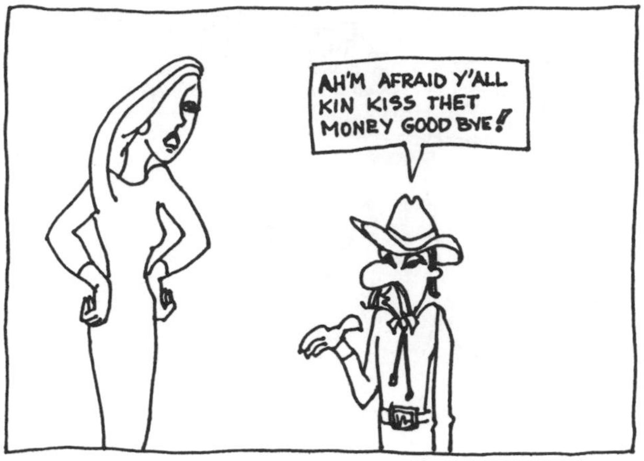
AH'M AFRAID Y'ALL KIN KISS THET MONEY GOOD BYE!

In the deep South, a southern drawl is as common as a bear looking for honey.

Speech Impediments

Speech impediments can be caused by hearing impairments, colds, physical and neurological disorders, interference from the background language and inexperience with the language because of youth or being a new student of that language. I used to get a big kick out of listening to young children recite the Lord's Prayer — "Our father, heart in heaven, Howard be thy name...." In this case, the impediment was simply unfamiliarity with the style of language used in the prayer.

28.

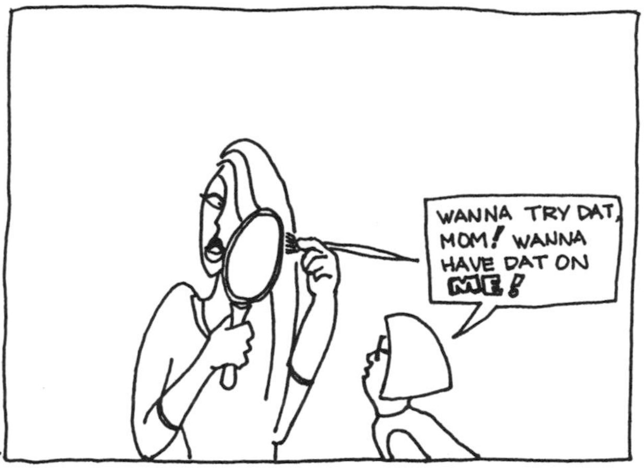
WANNA TRY DAT, MOM! WANNA HAVE DAT ON ME!

Here's your chance to examine common substitutions for various sounds in the English language (/d/ for /ð/, as in the *th* in *that*, for example).

29.

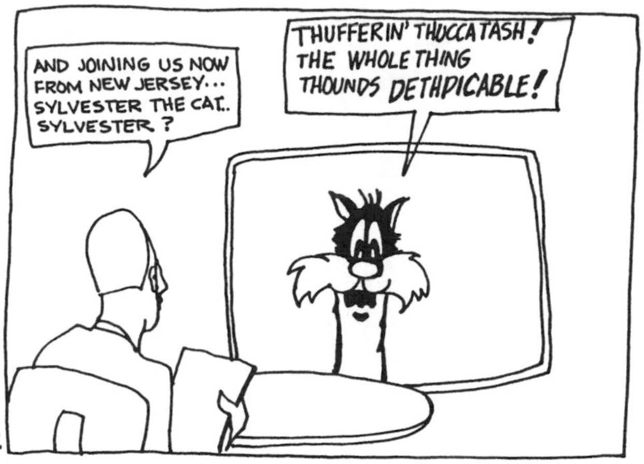
AND JOINING US NOW FROM NEW JERSEY... SYLVESTER THE CAT. SYLVESTER ?
THUFFERIN' THUCCATASH! THE WHOLE THING THOUNDS DETHPICABLE!

Sylvester's lisp is well-known among cartoon lovers.

30.

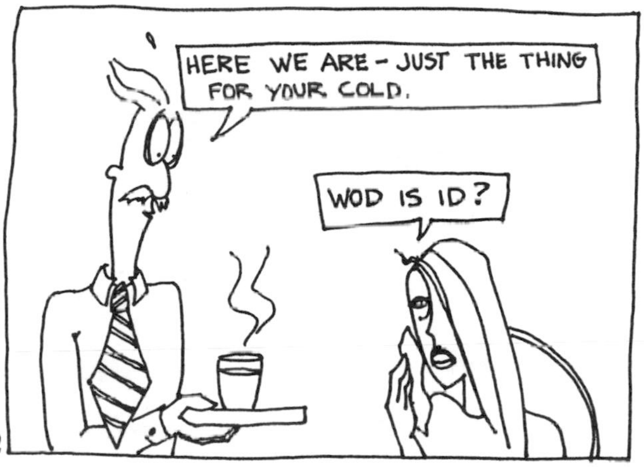
HERE WE ARE - JUST THE THING FOR YOUR COLD.
WOD IS ID?

Jessica's cold causes her to replace voiceless stops with voiced stops.

31.

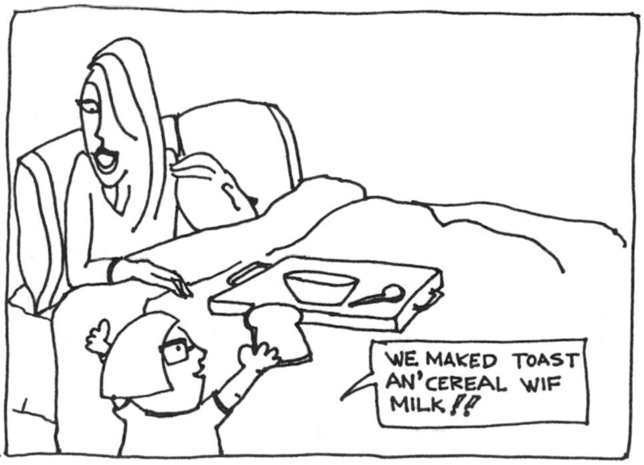
WE MAKED TOAST AN' CEREAL WIF MILK!!

The cursed interdental is a major problem for many youngsters and learners of English. Common substitutions include /f/ and /t/ for the unvoiced interdental (/θ/, pronounced like the *th* in *thin*) and /v/ and /d/ for the voiced interdental (/ð/, pronounced like the *th* in *this*).

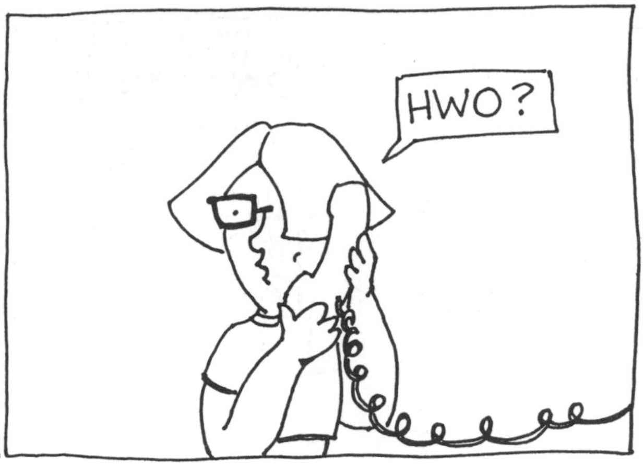
HWO?
32.

I challenge my students to decipher the last example by themselves. It is a young child answering the telephone with her version of "Hello."

Current Events

The examples here were current at the time this book was conceived. By the time you read this, however, some of them might be more appropriate for the historical events section.

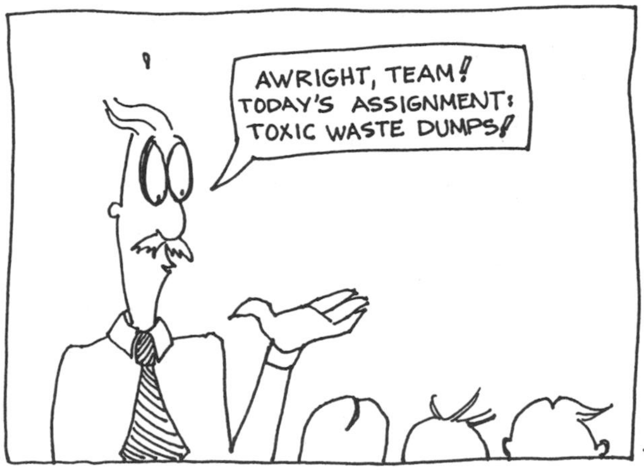
AWRIGHT, TEAM!
TODAY'S ASSIGNMENT:
TOXIC WASTE DUMPS!
33.

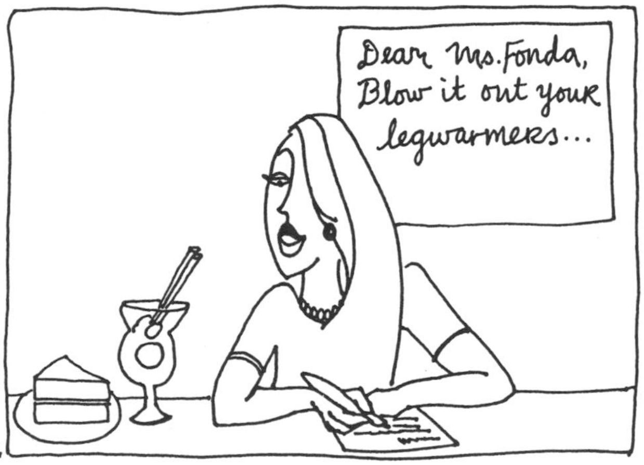
Dear Ms. Fonda,
Blow it out your
legwarmers...
34.

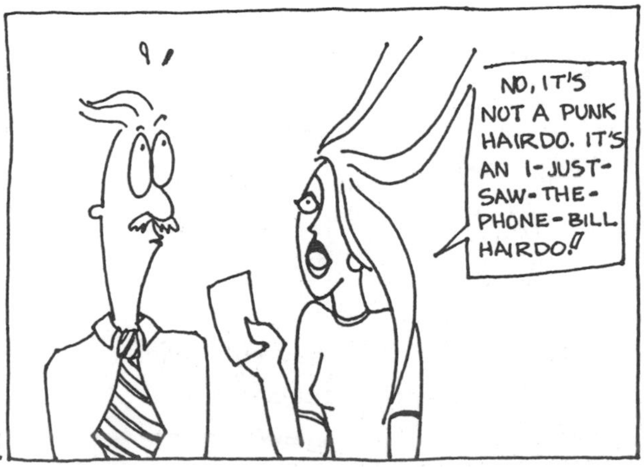
NO, IT'S NOT A PUNK HAIRDO. IT'S AN I-JUST-SAW-THE-PHONE-BILL HAIRDO!
35.

36.
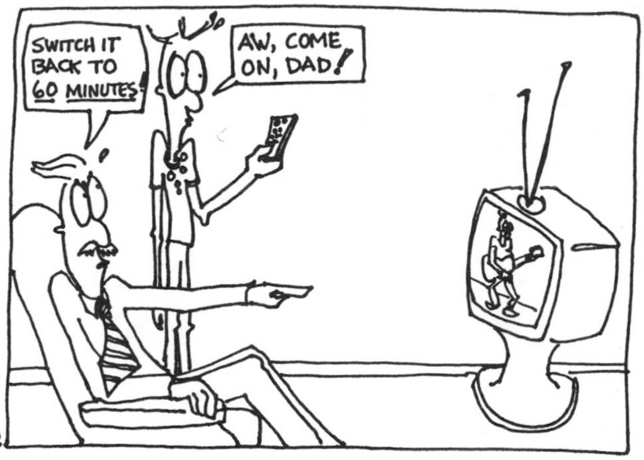
SWITCH IT BACK TO 60 MINUTES!
AW, COME ON, DAD!

37.
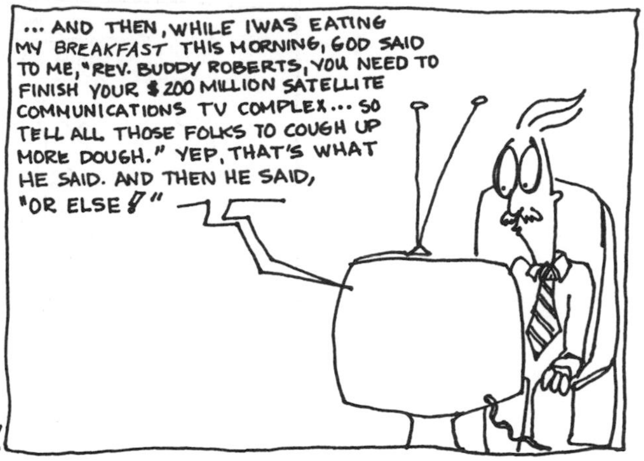
... AND THEN, WHILE I WAS EATING MY BREAKFAST THIS MORNING, GOD SAID TO ME, "REV. BUDDY ROBERTS, YOU NEED TO FINISH YOUR $200 MILLION SATELLITE COMMUNICATIONS TV COMPLEX... SO TELL ALL THOSE FOLKS TO COUGH UP MORE DOUGH." YEP, THAT'S WHAT HE SAID. AND THEN HE SAID, "OR ELSE!"

Toxic waste dumps, Jane Fonda's exercise video, punk styles, video games, the television program, *Sixty Minutes*, and evangelical ministers begging for donations on TV may all have disappeared by now. In some cases, I hope so; in others, I hope not. No matter, I'm sure you'll be able to find suitable, current examples for the students you're teaching.

Puns

About 300 years ago, John Dennis said that puns are the lowest form of wit. My response to that accusation is that puns may be terrible, but poetry is verse (get it?). I love puns. I feel that they show a true understanding of the language and a sharp sense of humor in catching the wittiness in the switch. I introduce the concept of puns by using this example: "My father thinks I'm so bright, he calls me sun." Students very quickly see the connection between bright and sun and, of course, between father and son.

Children love using puns. Here are a few from my childhood: What kind of rooms have no walls? (Mushrooms); Where do elephants keep their clothes? (In their trunks); How do you know when it's raining cats and dogs? (When you step in a poodle).

All the knock-knock jokes, too, were punny: Knock, knock. Who's there? Pencil. Pencil who? Pencil fall down if you don't wear a belt. Transit companies use them on the backs of their buses: Thanks for the brake! Even the highways department appreciates a good pun: Be patient today, not a patient tomorrow! William Shakespeare was so fond of puns that he used nearly 3,000 in his works and, if they were good enough for the immortal bard, who am I to denigrate them?

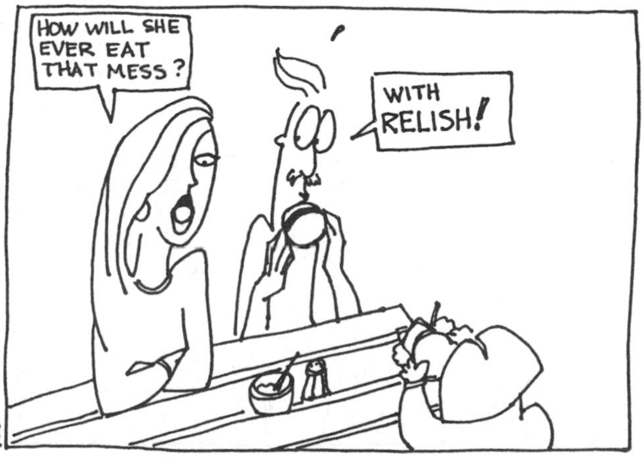
HOW WILL SHE EVER EAT THAT MESS?
WITH RELISH!
38.

The expression *with relish* means with enthusiasm. The pun here relates to how Katie will eat her monstrous hamburger.

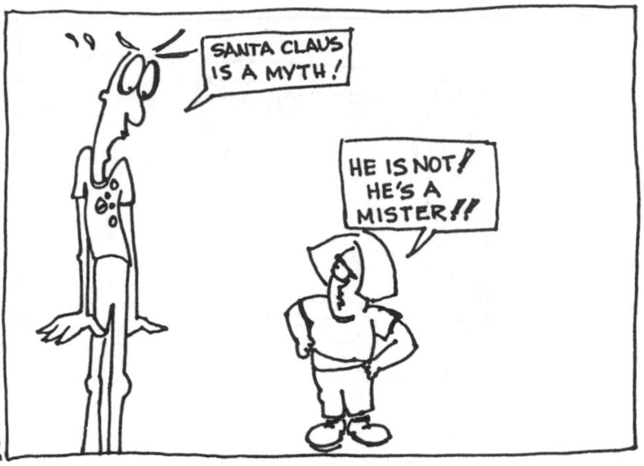
SANTA CLAUS IS A MYTH!
HE IS NOT! HE'S A MISTER!!
39.

Andy tries to tell Katie that Santa Claus doesn't really exist by declaring that Santa is a myth. Katie thinks she hears miss and tries to correct him by telling him that Santa is not a miss, he's a mister.

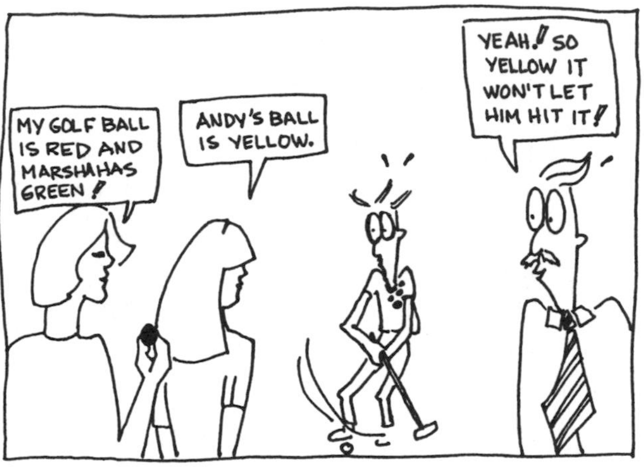
MY GOLF BALL IS RED AND MARSHA HAS GREEN!
ANDY'S BALL IS YELLOW.
YEAH! SO YELLOW IT WON'T LET HIM HIT IT!
40.

The expression *to be yellow* means to be afraid.

Foreign Words and Phrases

Many languages borrow words and phrases from other languages: English is probably the biggest borrower and may be the biggest lender, as well.

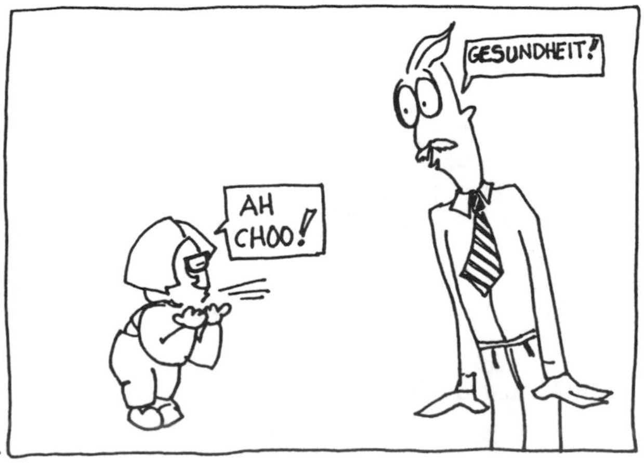
GESUNDHEIT!
AH CHOO!
41.

Gesundheit is German for bless you.

42.
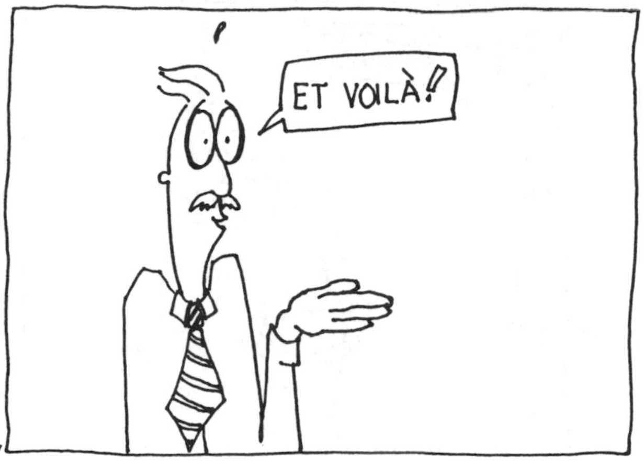
ET VOILÀ!

Et voilà! is French for and there you are, used when something has finally been complcted to one's satisfaction.

43.
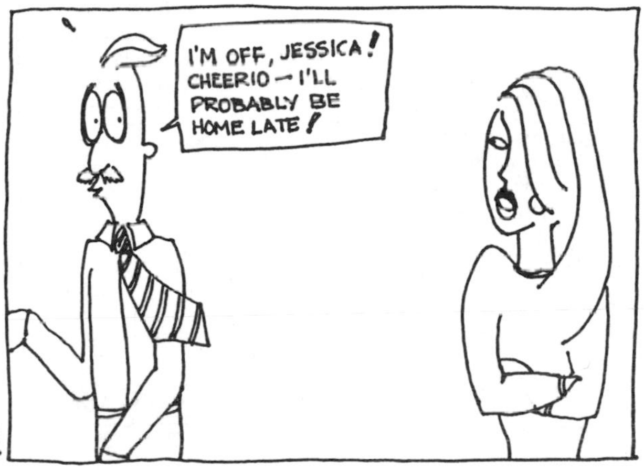
I'M OFF, JESSICA! CHEERIO – I'LL PROBABLY BE HOME LATE!

Cheerio is British English for good-bye.

44.
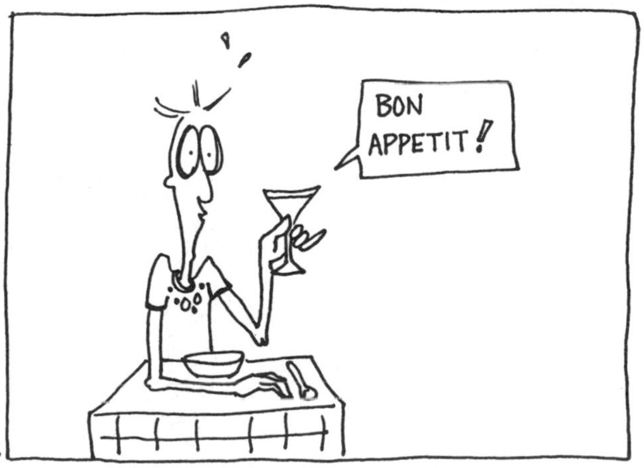
BON APPETIT!

Bon appetit! means enjoy your meal in French.

45. 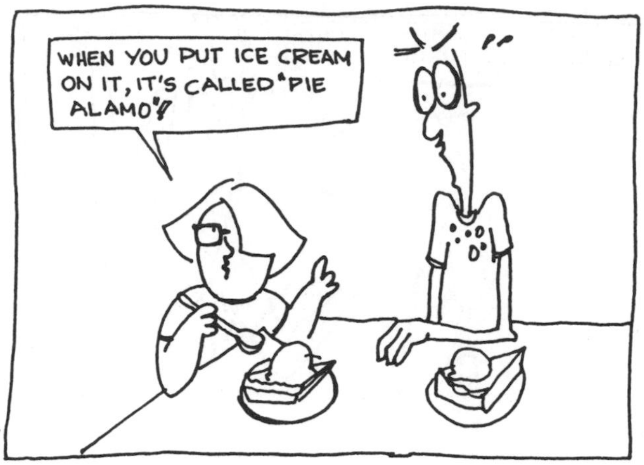
WHEN YOU PUT ICE CREAM ON IT, IT'S CALLED "PIE ALAMO"!

The final example is a pun arising from a foreign phrase. Pie *à la mode* means with ice cream (literally, in fashion in French).

Historical Events

46. 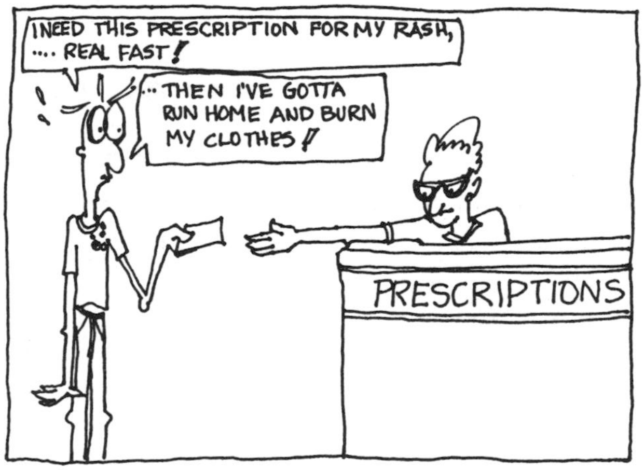
I NEED THIS PRESCRIPTION FOR MY RASH, ... REAL FAST!
... THEN I'VE GOTTA RUN HOME AND BURN MY CLOTHES!
PRESCRIPTIONS

The reference here, of course, is to the Black Death, the plague of the 14th century.

47. 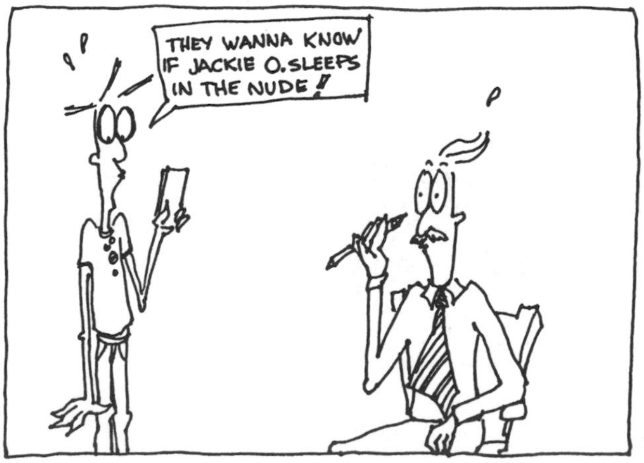
THEY WANNA KNOW IF JACKIE O. SLEEPS IN THE NUDE!

A photographer snapped Jackie Onassis (formerly Jackie Kennedy, wife of U.S. President John F. Kennedy) sunbathing in the nude.

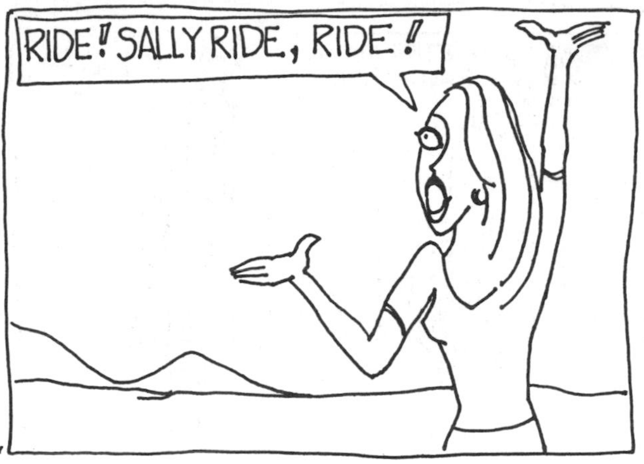
RIDE! SALLY RIDE, RIDE!

48.

Sally Ride was the first female NASA astronaut.

Dictionary Skills

Students often look up the meaning of unfamiliar words, then try, unsuccessfully, to apply the first definition listed to the context. I take great pains to teach them to examine the word in context and to determine which definition is most appropriate.

Other useful dictionary skills include ascertaining the correct pronunciation and spelling and learning how to use the word correctly in a sentence.

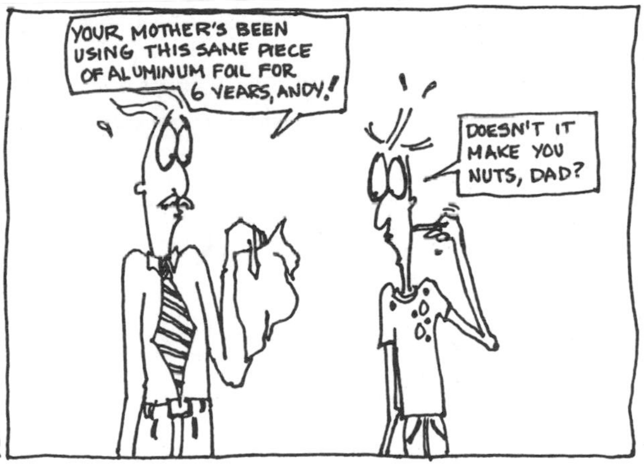
YOUR MOTHER'S BEEN USING THIS SAME PIECE OF ALUMINUM FOIL FOR 6 YEARS, ANDY!
DOESN'T IT MAKE YOU NUTS, DAD?

49.

The word *nut* (or *nuts*) can mean: 1) dry fruit or seeds with a hard shell and a firm inner kernel; 2) a metal block containing a threaded central hole designed to fit around a bolt or screw; 3) the ridge at the upper end of the fingerboard of a stringed musical instrument over which the strings pass; 4) a foolish, eccentric or crazy person. What do you think it means in this context?

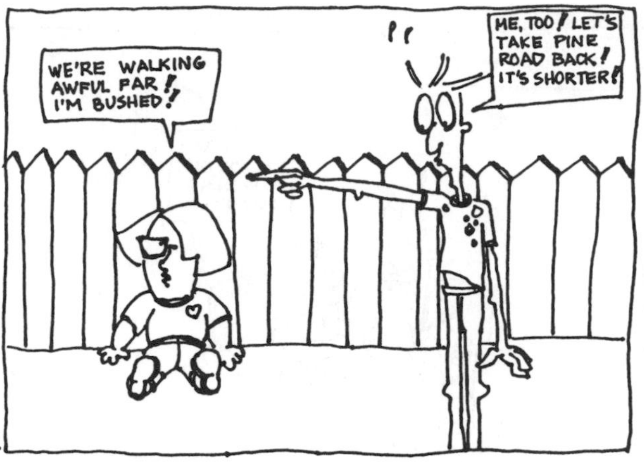
WE'RE WALKING AWFUL FAR! I'M BUSHED!
ME, TOO! LET'S TAKE PINE ROAD BACK! IT'S SHORTER!

50.

Awful is defined as: 1) inspiring awe or admiration; 2) extremely disagreeable; 3) very great. Which meaning is best in this context?

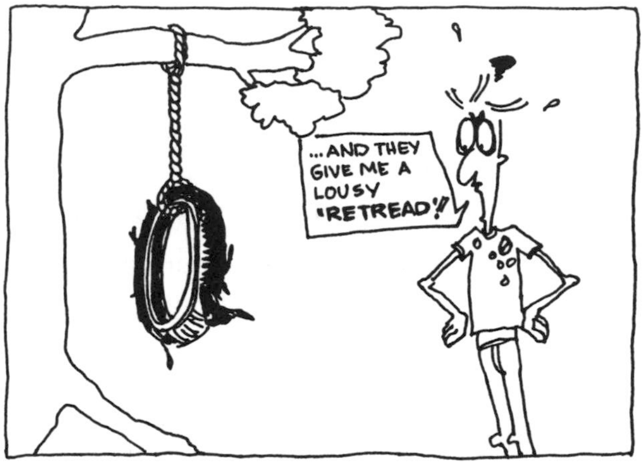
...AND THEY GIVE ME A LOUSY "RETREAD"!

51.

The dictionary defines *lousy* as: 1) infested with lice; 2) poor, inferior; 3) amply supplied (with money). Which meaning is most appropriate in this context?

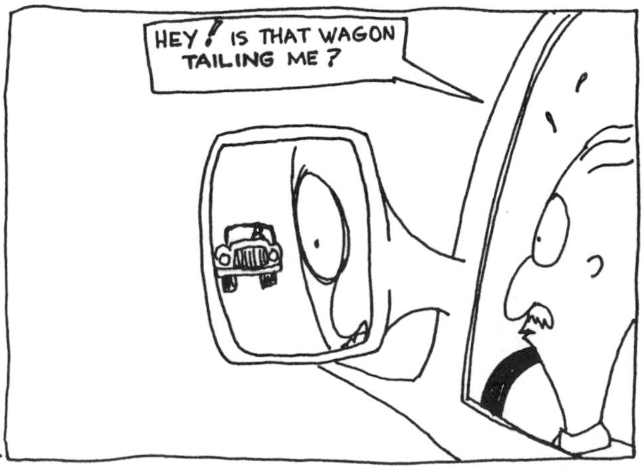
HEY! IS THAT WAGON TAILING ME?

52.

When used as a noun, the word *tail* usually means the appendage attached to the rear end of an animal. Here, it is used as a verb. Find the meaning of *tail*, as a verb, in your dictionary. Is it different from its meaning as a noun? Is it suitable in this context?

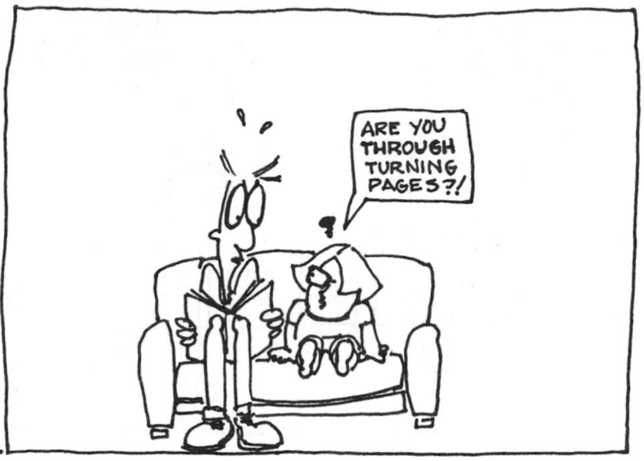
ARE YOU THROUGH TURNING PAGES?!

53.

Determine the part of speech of *through* as it is used in this context and find the appropriate meaning in a dictionary.

Oral Composition

The most useful comics and comic strips for eliciting oral compositions contain a certain amount of action but no captions (dialogue). You can remove the captions from any comic strip that uses action to portray what is happening.

Depending on the students' abilities, the examples here have been used to elicit stories using the simple present, present continuous, simple past, past continuous and simple future tenses.

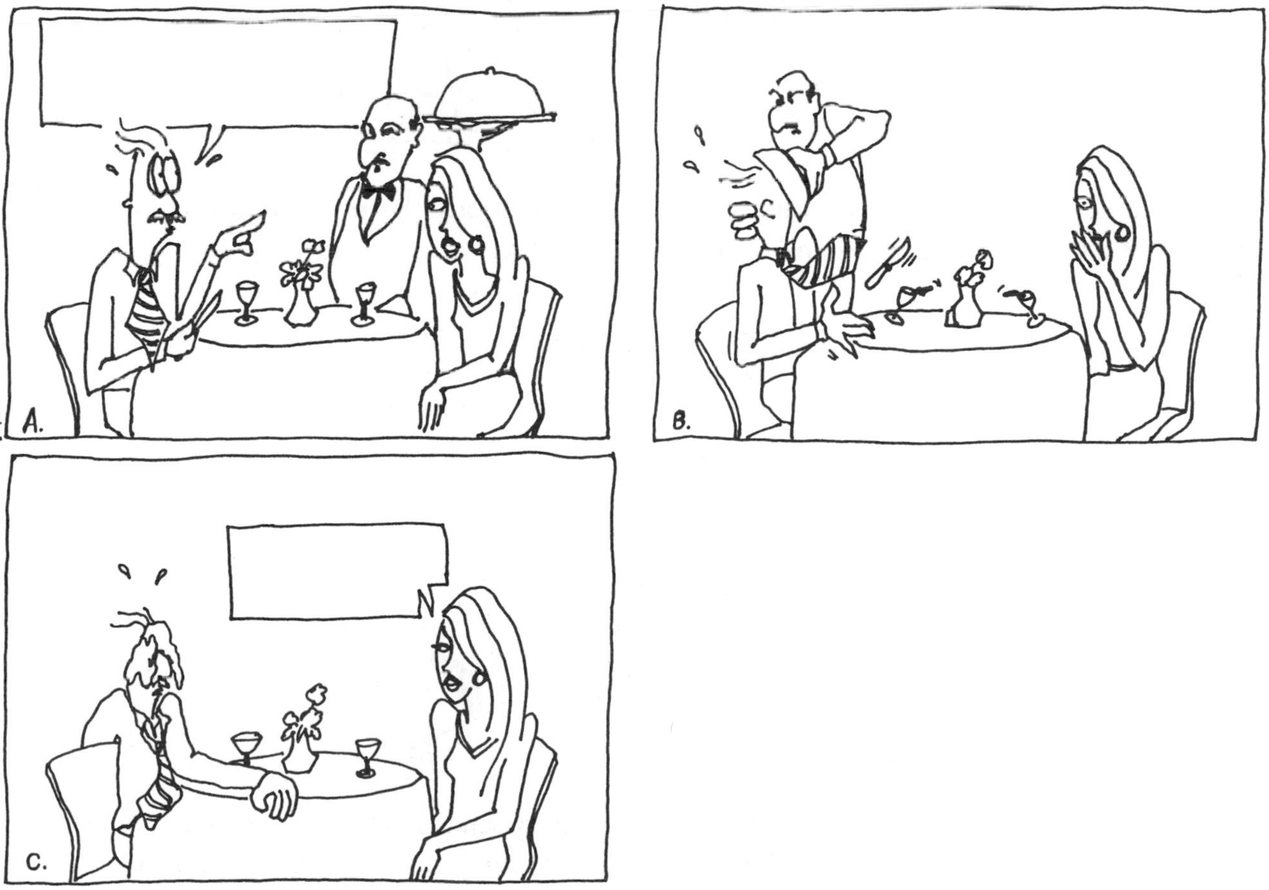

54. A. B. C.

John says something to the waiter that prompts the waiter to smash the salad into John's face. Then

Jessica says something to John in response to the incident. Students have a great time filling in the missing dialogue.

55.

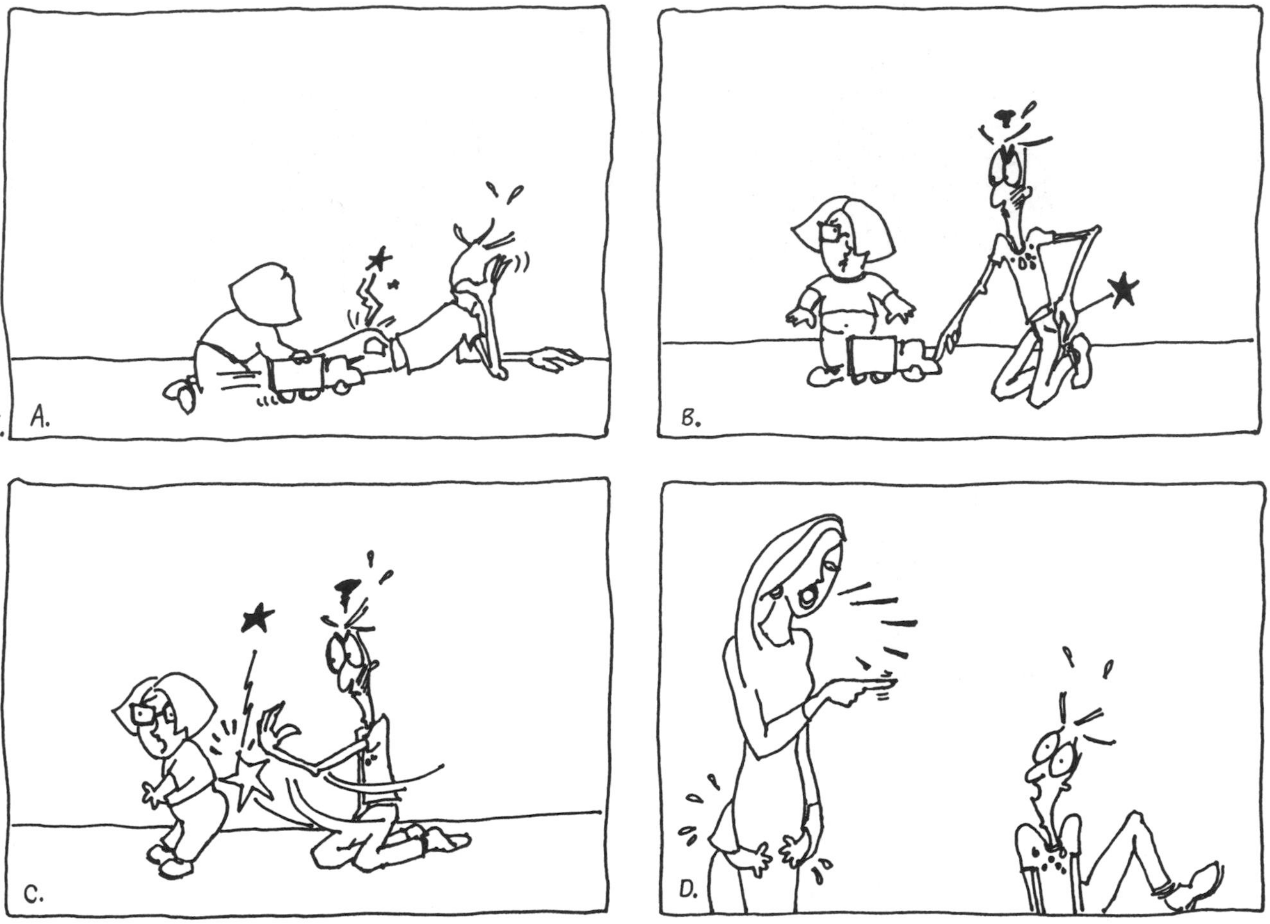
A.
B.
C.
D.

Katie smashes Andy with her sharp truck. Andy is hurt and smacks Katie. Katie runs, crying, to Mommy and Mommy scolds Andy for hitting his poor little sister. Similar situations arose frequently in our family when I was a kid. Are they common in your family? How about in the students' families?

56.

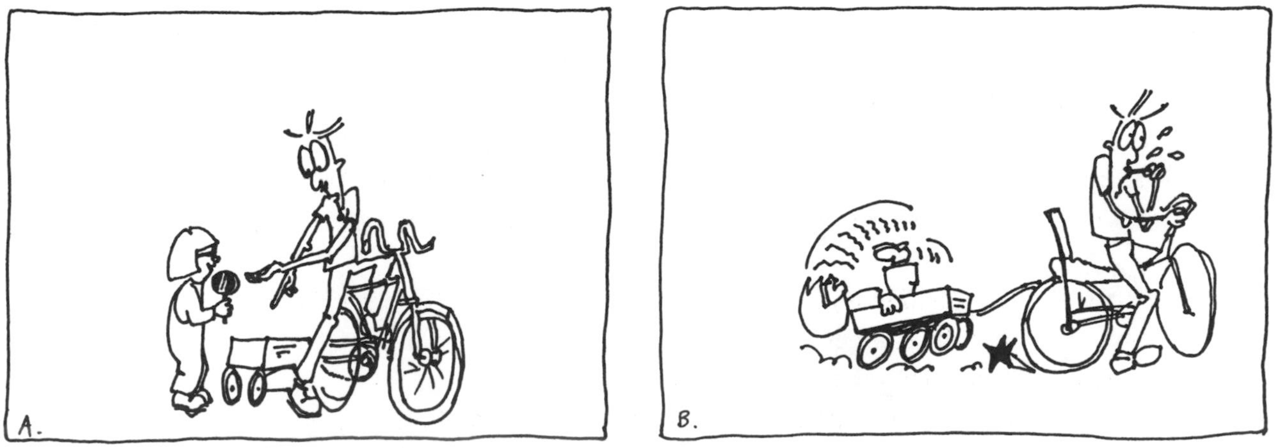
A.
B.

Andy offers to give Katie a ride in his wagon if she gives him her sucker. Andy takes off and jerks Katie around with sudden starts and stops. Katie gets out of the wagon, fed up with the jolting ride, and retrieves her sucker.

Sequence

To be able to place the frames of a comic strip in correct sequence, students must first understand the entire story. I start by giving the entire class a strip that is intact. Then, I shuffle the frames and challenge students to rearrange them in the correct order. To keep things simple at first, I use strips that are devoid of dialogue. Then, I introduce short strips with some captions before moving on to longer strips with full captions.

If the frames are numbered or lettered randomly, students can refer to them by number or letter, making it easier and faster to describe which they are referring to. Without numbers or letters on the frames, students must describe each well enough that others know which is being referred to.

To really challenge students, separate frames from two different episodes of the same strip and mix them together. In addition to deciding the correct order of the frames, students must first determine which frames belong to which episode.

Students can also put the frames into correct order and write the story.

As a follow-up activity, invite individual students to cut up a strip of their choice and challenge one another to arrange the frames in order.

57.

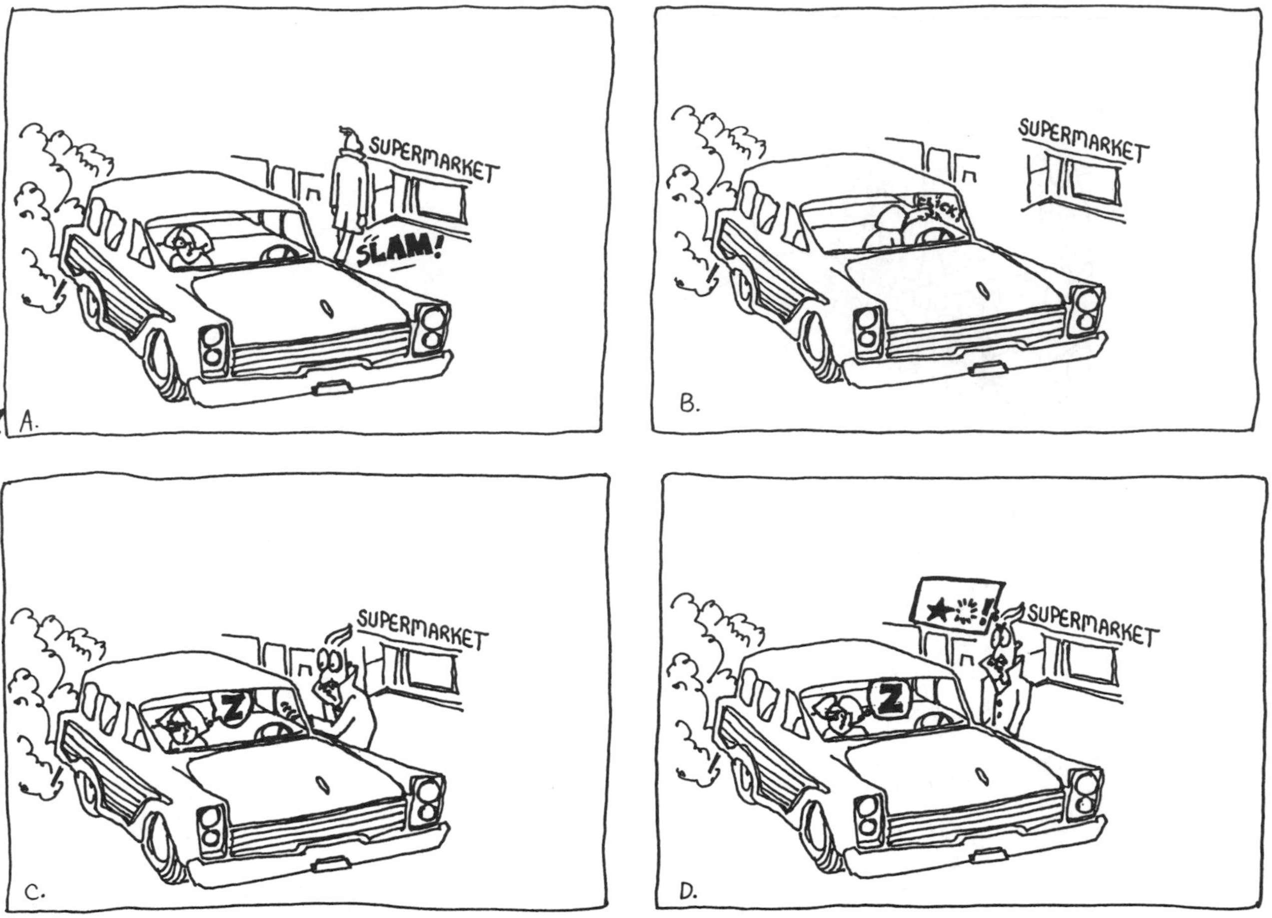
A.
SUPERMARKET
SLAM!
B.
SUPERMARKET
C.
SUPERMARKET
Z
D.
SUPERMARKET
Z

John stops at the supermarket and leaves little Katie in the car with the engine running, a thoughtless and dangerous act for several reasons: Katie could be kidnapped; she could play with the gear selector and cause an accident; she could become sick and die as heat builds up in the car; and so on. Fortunately, this time the worst that happens is that Katie locks the door and falls asleep. When John returns to the car, he can't open the door and has a hard time waking Katie.

58.

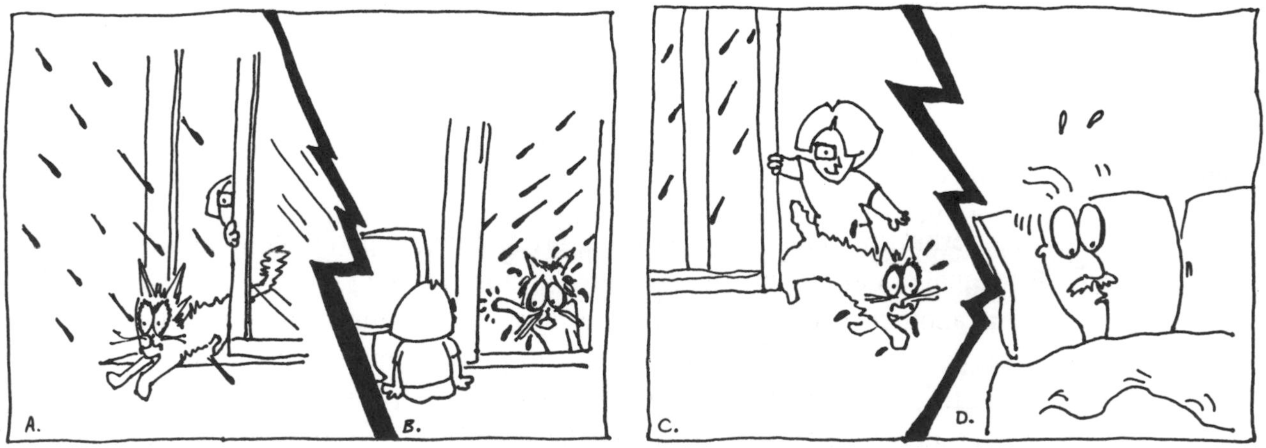
A.
B.
C.
D.

58. E.

Katie lets out Rocky, the cat, during a rain storm and then lets her back into the house. John wakes up in thc middle of the night to discover that he has a soaking wet cat in bed with him.

59. A.   B.   C.   D.

Katie is licking a sucker and Rocky, the cat, is playing with a toy mouse. The mouse rolls under the armchair and Katie helps her look for it. She places her sucker on the floor and reaches under the chair to fetch the mouse. After she retrieves it, she gives it to Rocky but can't find her sucker. It appears that Rocky sat on the sucker and it's now stuck to her behind.

Gestures

Also known as non-verbal communication, gestures are an integral part of communication and are specific to each language and culture. A particular gesture in one culture can have an entirely different meaning in another (sometimes with unfortunate results for the uninitiated!).

These exercises provide an excellent opportunity to share gestures with the class. Students — and teachers — are often amused, and sometimes shocked, when they discover what a particular gesture means in another culture. For example, the thumbs-up gesture, which has a positive meaning — okay or good — in western cultures, is considered quite rude in Iran and could get you into a fight, while the gesture meaning okay, made by making a ring with the thumb and index finger, with the other three fingers pointing up, has a rude sexual connotation in some cultures.

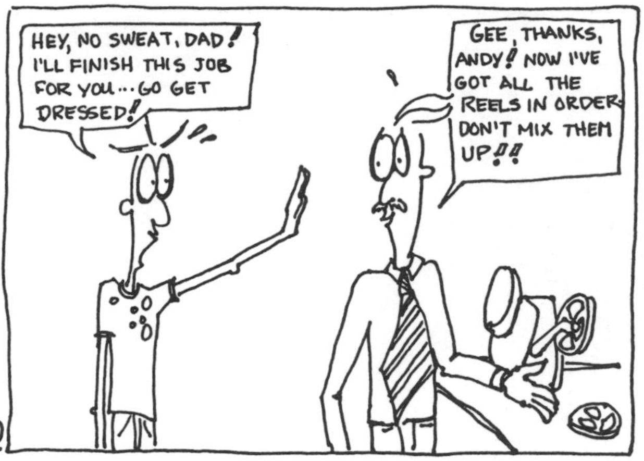
HEY, NO SWEAT, DAD! I'LL FINISH THIS JOB FOR YOU... GO GET DRESSED!
GEE, THANKS, ANDY! NOW I'VE GOT ALL THE REELS IN ORDER. DON'T MIX THEM UP!!

60.

In western cultures, an upraised, vertical palm indicates that you want someone not to do, or to stop doing, something.

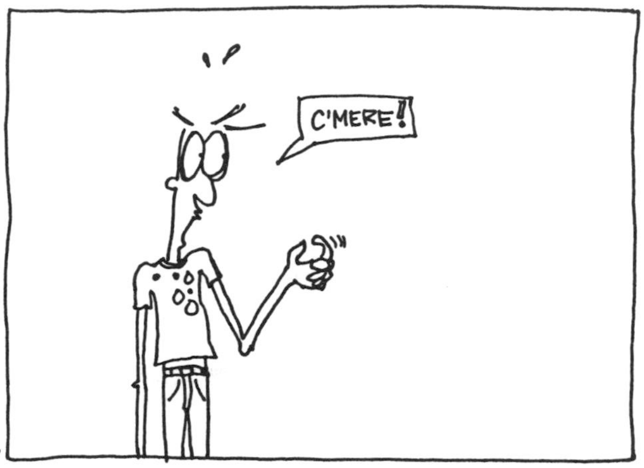
C'MERE!

61.

An upturned palm, with a finger (usually the index) or fingers curling up and back towards the gesturer signifies that you want the person to come to you. In some cultures, the palm is down with the same meaning.

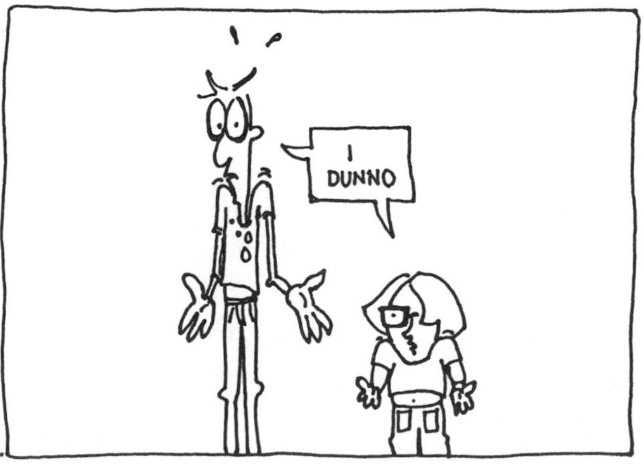
I DUNNO

62.

Hunching the shoulders and raising the arms demonstrates lack of knowledge or concern, as in I don't know and I don't care.

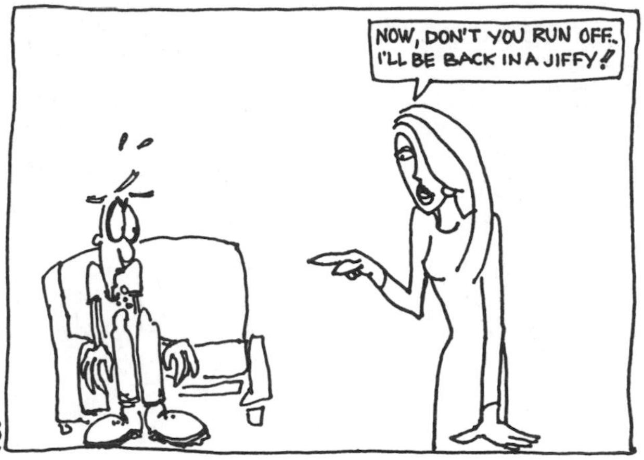
NOW, DON'T YOU RUN OFF. I'LL BE BACK IN A JIFFY!

63.

When giving orders, especially strict orders, it is customary to point the index finger at the listener, a custom considered quite rude in many cultures.

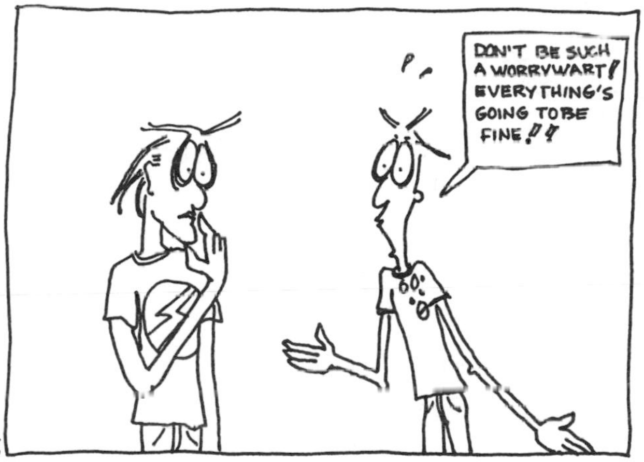
DON'T BE SUCH A WORRYWART! EVERYTHING'S GOING TO BE FINE!!

64.

When pleading with another person or trying to reassure her, we often shake our upturned, open palms up and down.

Ethics and Morals

65.

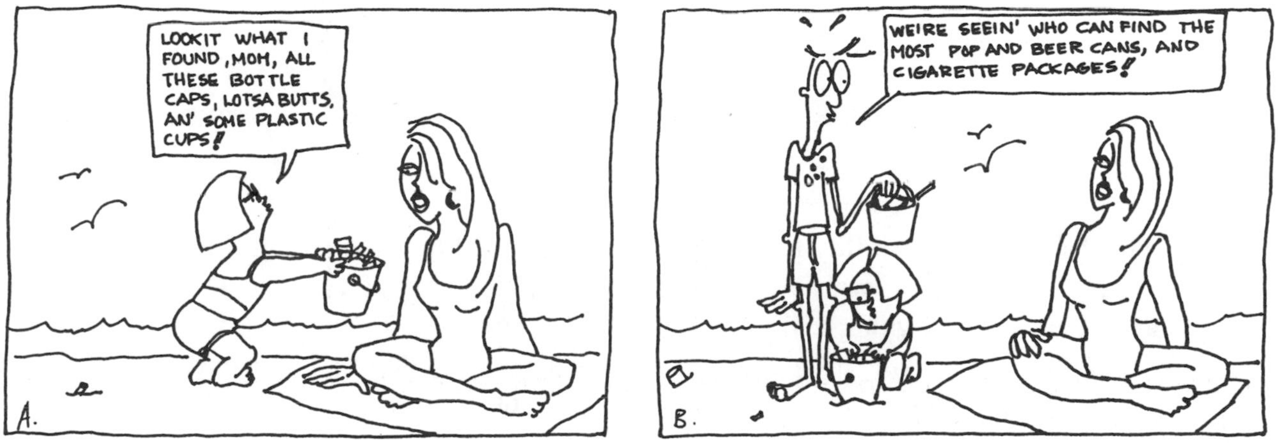
A.
LOOKIT WHAT I FOUND, MOM, ALL THESE BOTTLE CAPS, LOTSA BUTTS, AN' SOME PLASTIC CUPS!
B.
WE'RE SEEIN' WHO CAN FIND THE MOST POP AND BEER CANS, AND CIGARETTE PACKAGES!

65.

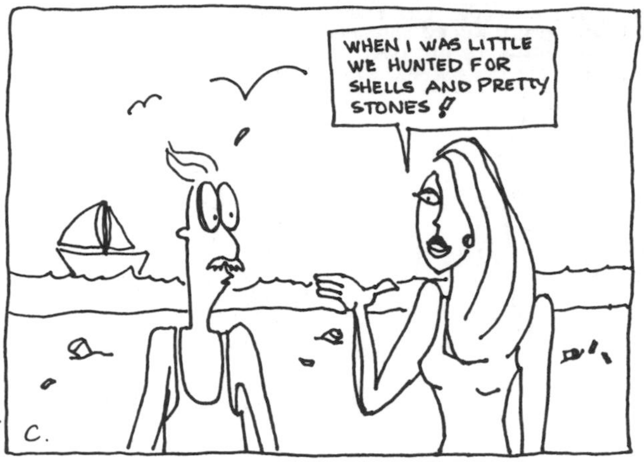
WHEN I WAS LITTLE WE HUNTED FOR SHELLS AND PRETTY STONES!!
C.

Different cultures have different ethical values. In some places in the world, no one would be shocked or even upset at seeing someone throw garbage in the street, park or on the beach. On the other hand, most people in North America frown upon the improper disposal of garbage and most municipalities levy fines against litterers.

66.

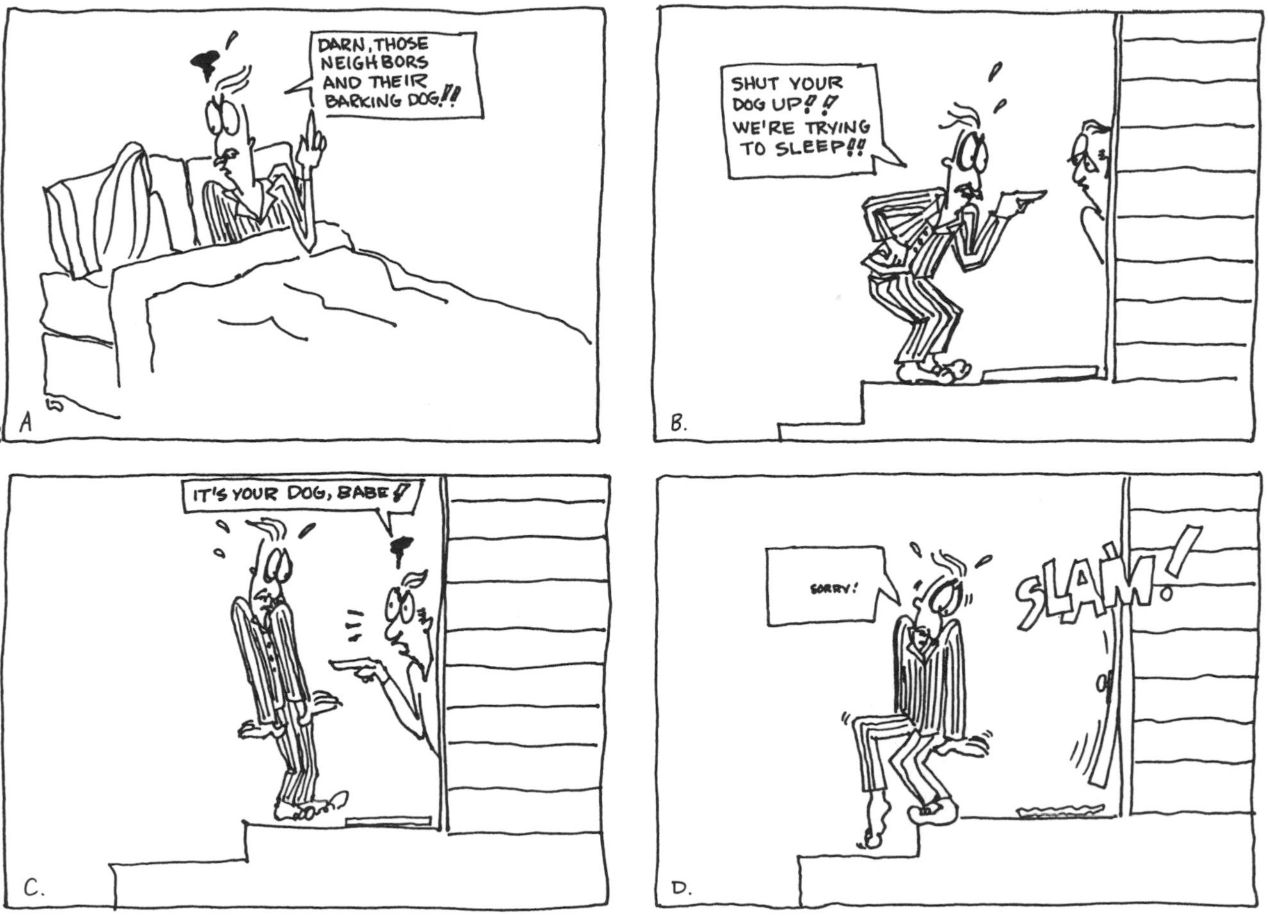
A
DARN, THOSE NEIGHBORS AND THEIR BARKING DOG!!
B.
SHUT YOUR DOG UP!! WE'RE TRYING TO SLEEP!!
C.
IT'S YOUR DOG, BABE!!
D.
SORRY!
SLAM!

Most people assume responsibility for the behavior of their children and pets. If, for example, your neighbor's child breaks your window, your neighbor would likely offer to pay for the repairs. If your dog dug up your neighbor's flowers, you would, somehow, make restitution. John's dog, Babe, is barking late at night. John assumes it is his neighbor's dog that is disturbing his sleep. When he scolds his neighbor for being irresponsible and not controlling his dog, he is embarrassed when it is pointed out that it is his dog that is causing the ruckus.

67. 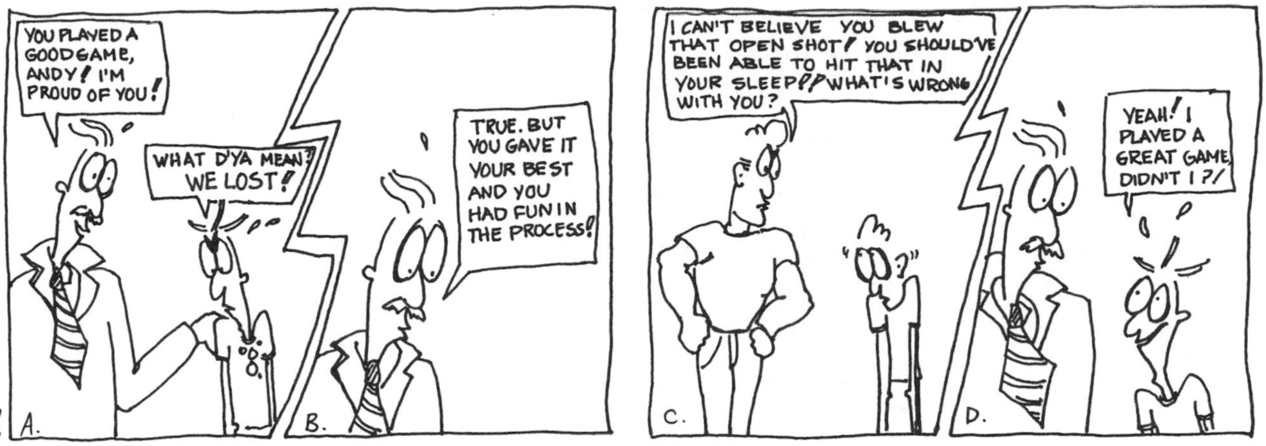
A.
YOU PLAYED A GOODGAME, ANDY! I'M PROUD OF YOU!
WHAT D'YA MEAN? WE LOST!
B.
TRUE. BUT YOU GAVE IT YOUR BEST AND YOU HAD FUN IN THE PROCESS!
C.
I CAN'T BELIEVE YOU BLEW THAT OPEN SHOT! YOU SHOULD'VE BEEN ABLE TO HIT THAT IN YOUR SLEEP!! WHAT'S WRONG WITH YOU?
D.
YEAH! I PLAYED A GREAT GAME, DIDN'T I?!

It's more important to play hard and fairly and to enjoy playing than to win; as the adage goes, It's not whether you win or lose, but how you play the game. Too many parents push their children to win at any cost.

Jargon

Jargon is technical, professional or specialized language that may be appropriate in certain situations, but is totally out of place in othcrs.

68. 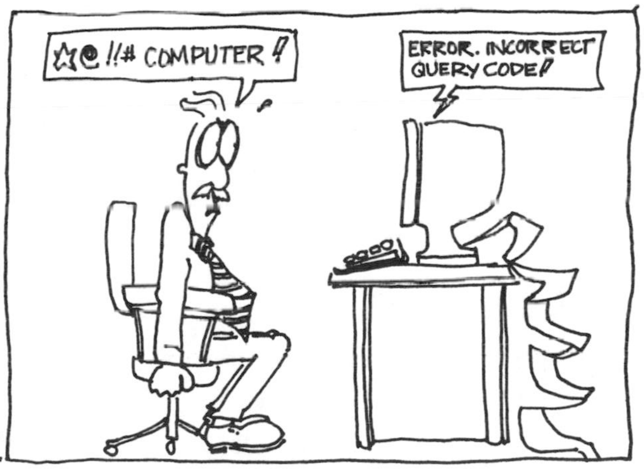
@!!# COMPUTER!
ERROR. INCORRECT QUERY CODE!

We are being inundated with brand-new jargon by the computer industry.

69. 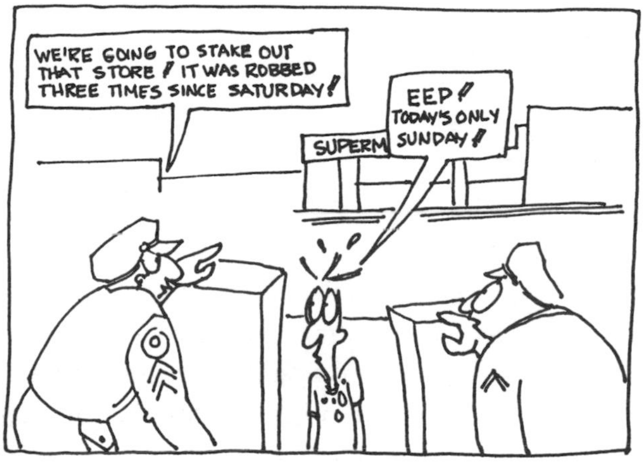
WE'RE GOING TO STAKE OUT THAT STORE! IT WAS ROBBED THREE TIMES SINCE SATURDAY!
SUPERM
EEP! TODAY'S ONLY SUNDAY!

Police use their own peculiar jargon, as do criminals.

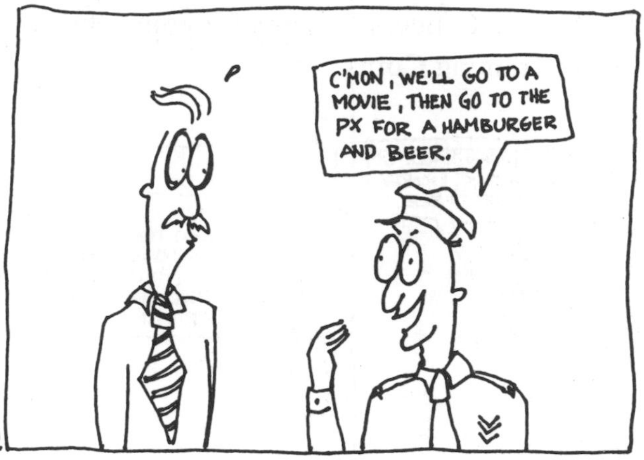
C'MON, WE'LL GO TO A MOVIE, THEN GO TO THE PX FOR A HAMBURGER AND BEER.

70.

The military use theirs. In the Canadian Forces, the general store is known as the Canex.

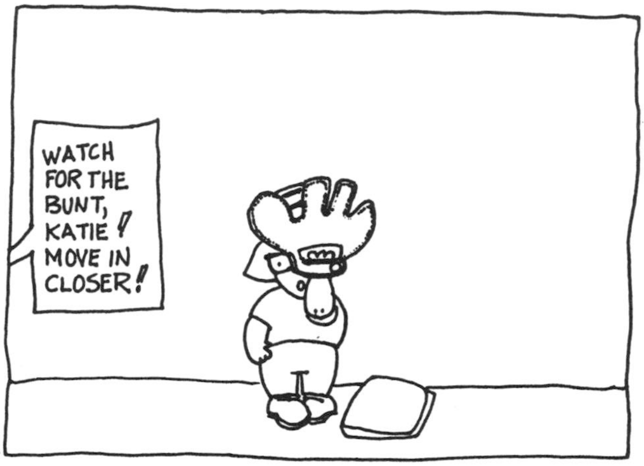
WATCH FOR THE BUNT, KATIE! MOVE IN CLOSER!

71.

And each sport has its own.

Abbreviations and Acronyms

Abbreviations are frequently used to reduce the amount of verbiage in both writing and speech. For example, few people refer to the AFL-CIO by its full name (American Federation of Labor-Congress of Industrial Organizations — that is a mouthful!) and acronyms are simply pronounceable abbreviations, such as NATO (North Atlantic Treaty Organization), or UNICEF (United Nations Children's Fund, formerly United Nations International Children's Emergency Fund).

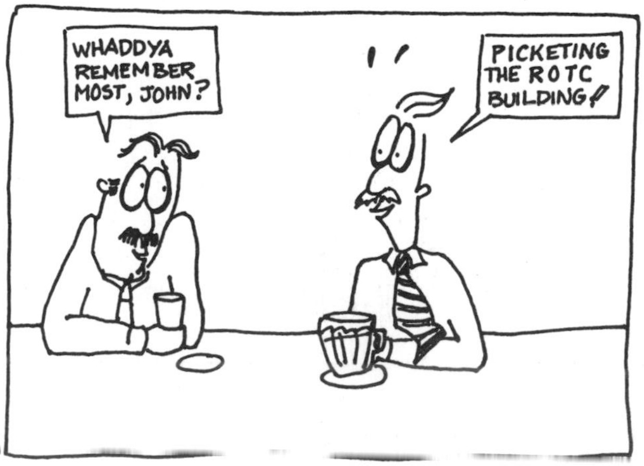
WHADDYA REMEMBER MOST, JOHN?
PICKETING THE ROTC BUILDING!

72.

In Canada, ROTP stands for Regular Officers Training Program while in the United States, ROTC stands for the Reserve Officers Training Corps.

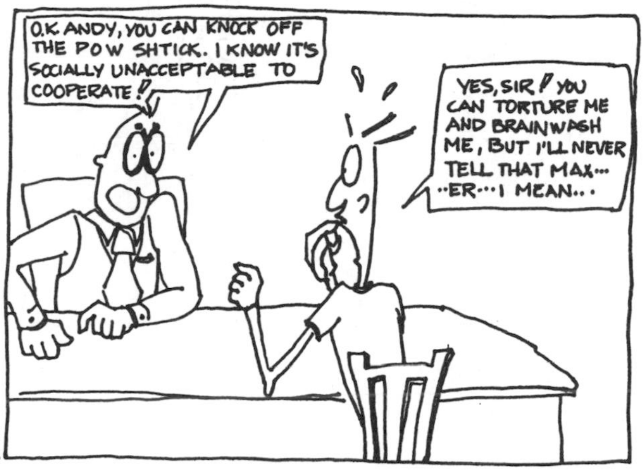
O.K. ANDY, YOU CAN KNOCK OFF THE POW SHTICK. I KNOW IT'S SOCIALLY UNACCEPTABLE TO COOPERATE!
YES, SIR! YOU CAN TORTURE ME AND BRAINWASH ME, BUT I'LL NEVER TELL THAT MAX... ..ER... I MEAN...

73.

A PoW is a prisoner of war.

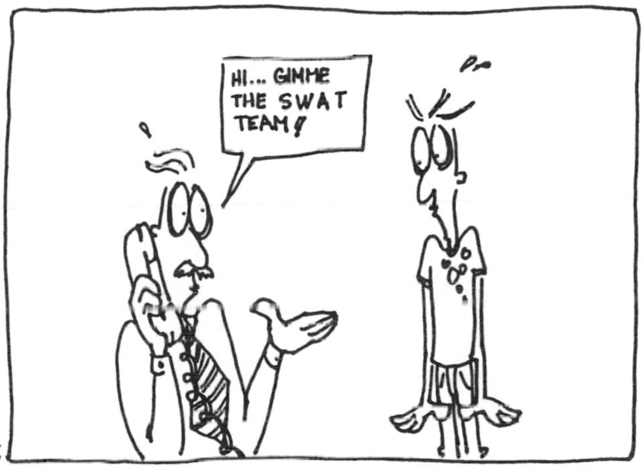
HI... GIMME THE SWAT TEAM!

74.

SWAT stands for special weapons and tactics.

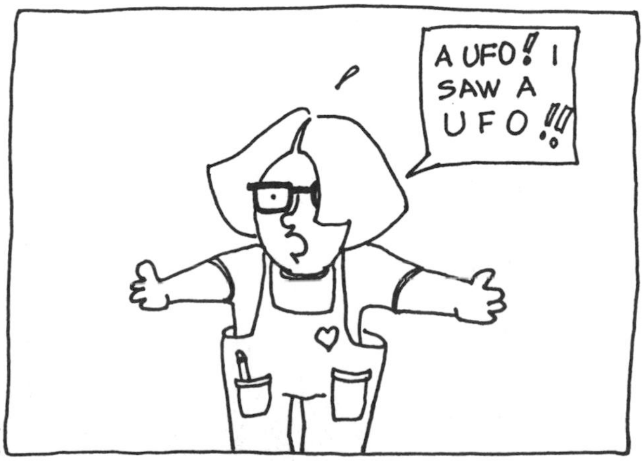
A UFO! I SAW A UFO!!!

75.

Unidentified flying objects are commonly called UFOs.

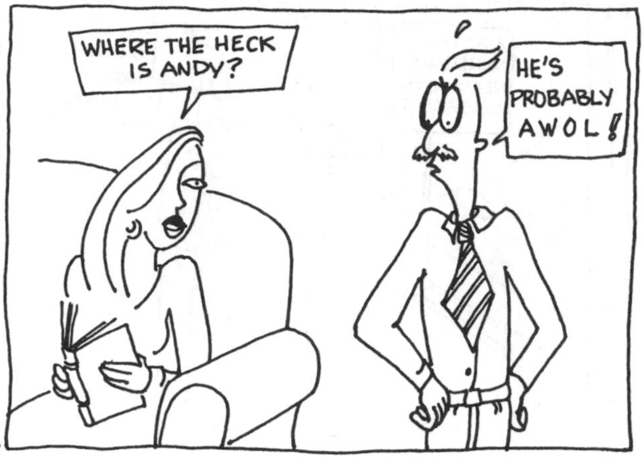
WHERE THE HECK IS ANDY?
HE'S PROBABLY AWOL!
76.

In the U.S. military, if you go away without permission, you are absent without leave (AWOL). In Canada, you are AWL.

Vocal Segregates

Students love learning vocal segregates and I, for one, love teaching them. They express a great deal without saying a word. The discussion arising from this series of comics is an excellent chance to find out what is used in other languages to convey various emotions and sentiments.

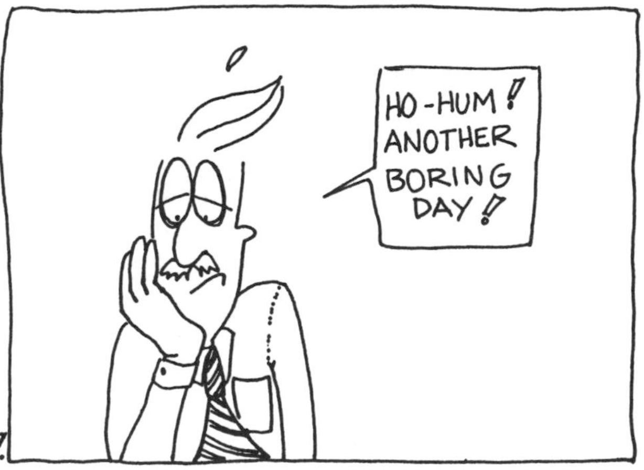
HO-HUM! ANOTHER BORING DAY!
77.

Ho-hum or a sigh indicates boredom.

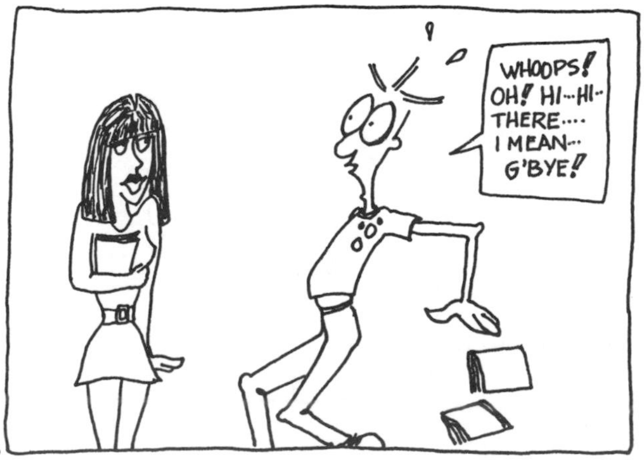
WHOOPS! OH! HI-HI- THERE.... I MEAN-- G'BYE!
78.

Whoops! or *oops*! implies that a mistake has been made or an accident has happened.

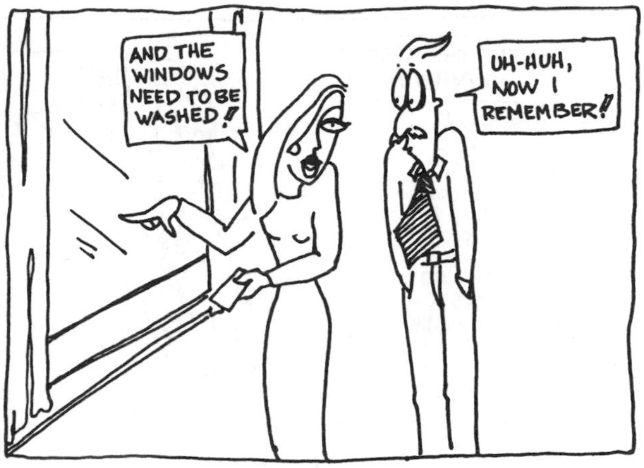
AND THE WINDOWS NEED TO BE WASHED!
UH-HUH, NOW I REMEMBER!

79.

Uh-huh (with rising intonation) conveys agreement or a positive response while *uh-uh* (with falling intonation) indicates disagreement or a negative.

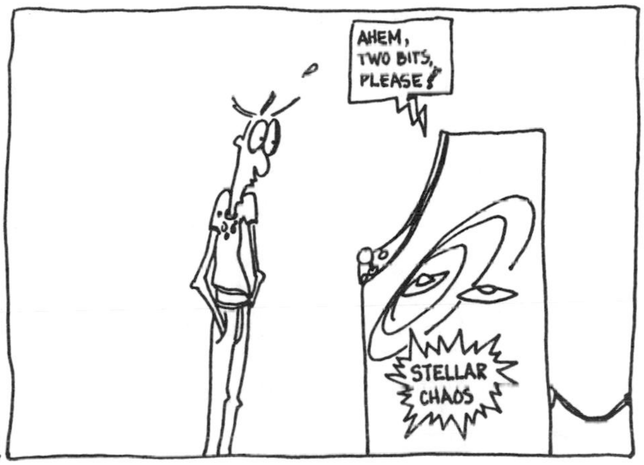
AHEM, TWO BITS, PLEASE!
STELLAR CHAOS

80.

Clearing one's throat (*ahem*!) is often used to get someone's attention.

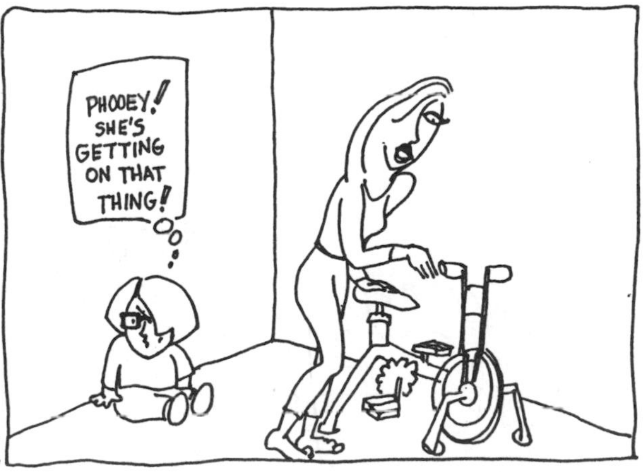
PHOOEY! SHE'S GETTING ON THAT THING!

81.

Phooey! implies disgust or disappointment.

Gambits

Gambits are openers, polite tools used to pry open a conversation and allow the other person to jump in. They are also used to get people's attention so that they will be listening to you by the time you start saying something meaningful.

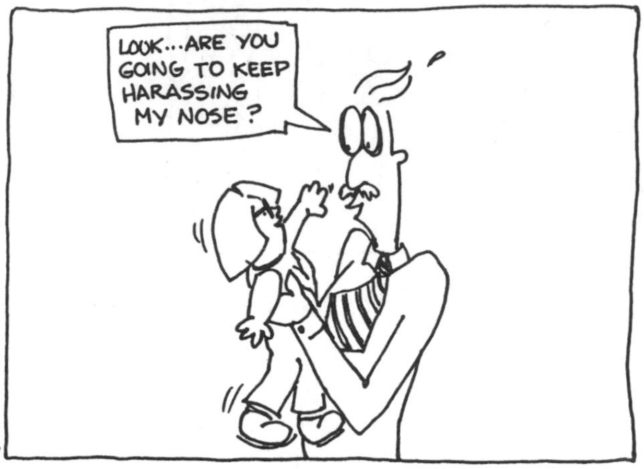
LOOK...ARE YOU GOING TO KEEP HARASSING MY NOSE?

82.

When used as a gambit, *look* doesn't mean please watch this.

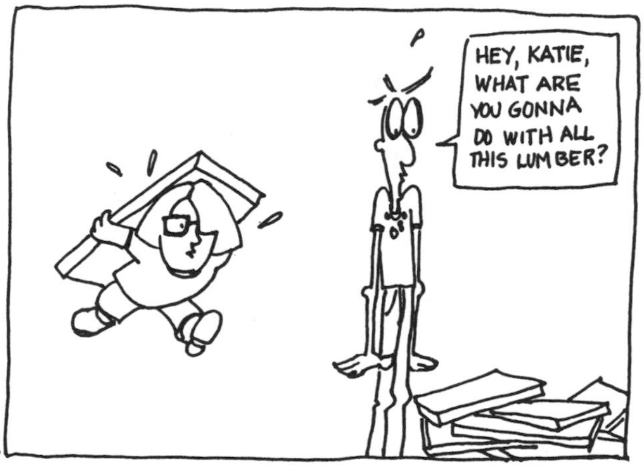
HEY, KATIE, WHAT ARE YOU GONNA DO WITH ALL THIS LUMBER?

83.

Hey is a simple opener.

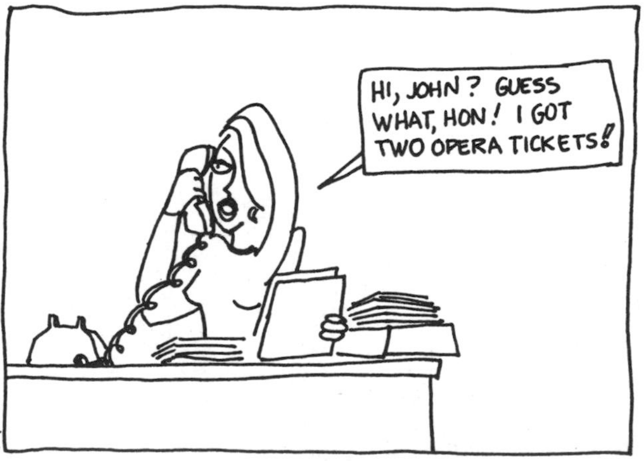
HI, JOHN? GUESS WHAT, HON! I GOT TWO OPERA TICKETS!

84.

When we want someone to become interested in what we are going to say, we often say, "Guess what!" Of course, the other person is highly unlikely to guess what's on your mind, but now you do have her attention.

MY, WHAT A CUTE LITTLE GIRL!

85.

My! shows interest, sometimes surprise. It has no possessive meaning when used as a gambit.

GEE, ANDY, MY LEGS WANNA TAKE A NAP!
BUT WE'RE ONLY ON THE FOURTH FLOOR!

86.

Gee!, like *my!*, is used to show interest or surprise and sorrow or disappointment.

Onomatopoeia

Isn't it odd that dogs bark differently in different languages! In English, they say, "Arf" or "Bow-wow." What do they say in other languages? How about cats? What sound does a wind-up clock make? What do you hear when you hit the table with your open hand? How do you show the sound made by two cars crashing together? When someone jumps into a swimming pool, what sound do you hear?

KATIE, WHAT ARE YOU DOING?!
BASH!
BAM!
BOP!

87.

What sound does a hammer make on a wooden floor? A concrete floor? A window?

Universals

88.

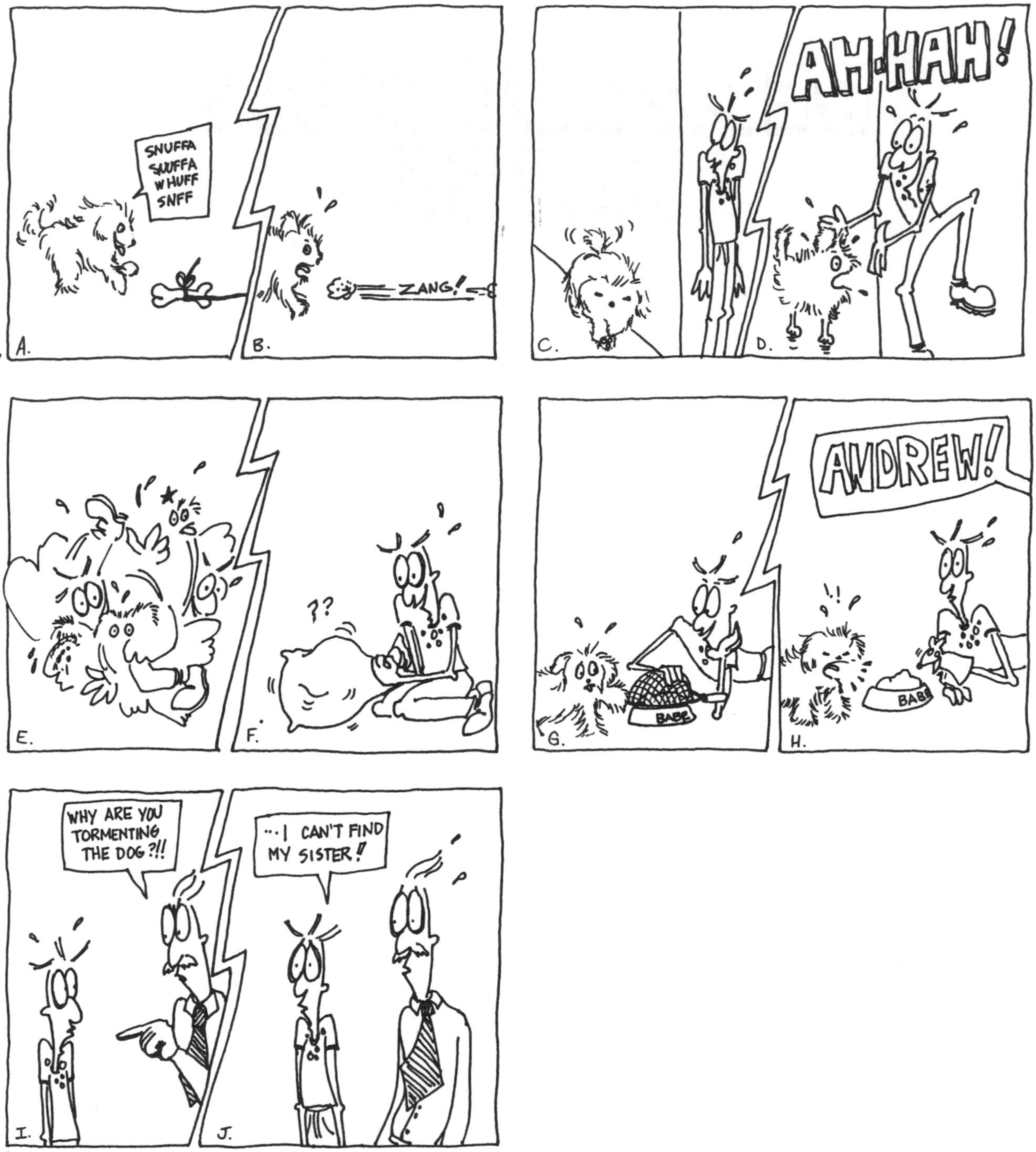
SNUFFA SNUFFA WHUFF SNFF
ZANG!
AH-HAH!
??
ANDREW!
BABE
WHY ARE YOU TORMENTING THE DOG?!!
...I CAN'T FIND MY SISTER!

Is there a place in the world where older siblings don't like to pick on younger ones? I doubt it!

I hope you and your students have as much fun using comics in the classroom as my students and I do.

REPRODUCIBLE PAGES

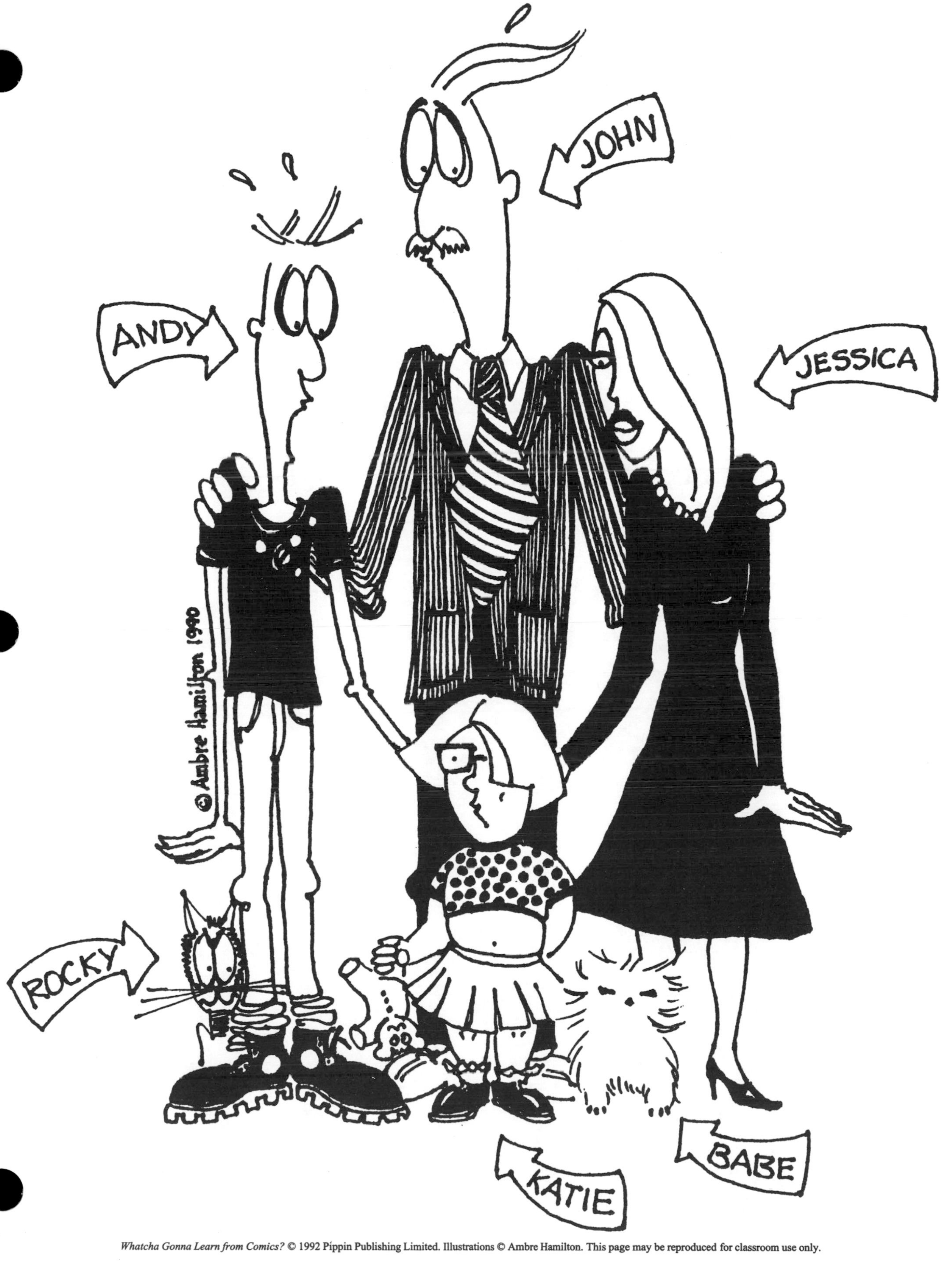
JOHN
ANDY
JESSICA
© Ambre Hamilton 1990
ROCKY
KATIE
BABE

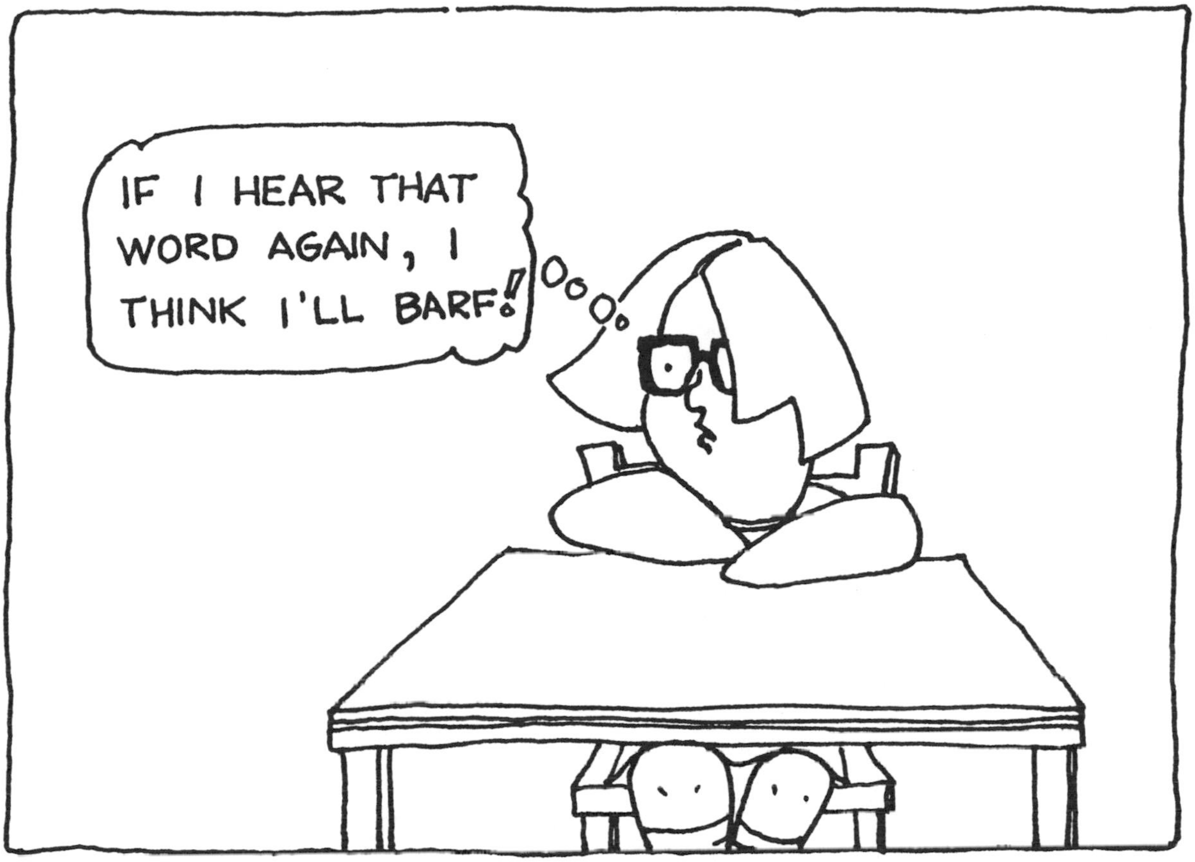
IF I HEAR THAT WORD AGAIN, I THINK I'LL BARF!

1.

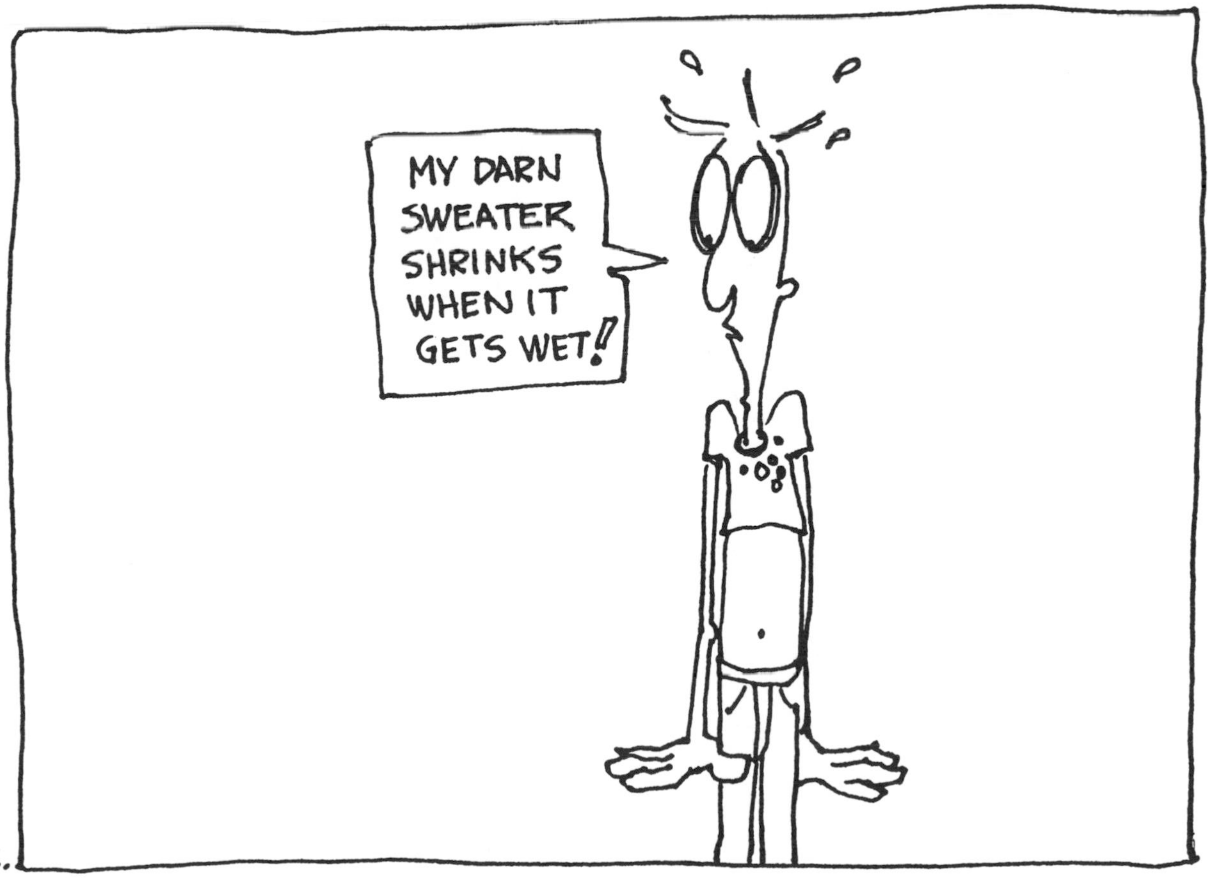
MY DARN SWEATER SHRINKS WHEN IT GETS WET!

2.

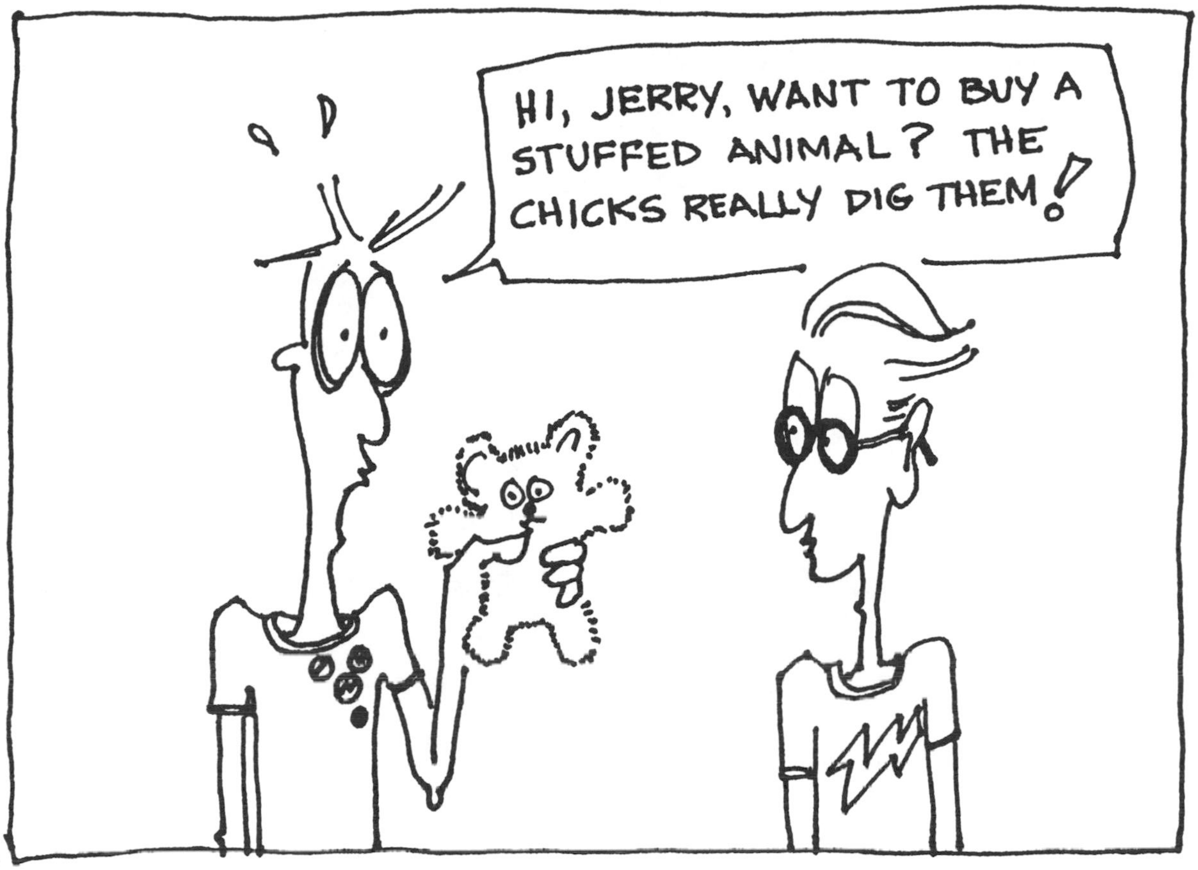
HI, JERRY, WANT TO BUY A STUFFED ANIMAL? THE CHICKS REALLY DIG THEM!

3.

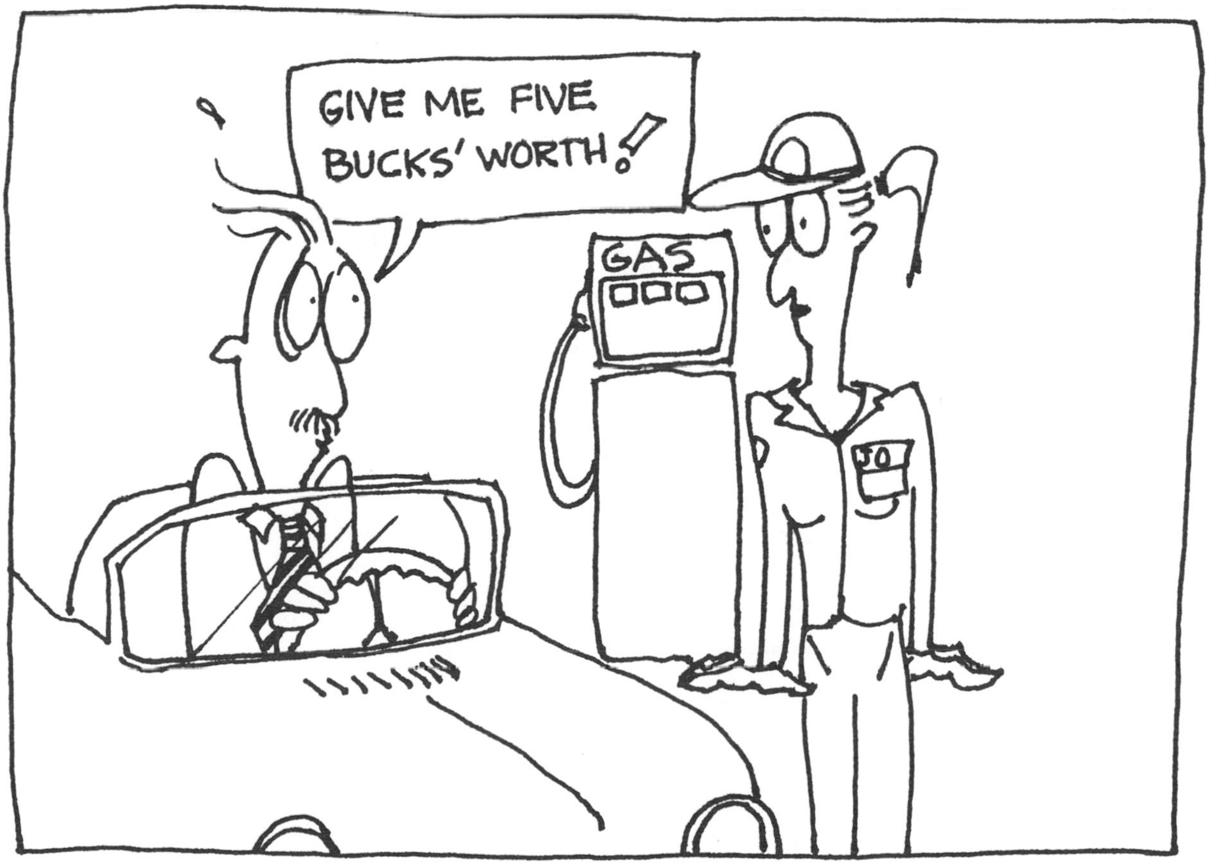
GIVE ME FIVE BUCKS' WORTH!
GAS
JO

4.

10.

11.

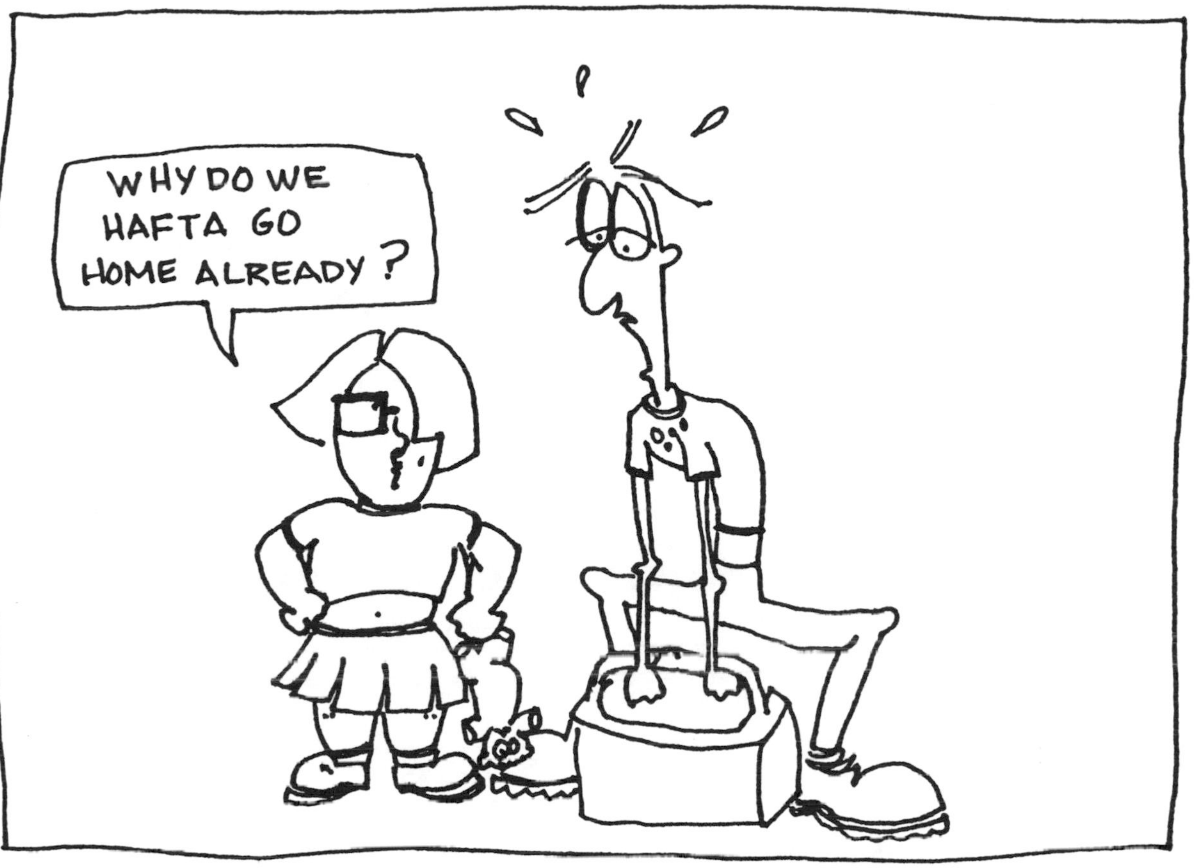
WHY DO WE HAFTA GO HOME ALREADY?

12.

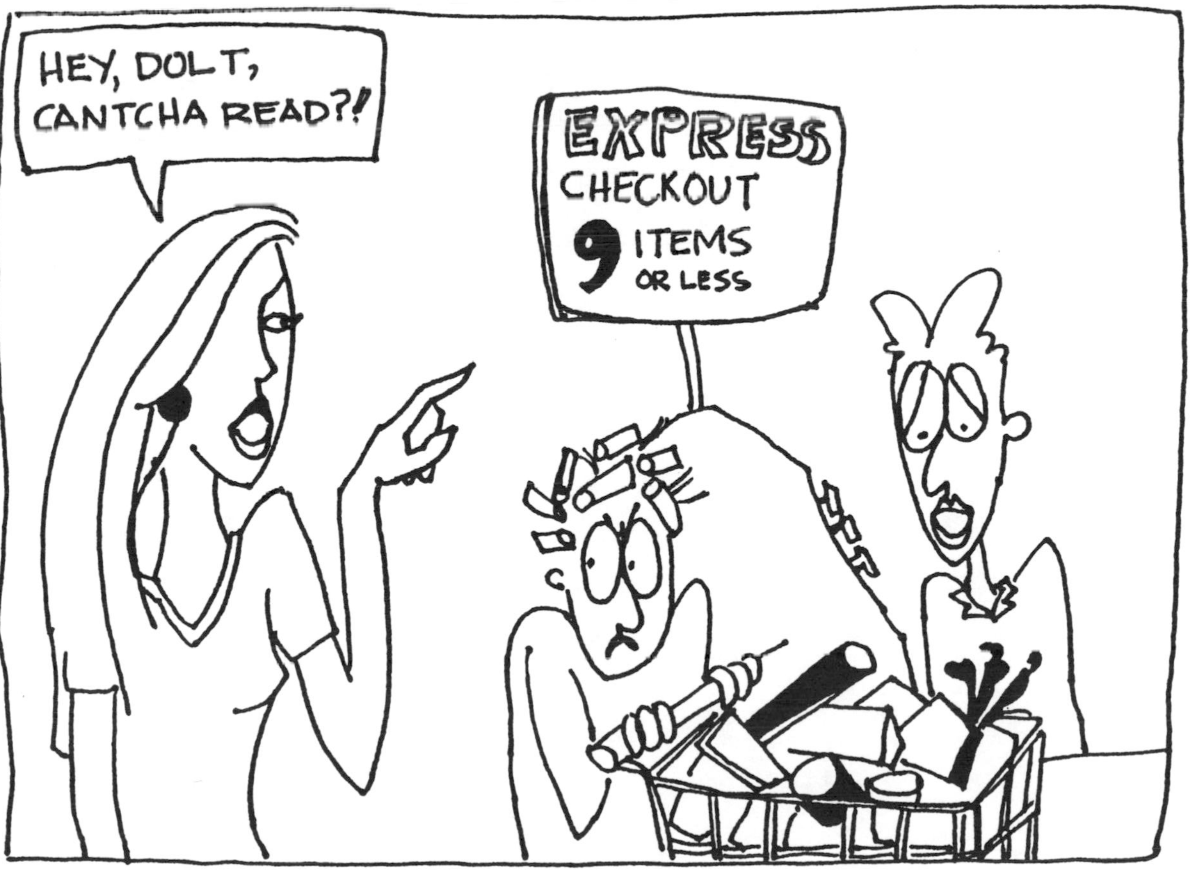
HEY, DOLT, CANTCHA READ?!
EXPRESS
CHECKOUT
9 ITEMS OR LESS

13.

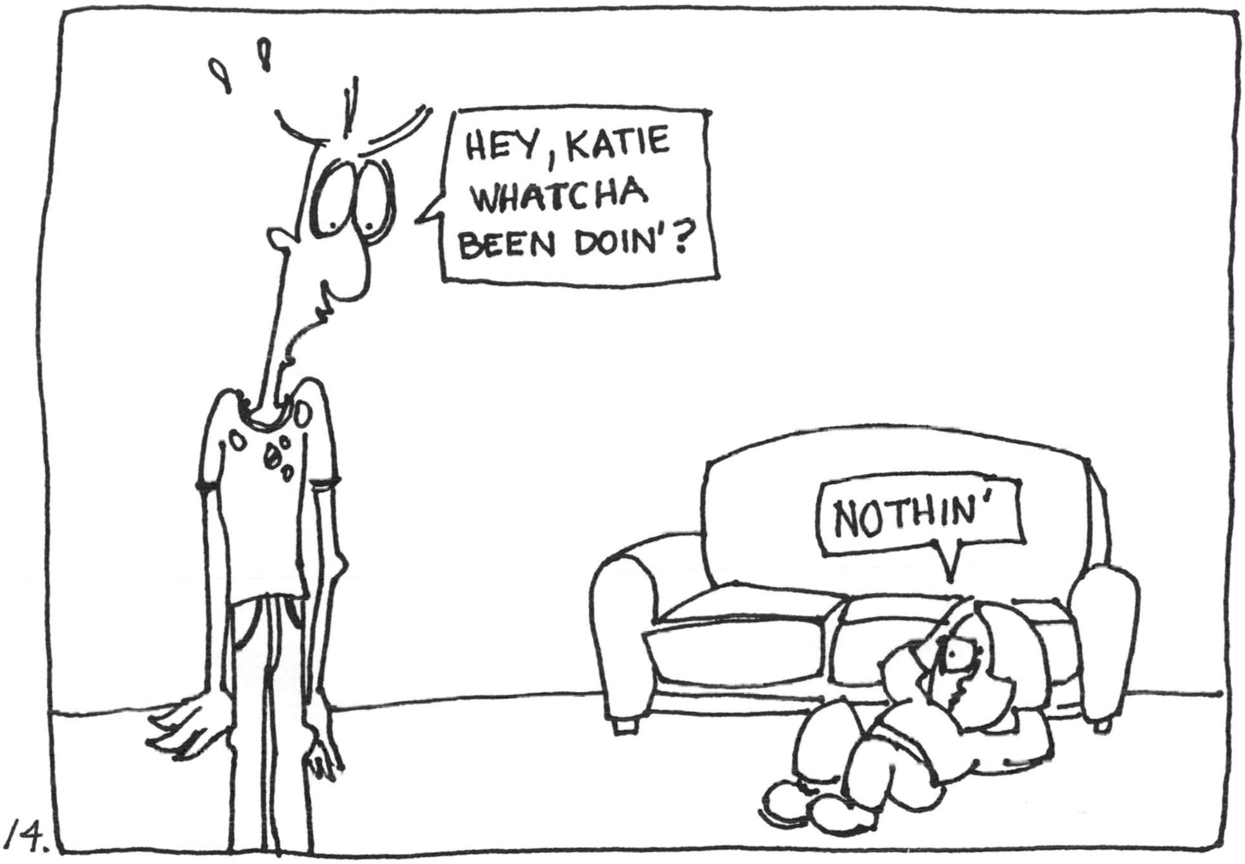
HEY, KATIE WHATCHA BEEN DOIN'?
NOTHIN'

15.

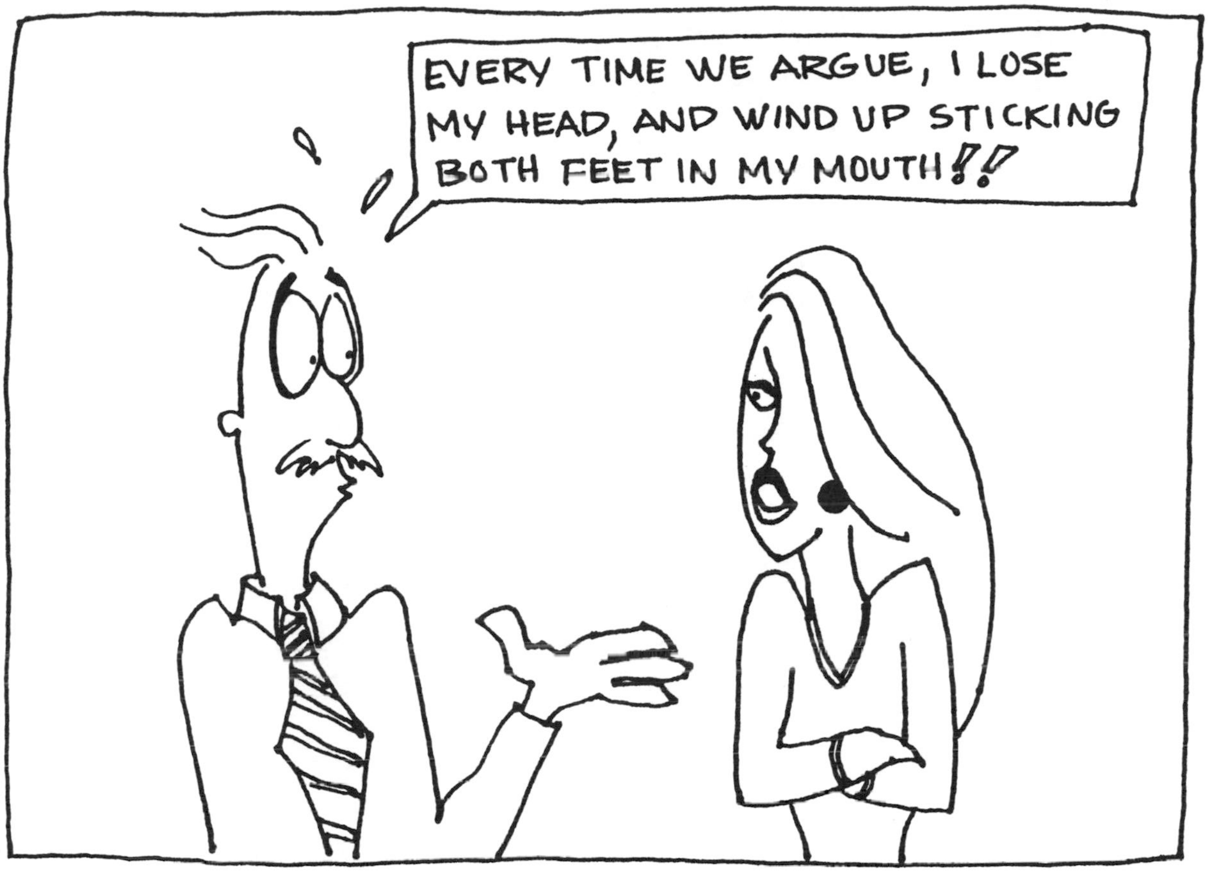
EVERY TIME WE ARGUE, I LOSE MY HEAD, AND WIND UP STICKING BOTH FEET IN MY MOUTH!!

16.

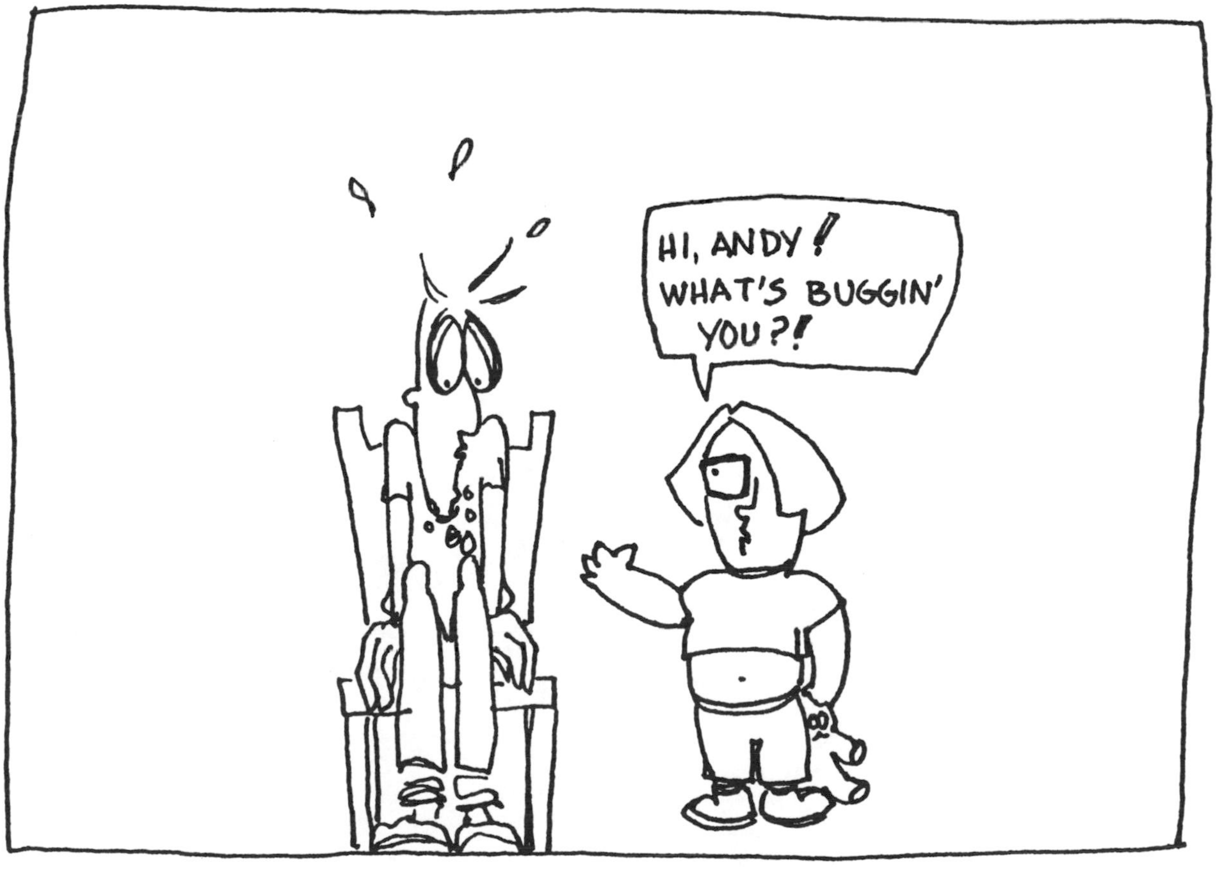
HI, ANDY! WHAT'S BUGGIN' YOU?!

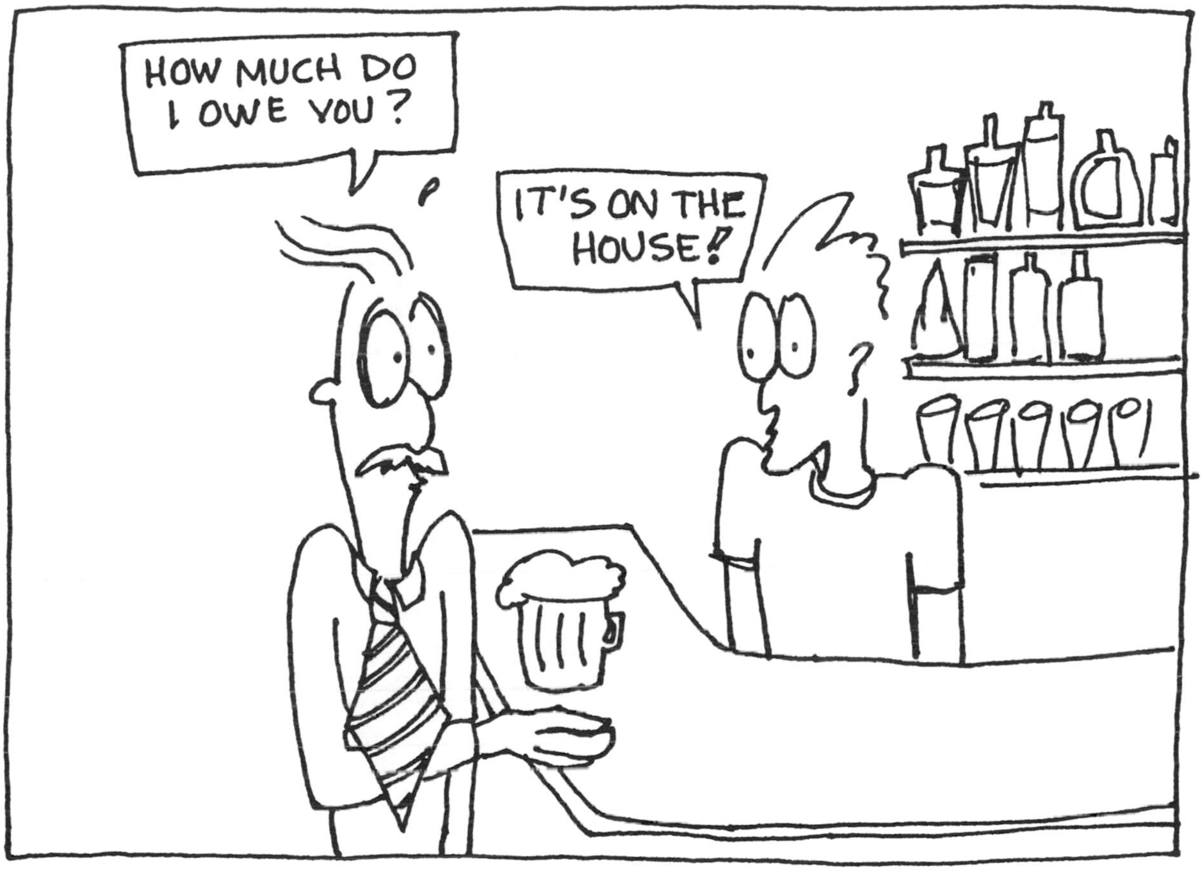
HOW MUCH DO I OWE YOU?
IT'S ON THE HOUSE!

17.

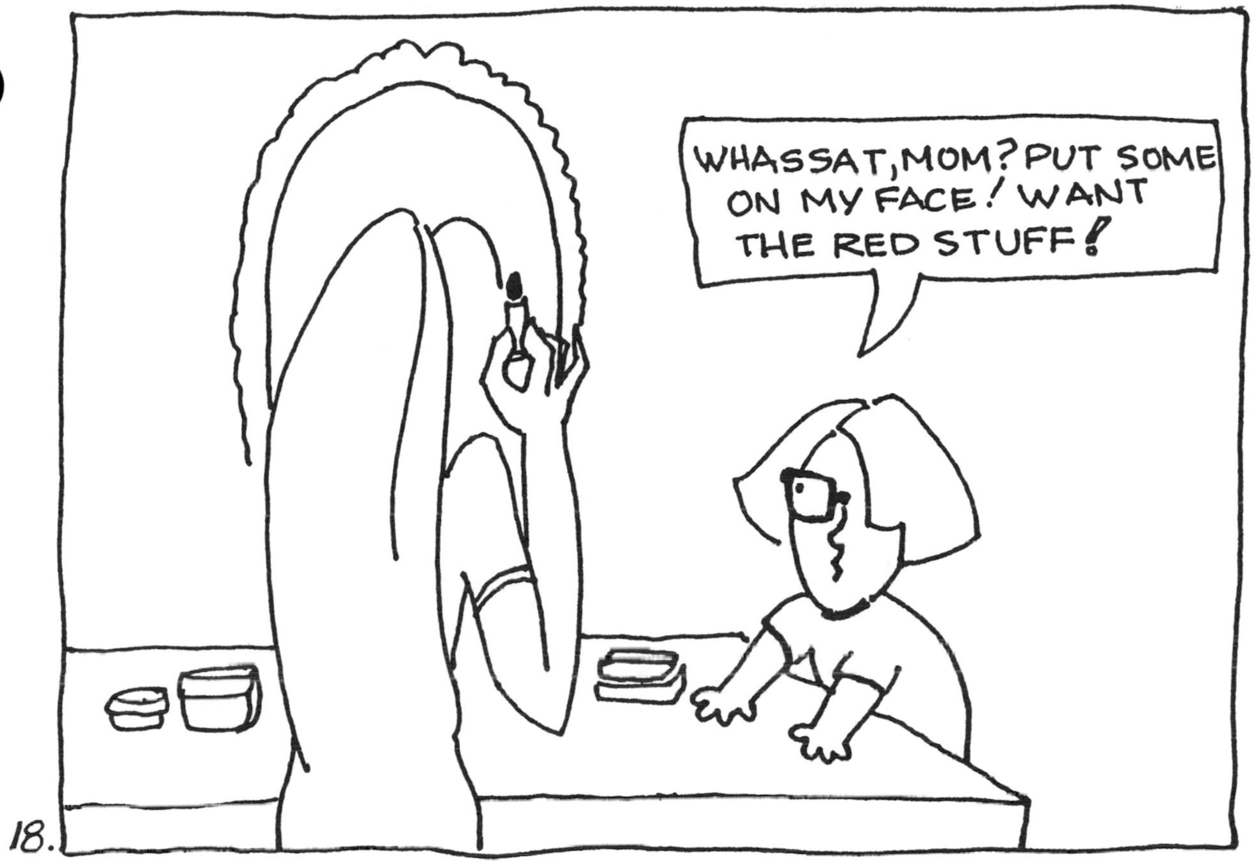
WHASSAT, MOM? PUT SOME ON MY FACE! WANT THE RED STUFF!
18.

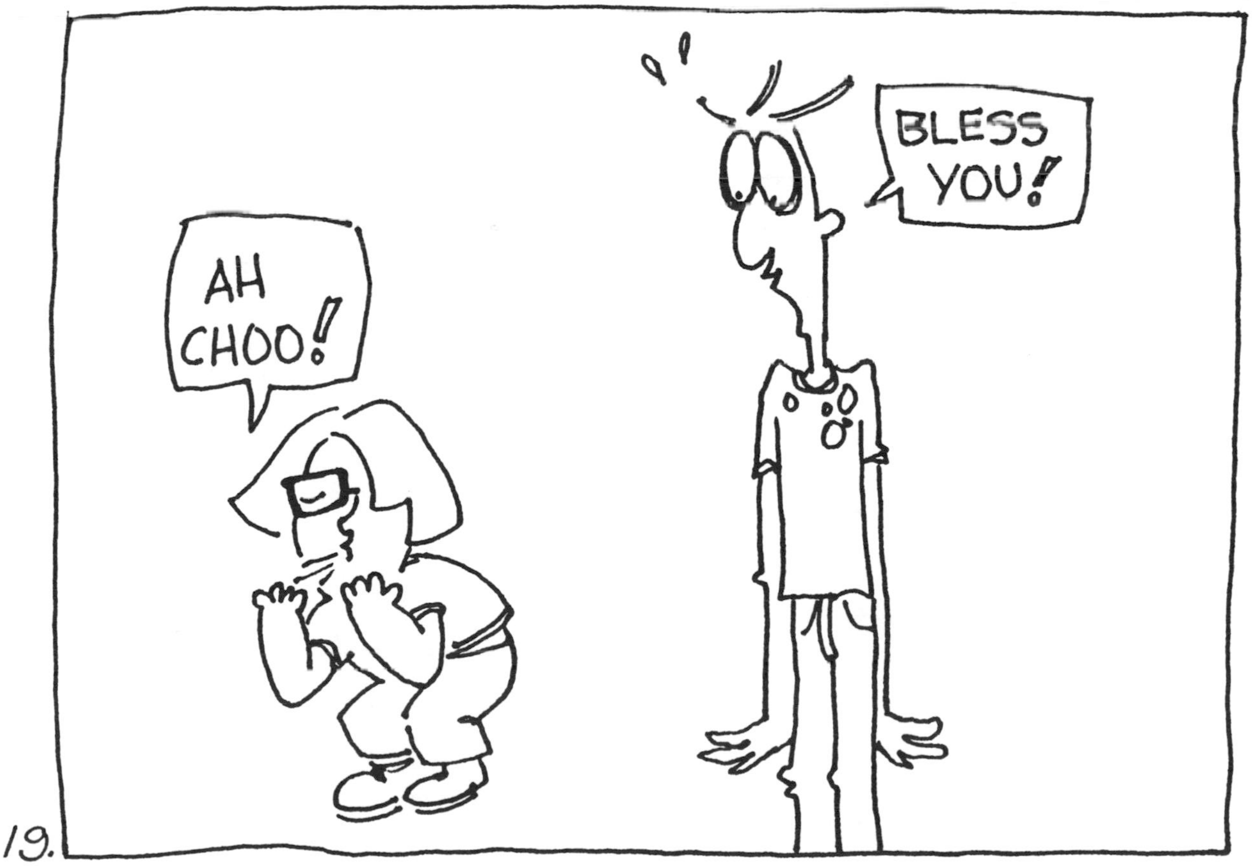
AH CHOO!
BLESS YOU!
19.

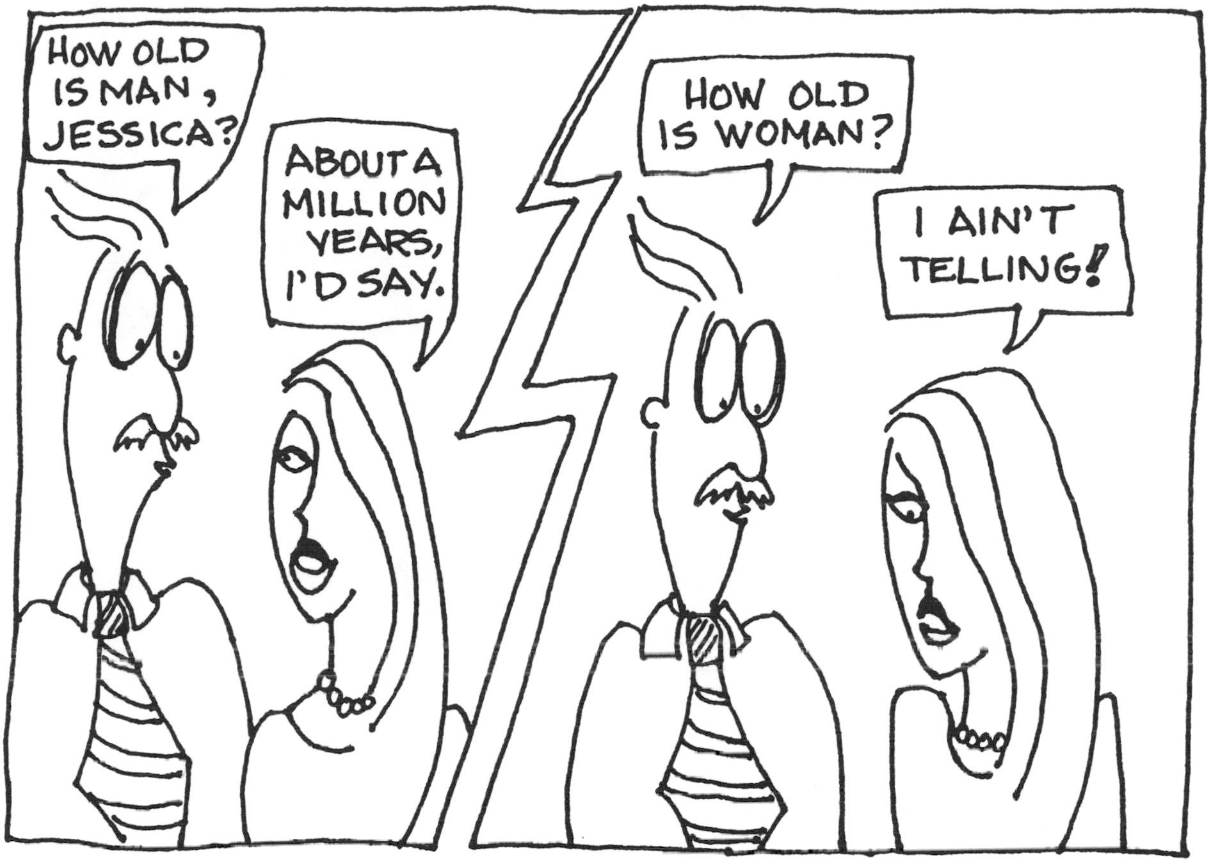
HOW OLD IS MAN, JESSICA?
ABOUT A MILLION YEARS, I'D SAY.
HOW OLD IS WOMAN?
I AIN'T TELLING!

20.

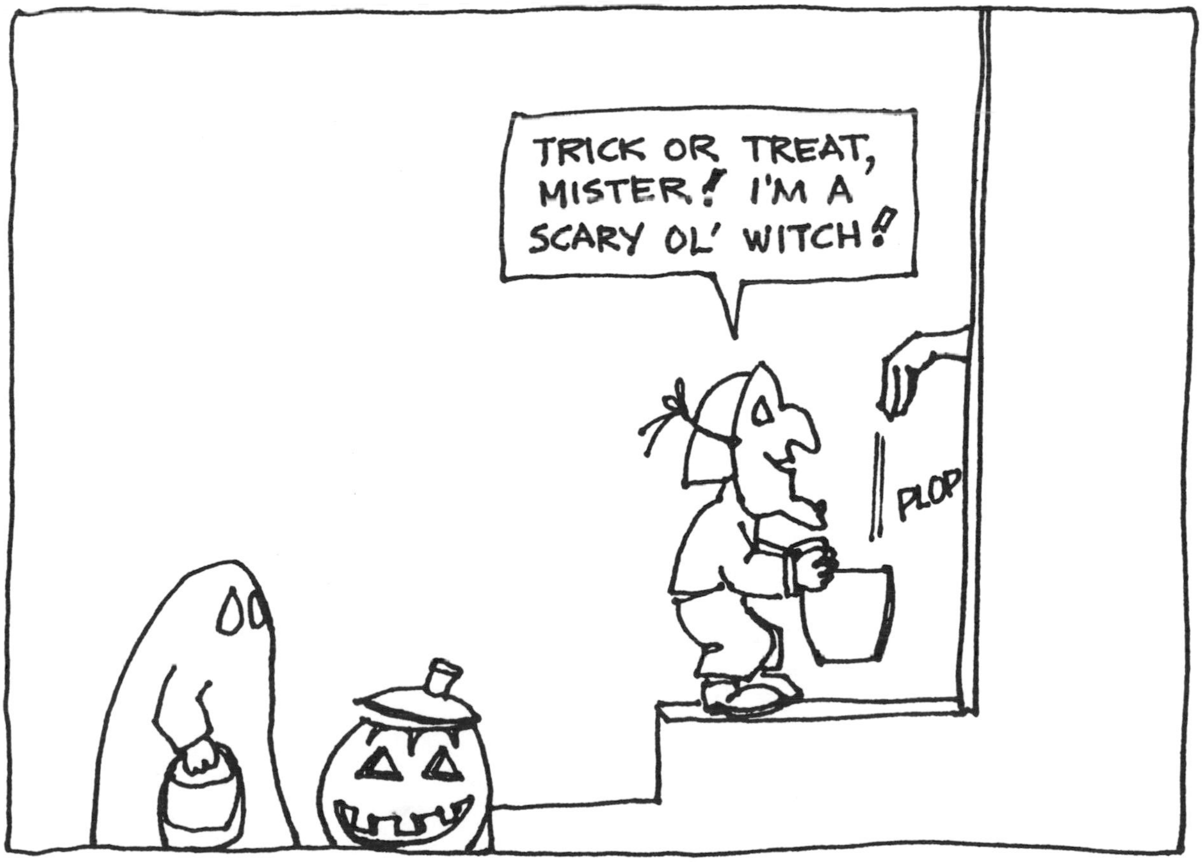
TRICK OR TREAT, MISTER! I'M A SCARY OL' WITCH!
PLOP

21.

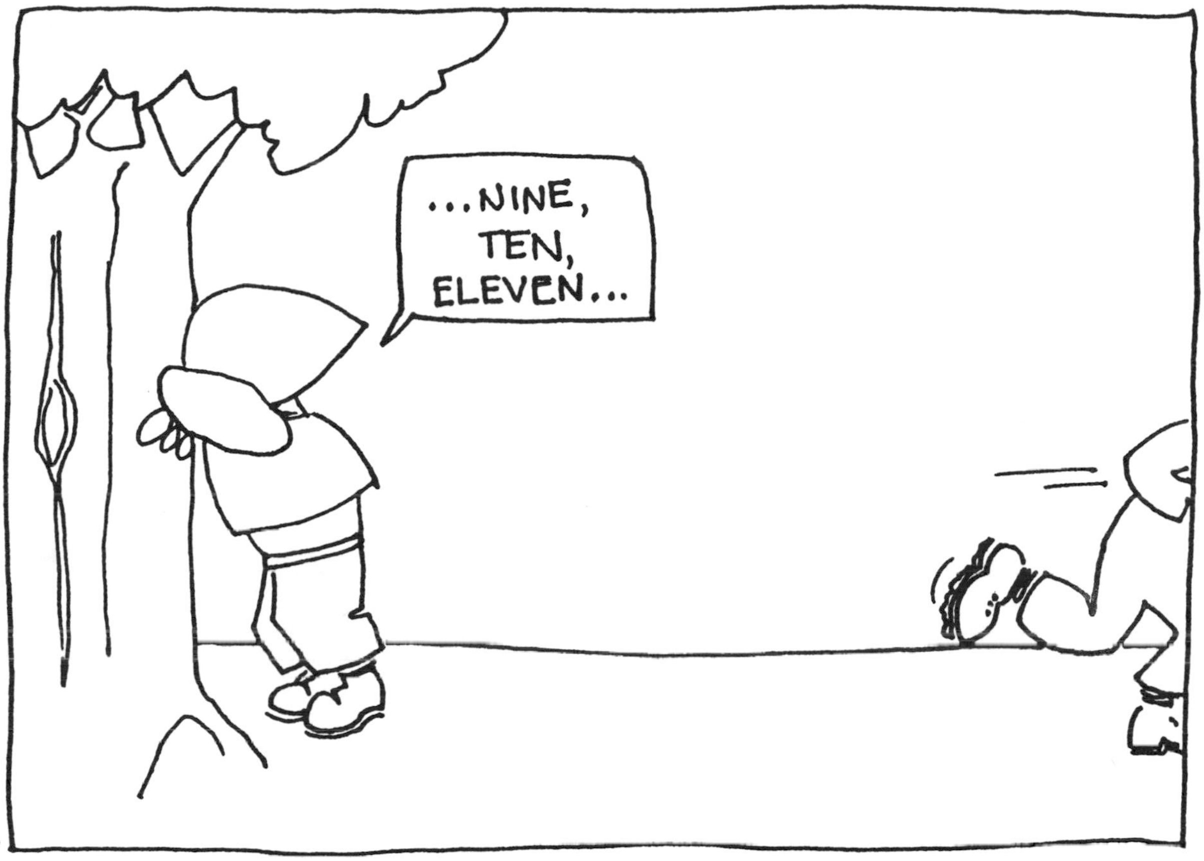
...NINE,
TEN,
ELEVEN...

22.

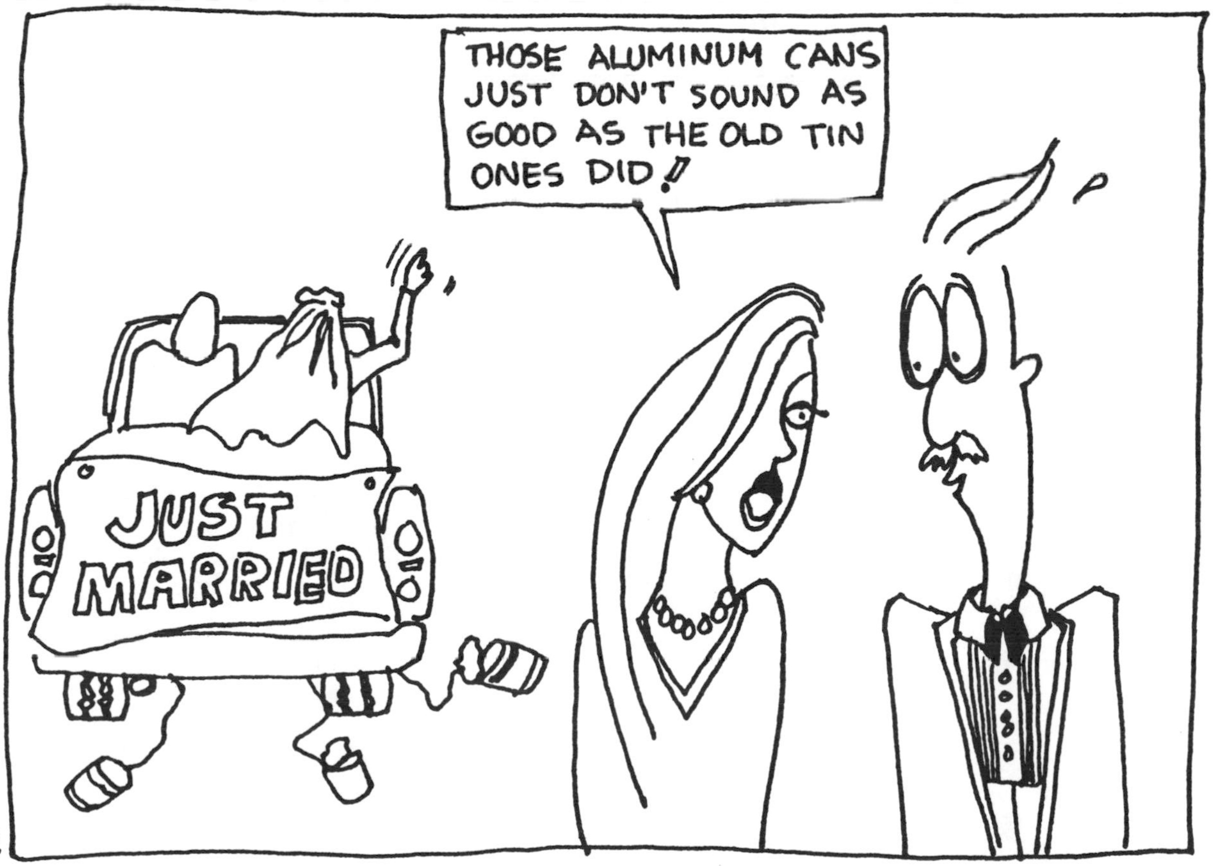
THOSE ALUMINUM CANS JUST DON'T SOUND AS GOOD AS THE OLD TIN ONES DID!
JUST MARRIED

23.

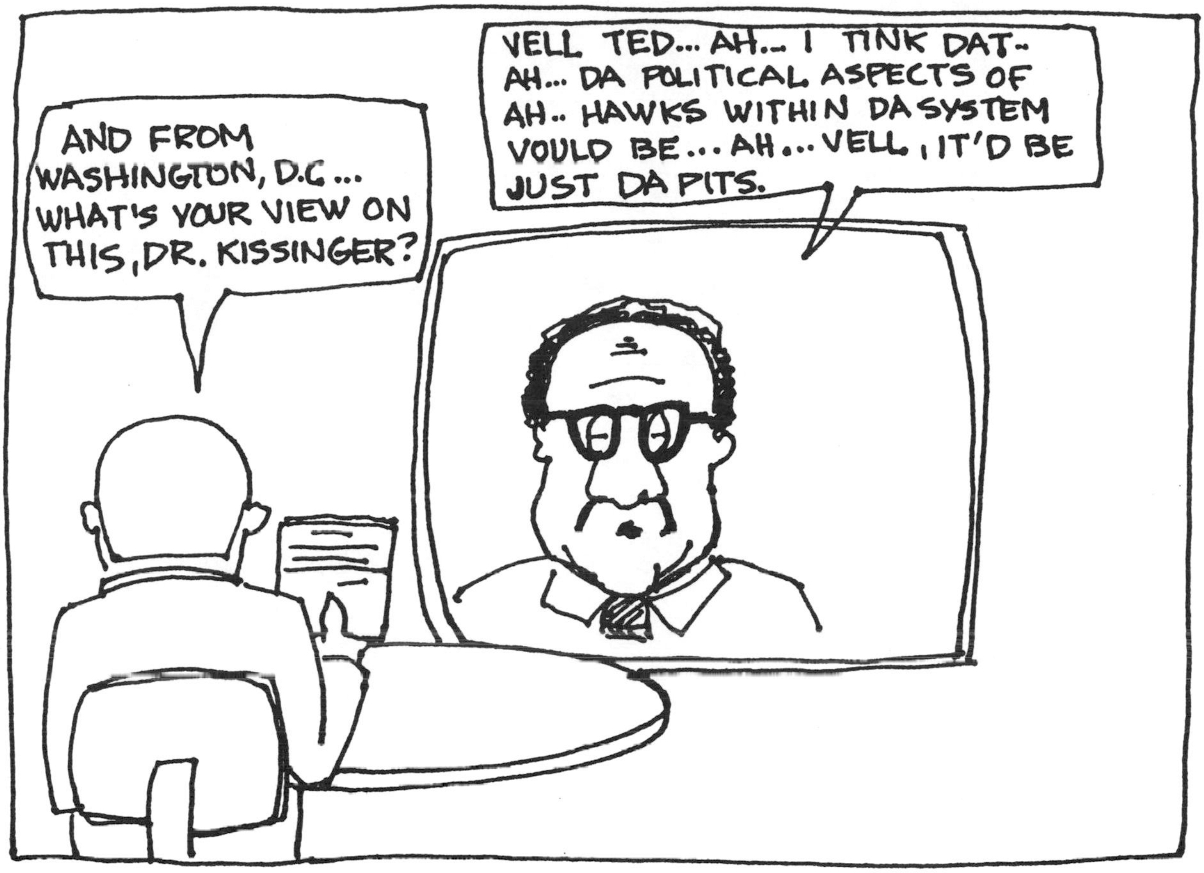
AND FROM WASHINGTON, D.C... WHAT'S YOUR VIEW ON THIS, DR. KISSINGER?
VELL TED... AH... I TINK DAT- AH... DA POLITICAL ASPECTS OF AH.. HAWKS WITHIN DA SYSTEM VOULD BE... AH... VELL, IT'D BE JUST DA PITS.

24.

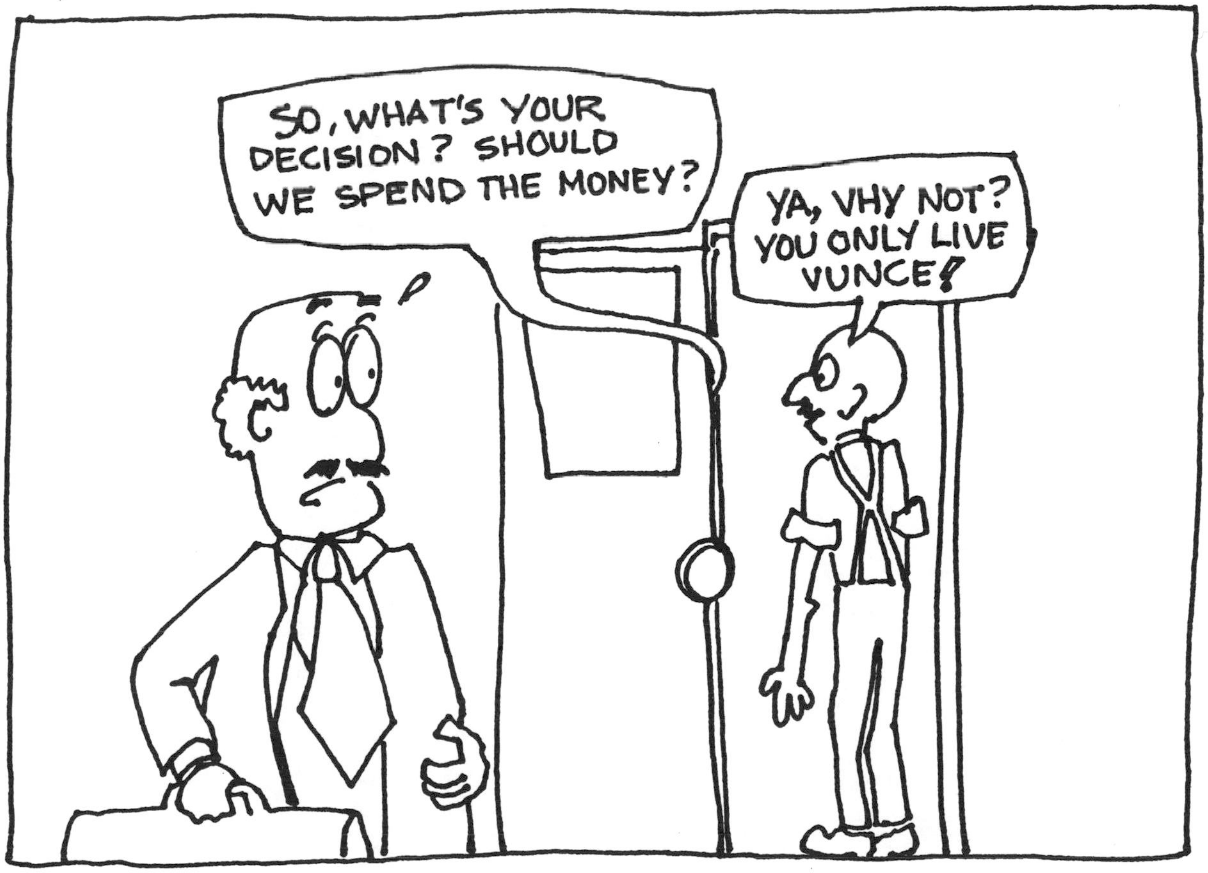
SO, WHAT'S YOUR DECISION? SHOULD WE SPEND THE MONEY?
YA, VHY NOT? YOU ONLY LIVE VUNCE!

25.

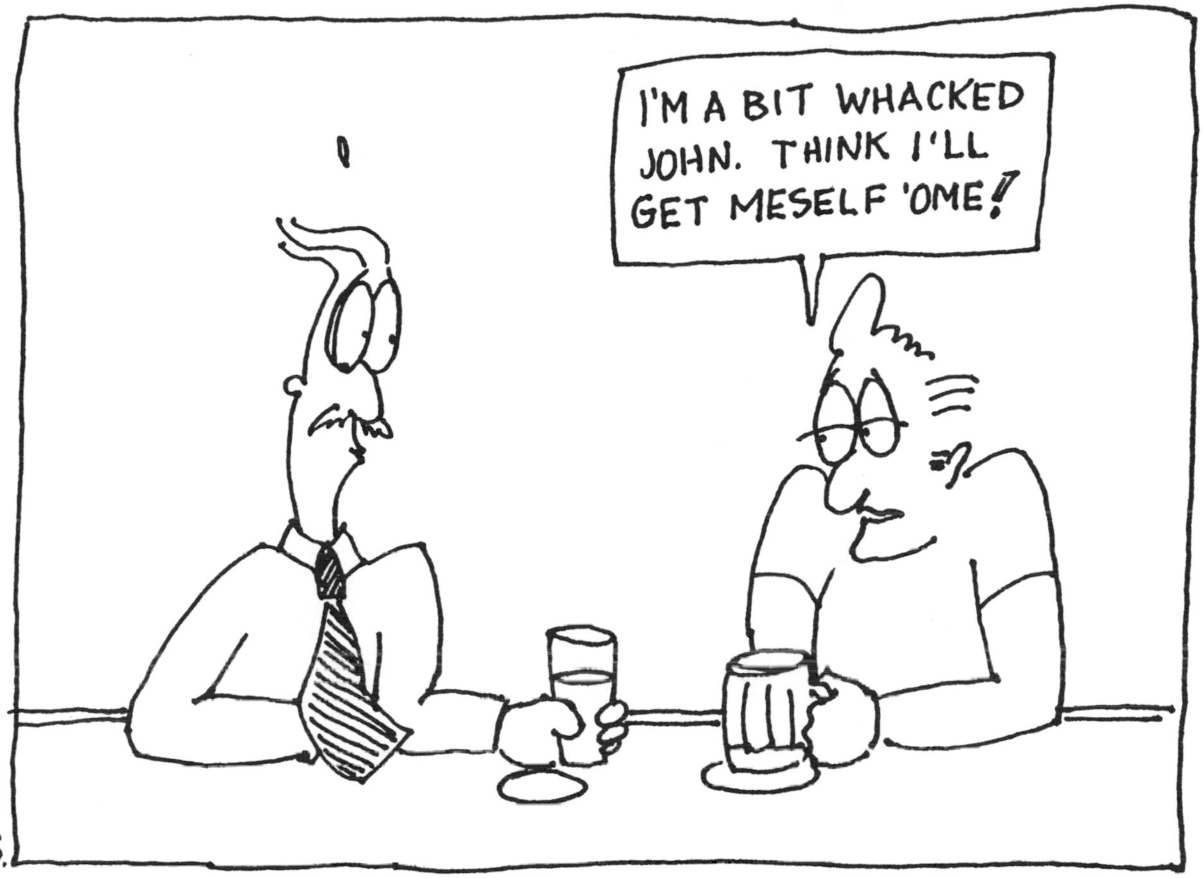
I'M A BIT WHACKED JOHN. THINK I'LL GET MESELF 'OME!

26.

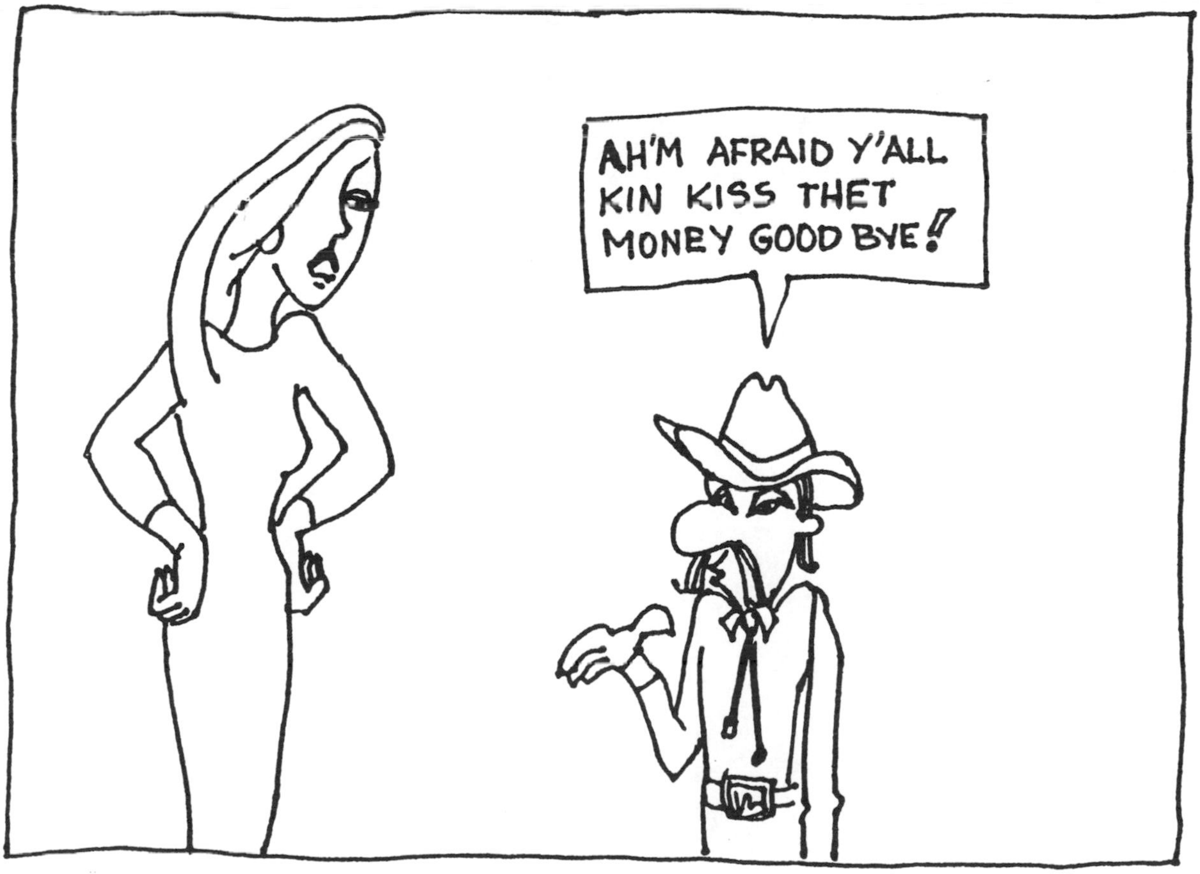
AH'M AFRAID Y'ALL KIN KISS THET MONEY GOOD BYE!

27.

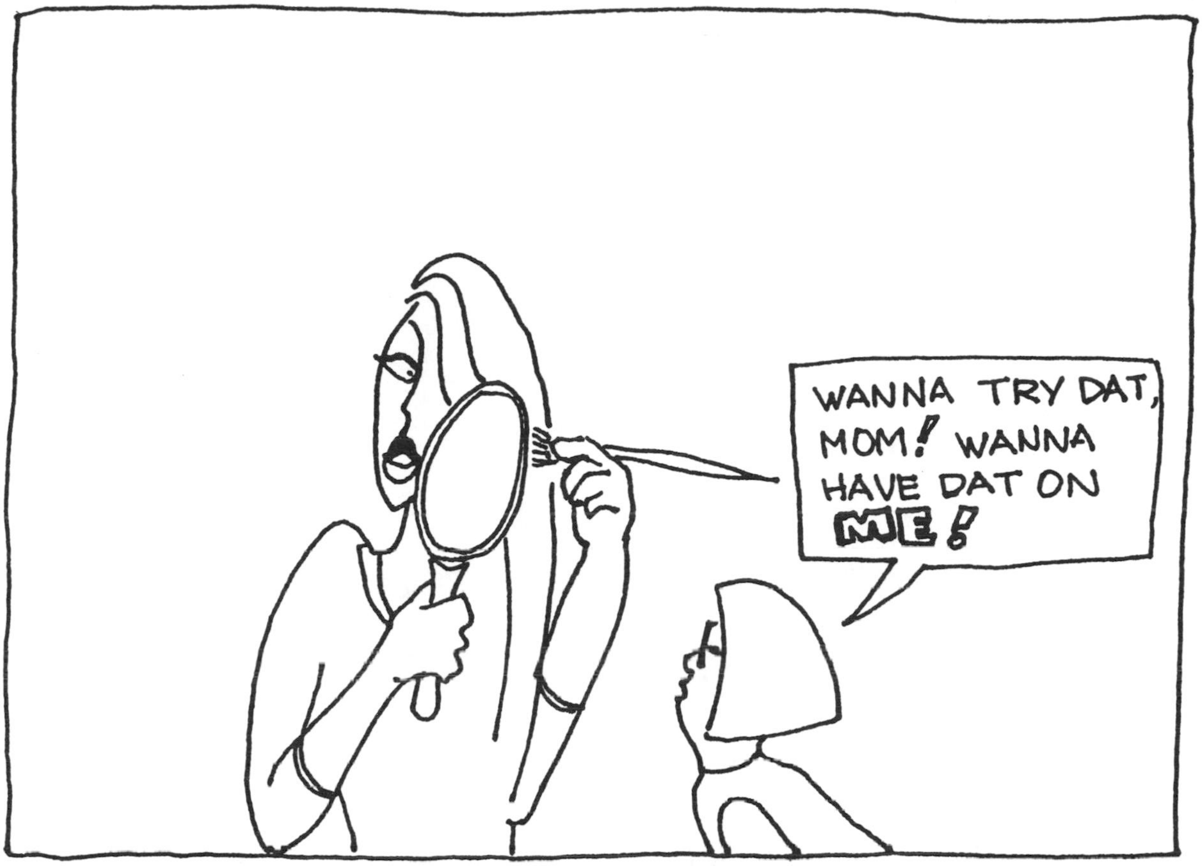
WANNA TRY DAT, MOM! WANNA HAVE DAT ON ME!

28.

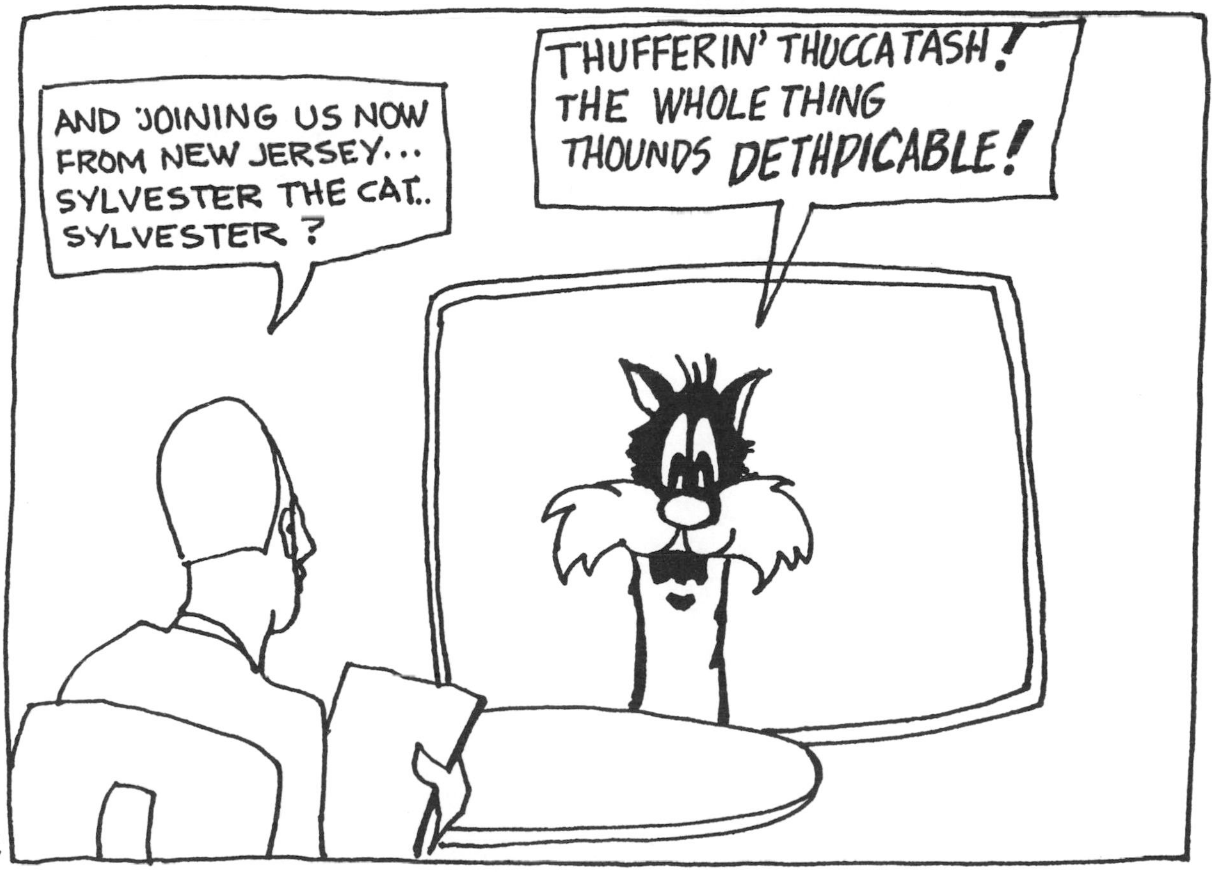
AND JOINING US NOW FROM NEW JERSEY... SYLVESTER THE CAT.. SYLVESTER?
THUFFERIN' THUCCATASH! THE WHOLE THING THOUNDS DETHPICABLE!

29.

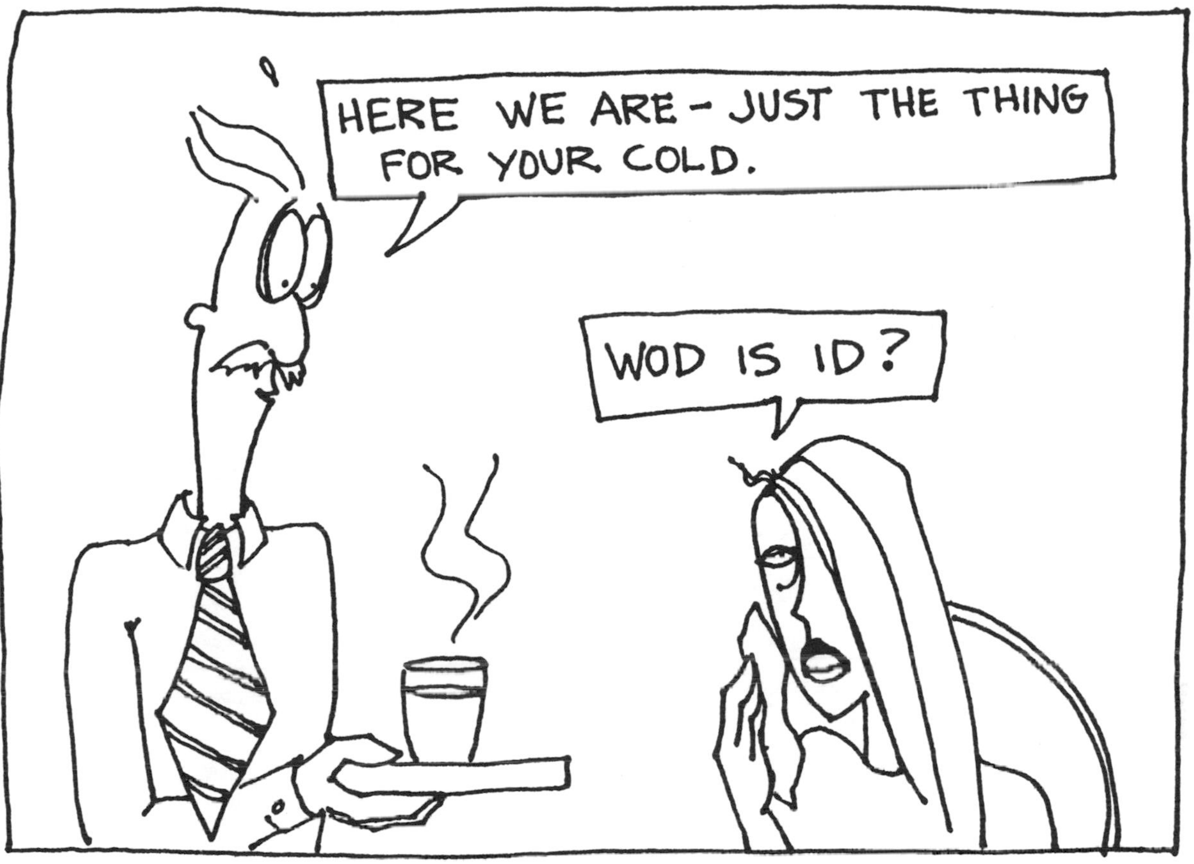
HERE WE ARE - JUST THE THING FOR YOUR COLD.
WOD IS ID?

30.

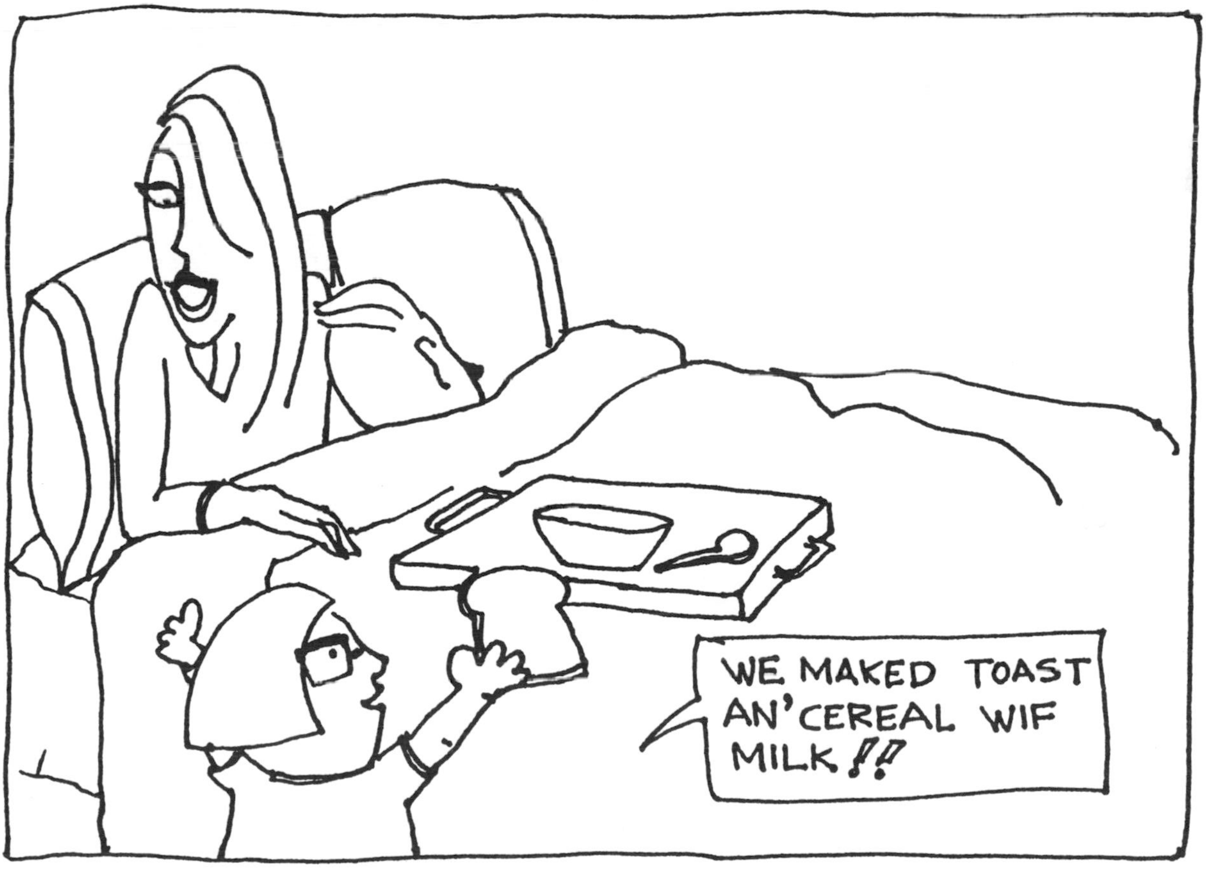
WE MAKED TOAST AN'CEREAL WIF MILK!!!

31.

32.

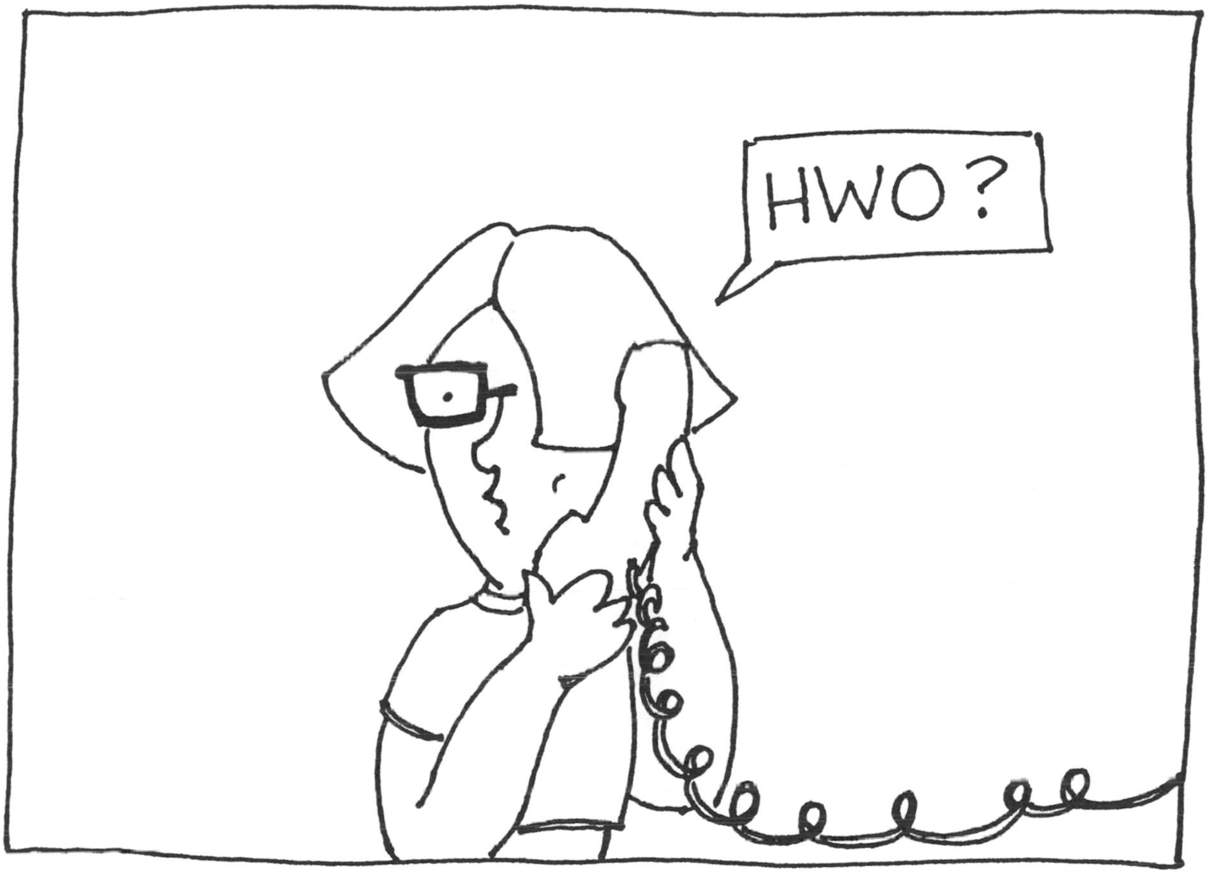
HWO?

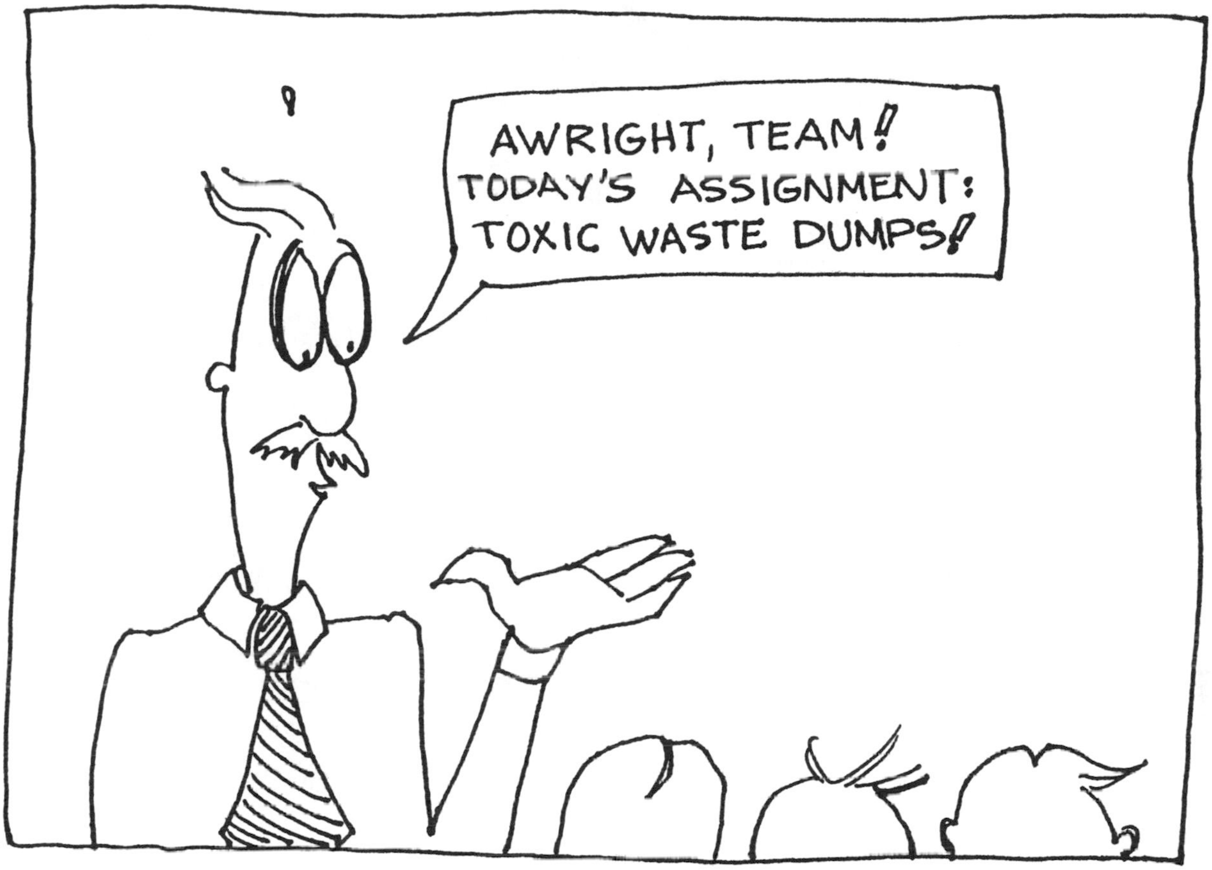
AWRIGHT, TEAM! TODAY'S ASSIGNMENT: TOXIC WASTE DUMPS!

33.

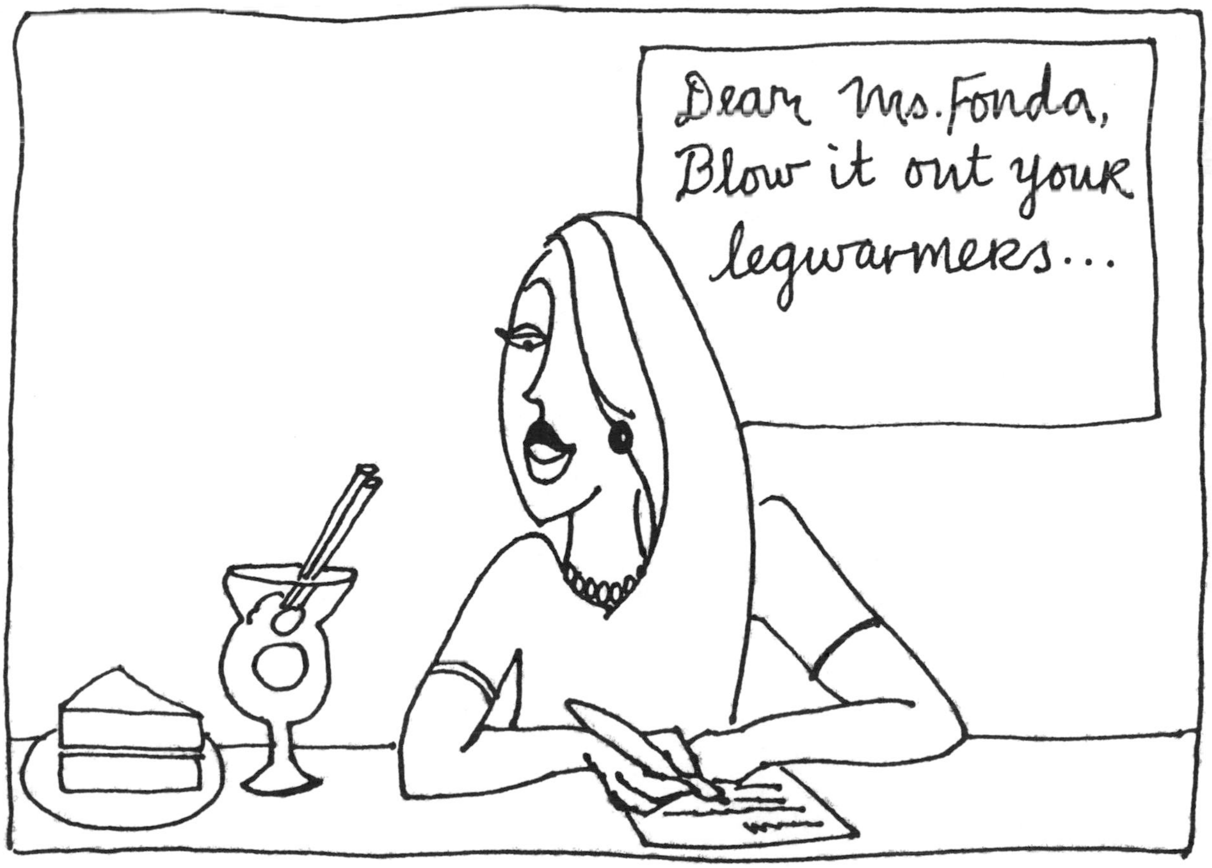
Dear Ms. Fonda, Blow it out your legwarmers...

34.

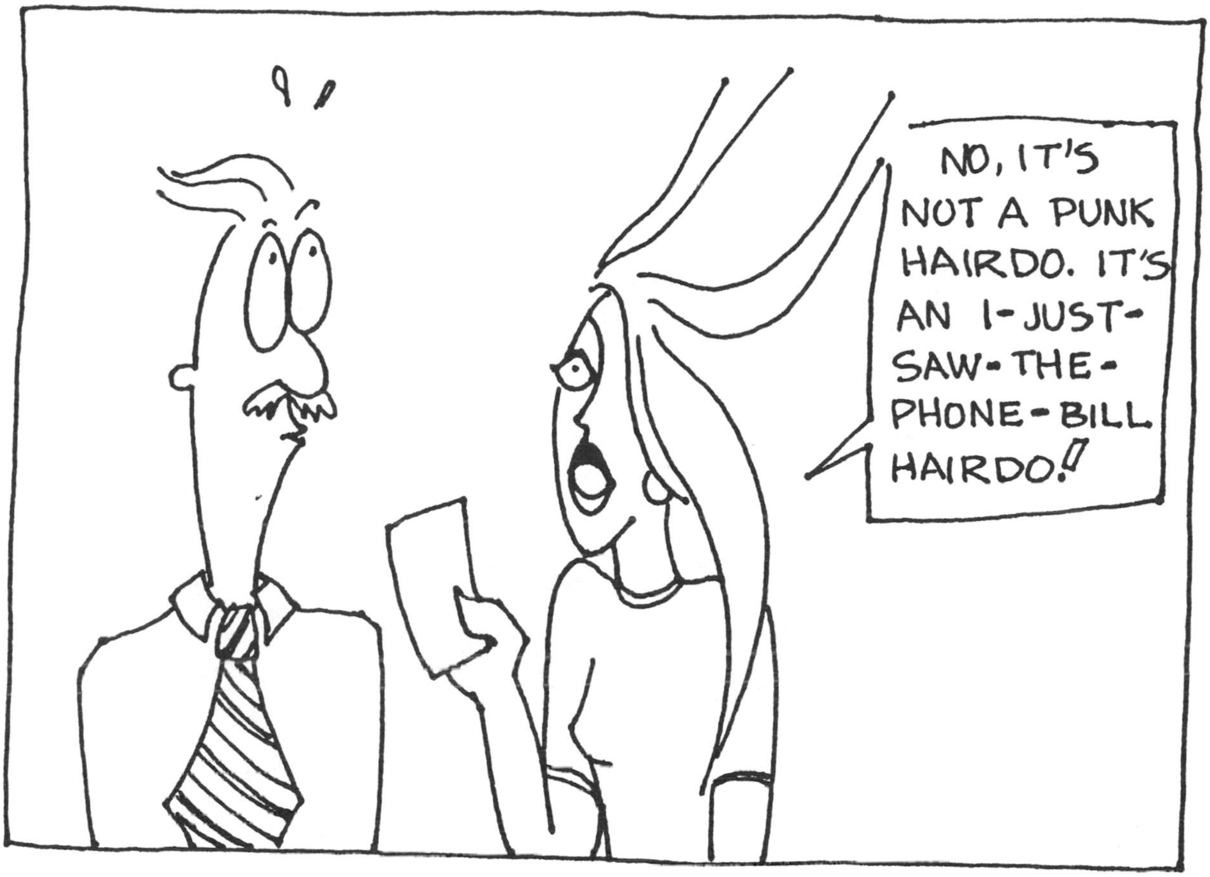
NO, IT'S NOT A PUNK HAIRDO. IT'S AN I-JUST-SAW-THE-PHONE-BILL HAIRDO!

35.

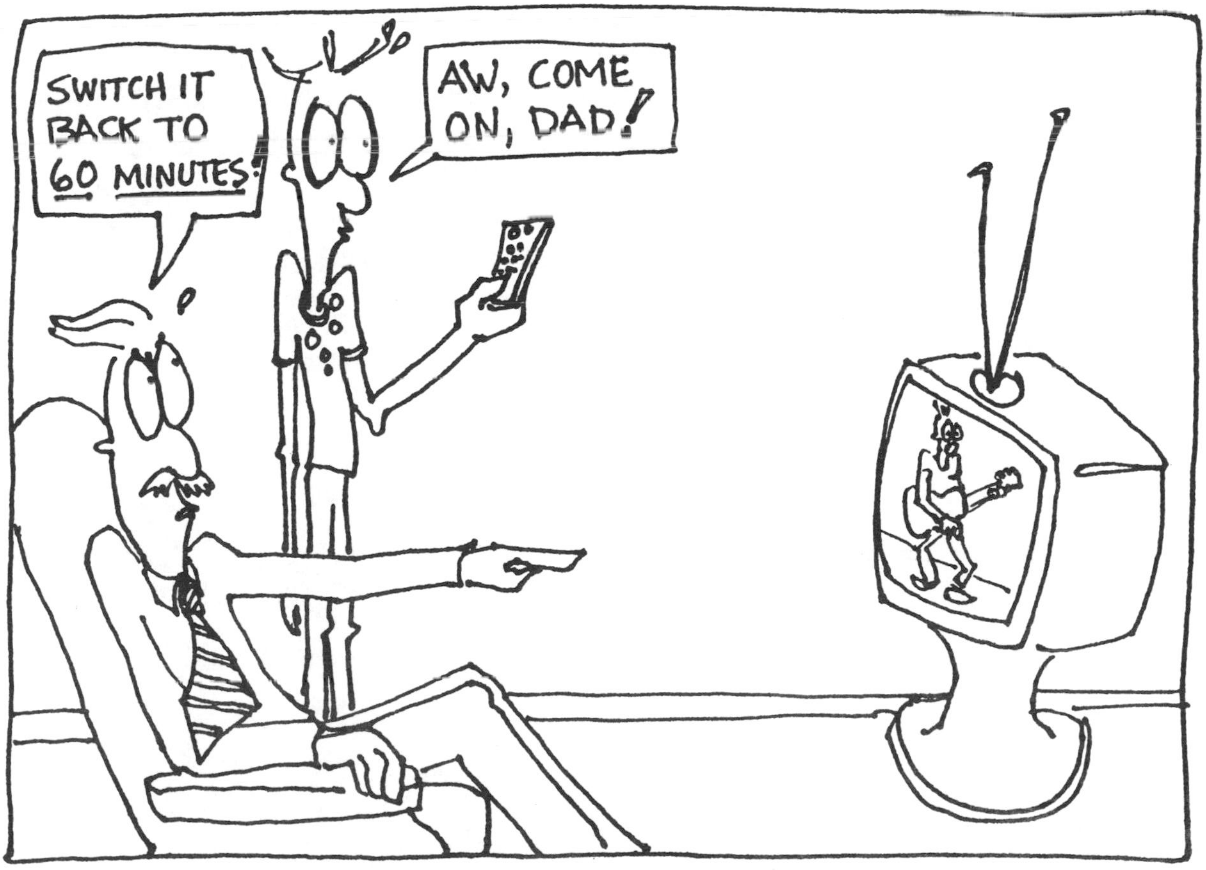
SWITCH IT BACK TO 60 MINUTES!
AW, COME ON, DAD!

36.

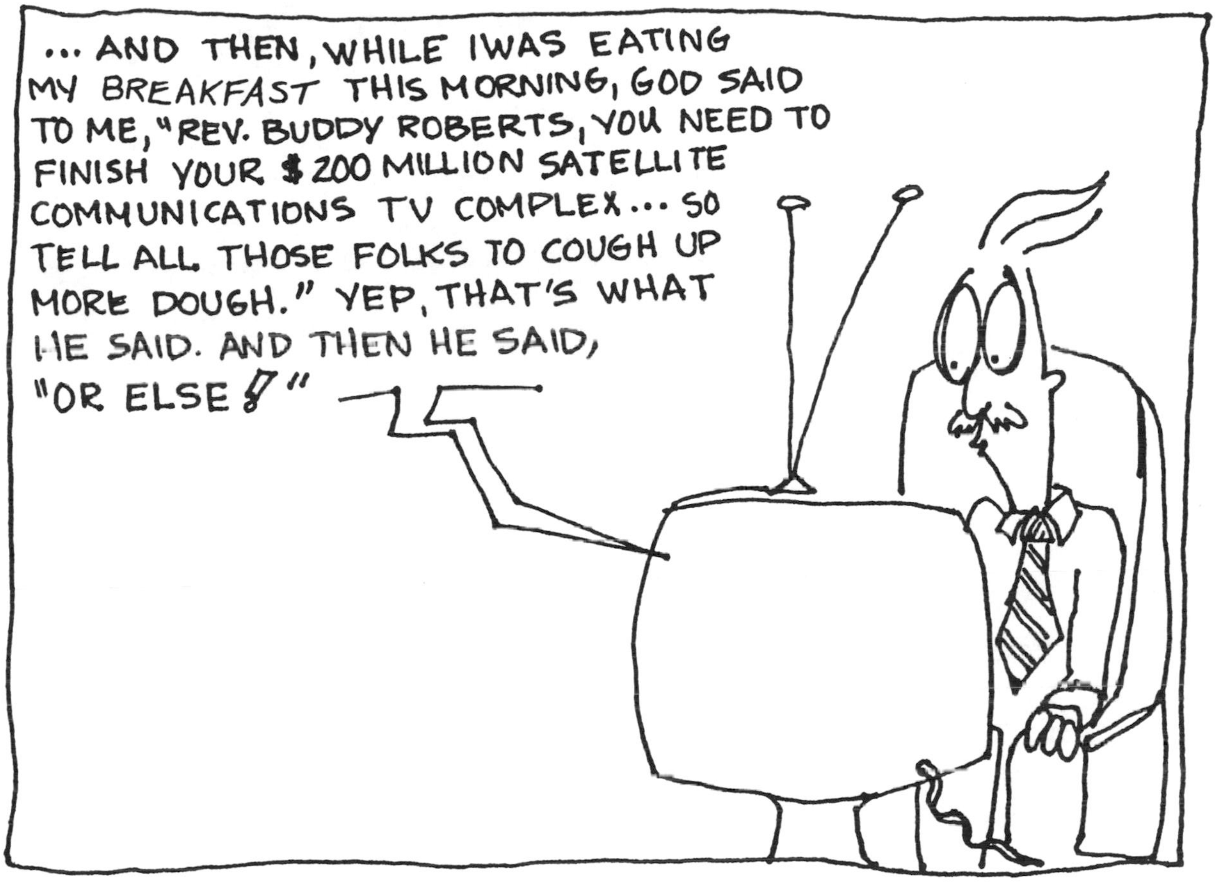
... AND THEN, WHILE I WAS EATING MY BREAKFAST THIS MORNING, GOD SAID TO ME, "REV. BUDDY ROBERTS, YOU NEED TO FINISH YOUR $200 MILLION SATELLITE COMMUNICATIONS TV COMPLEX... SO TELL ALL THOSE FOLKS TO COUGH UP MORE DOUGH." YEP, THAT'S WHAT HE SAID. AND THEN HE SAID, "OR ELSE!"

37.

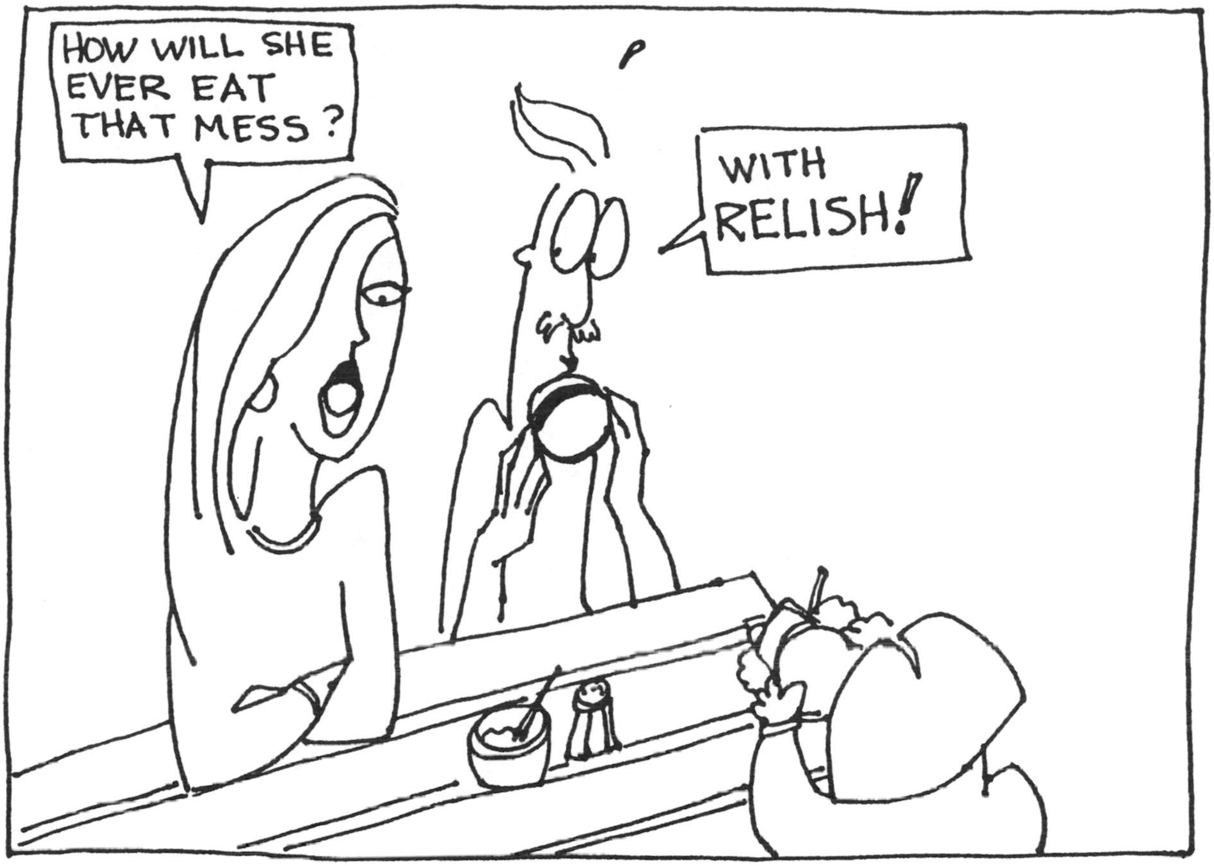
HOW WILL SHE EVER EAT THAT MESS?
WITH RELISH!

38.

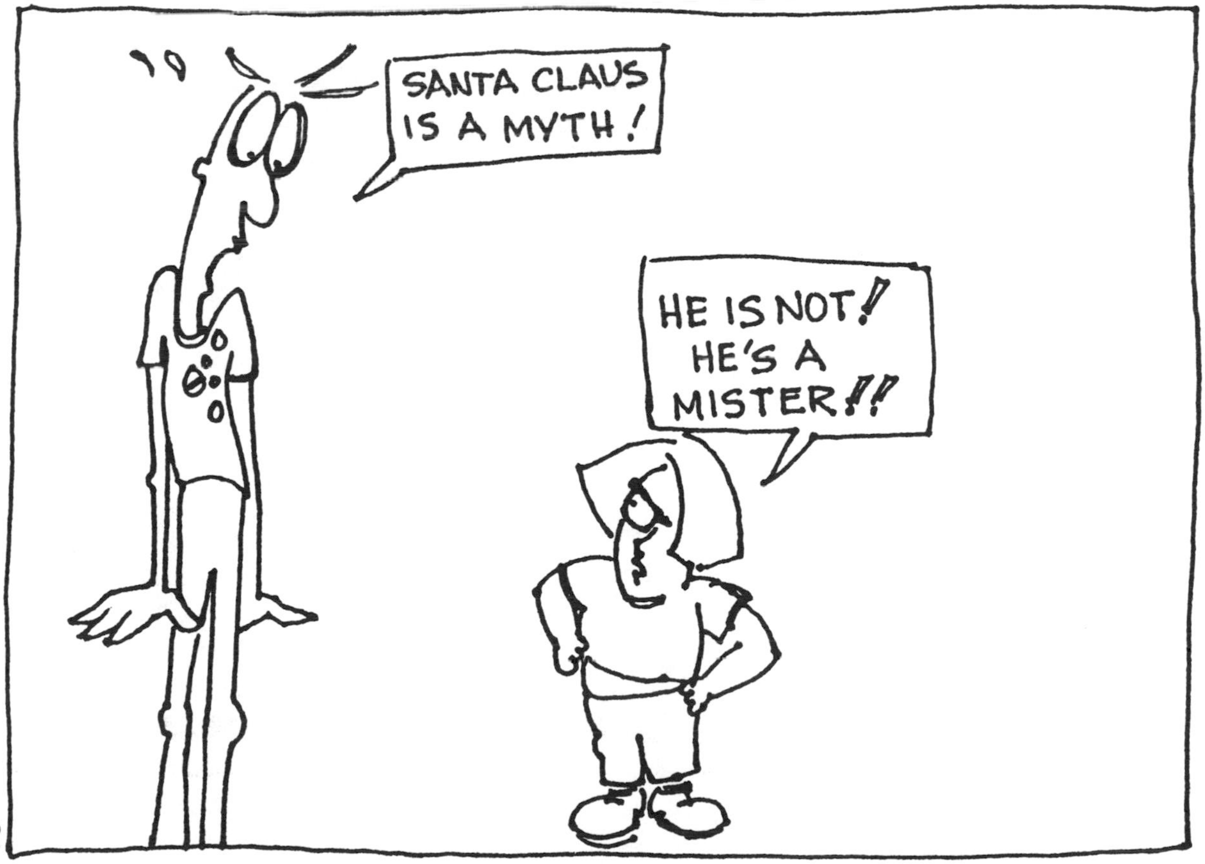
SANTA CLAUS IS A MYTH!
HE IS NOT! HE'S A MISTER!!

39.

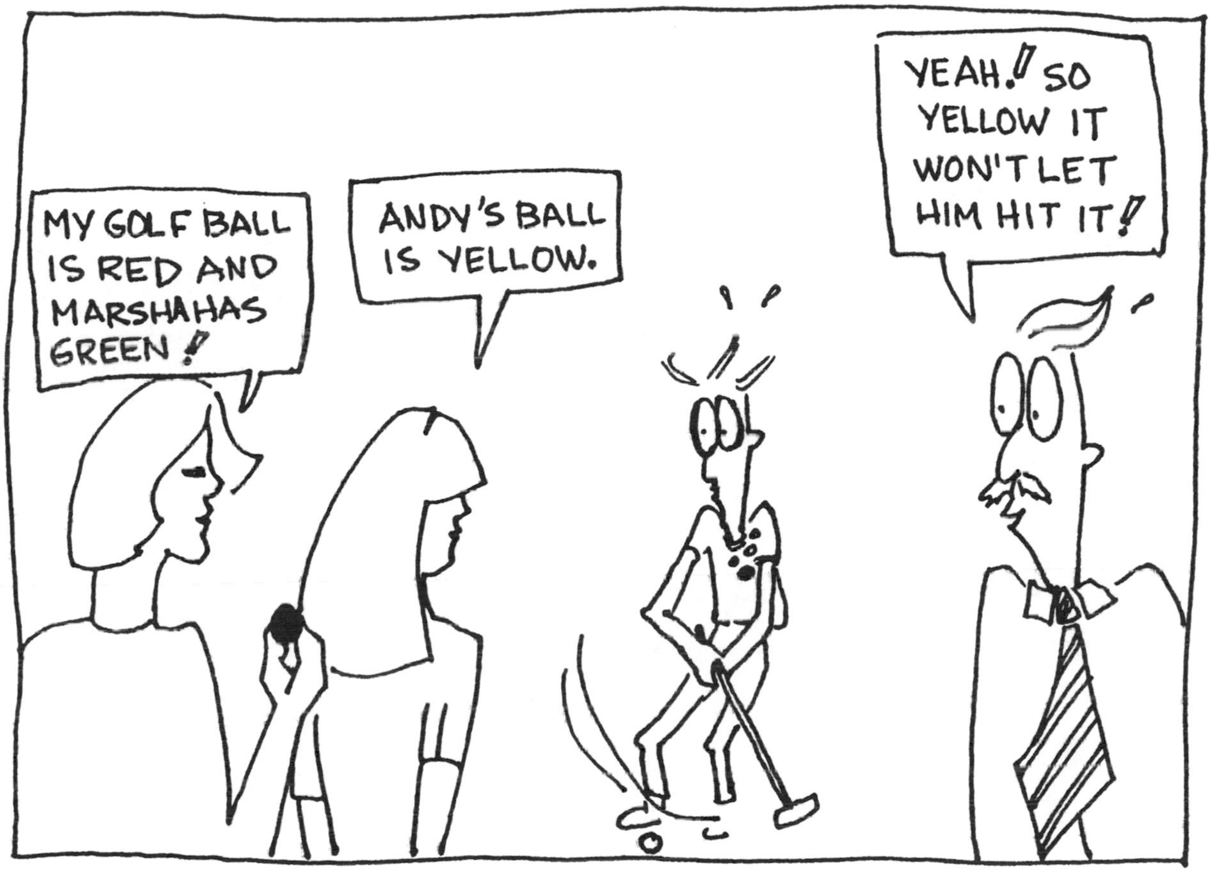
MY GOLF BALL IS RED AND MARSHA HAS GREEN!
ANDY'S BALL IS YELLOW.
YEAH!! SO YELLOW IT WON'T LET HIM HIT IT!!

40.

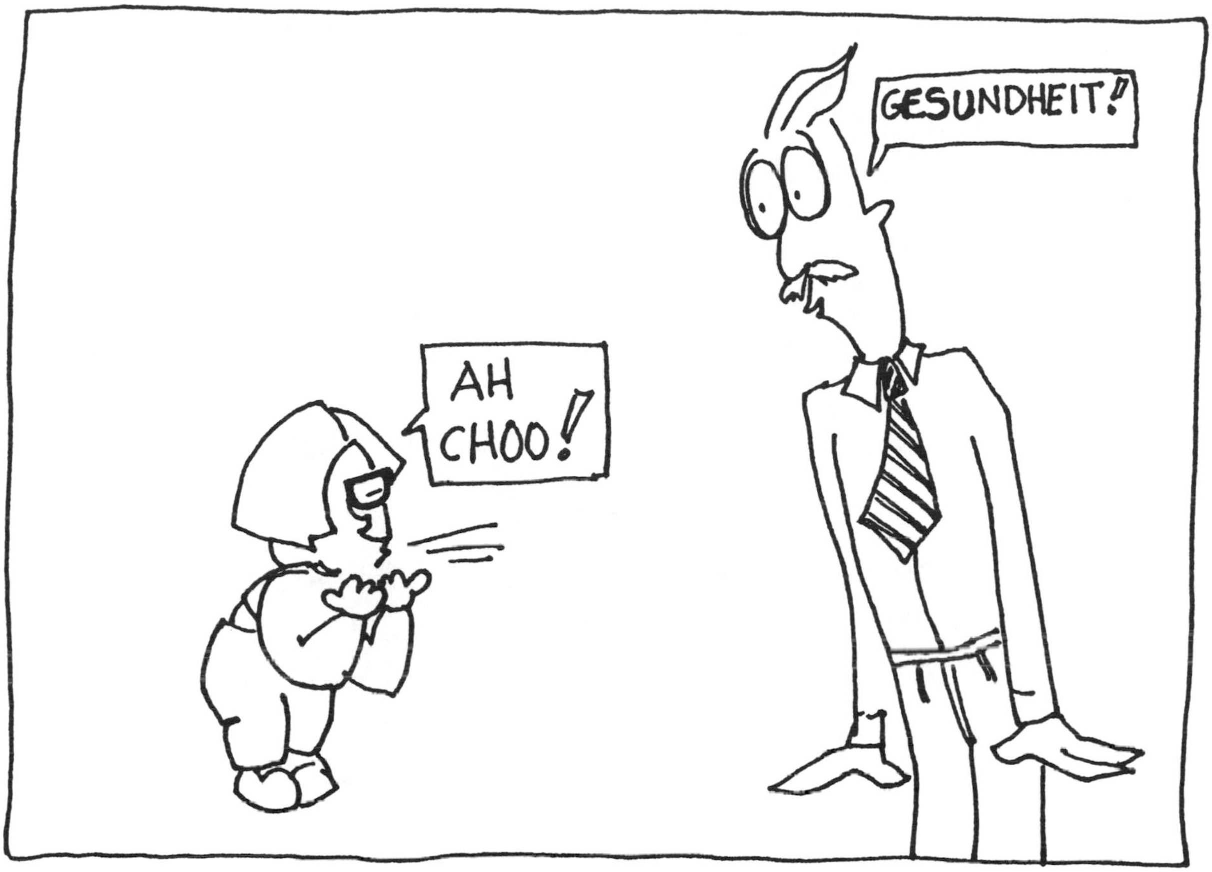
AH CHOO!
GESUNDHEIT!

41.

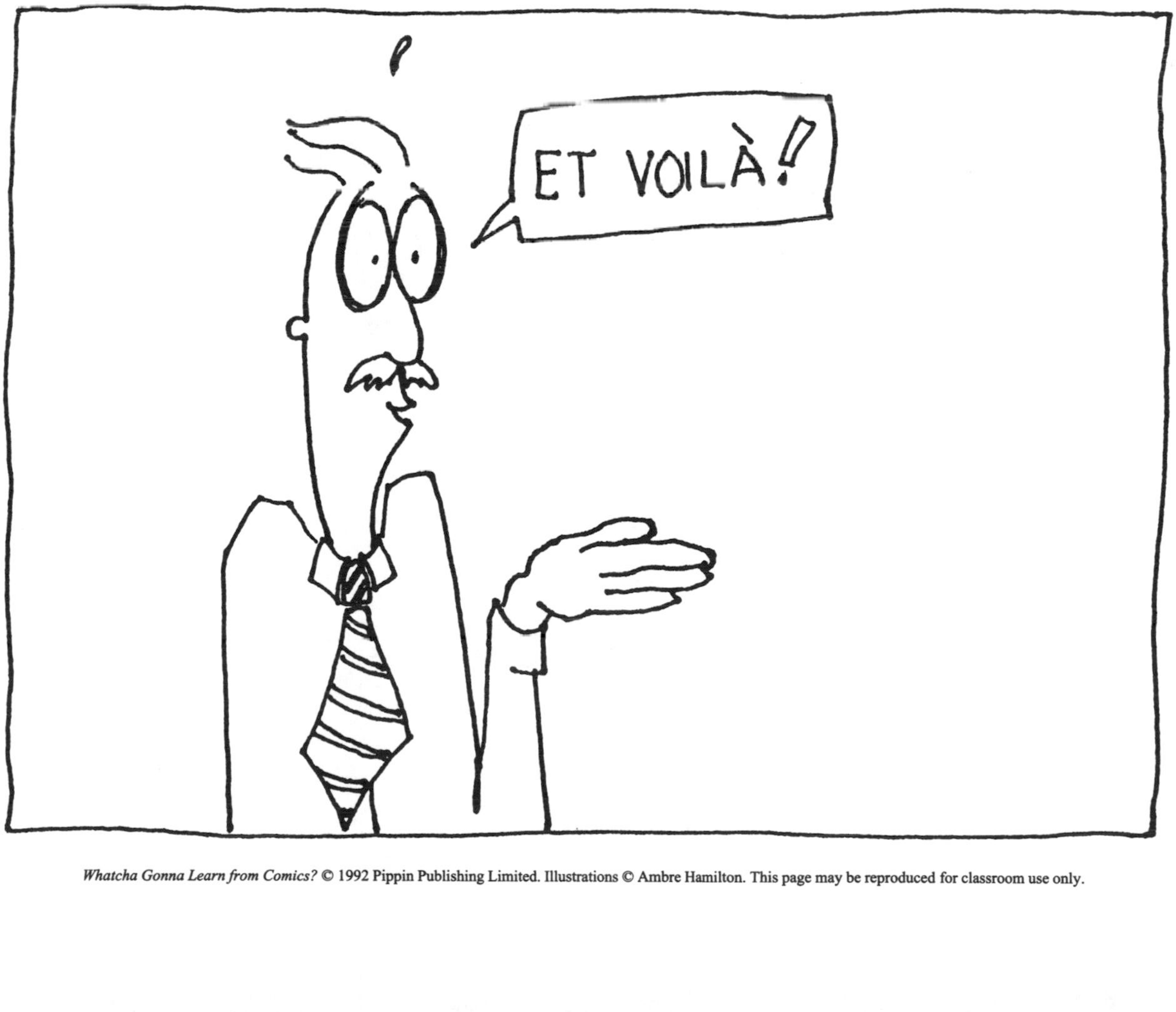
ET VOILÀ!

42.

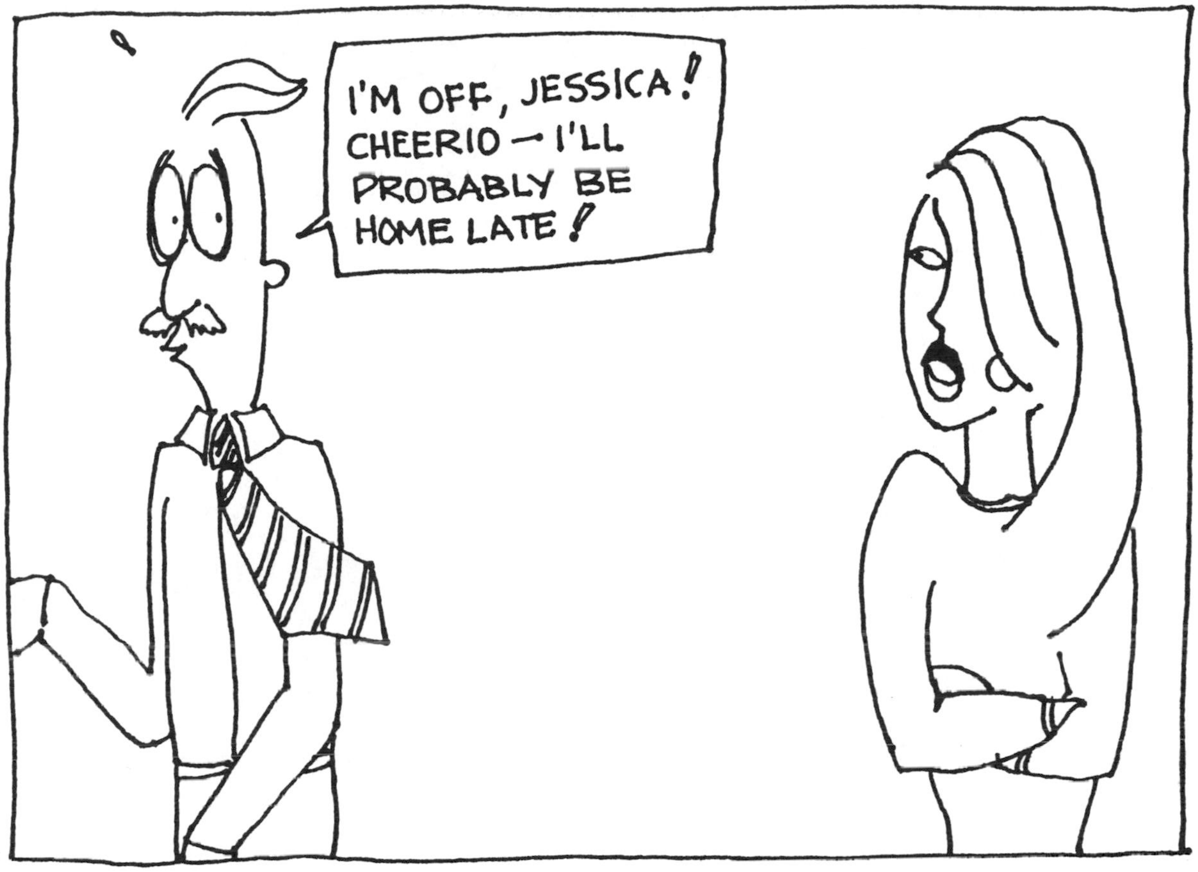
I'M OFF, JESSICA! CHEERIO – I'LL PROBABLY BE HOME LATE!

43.

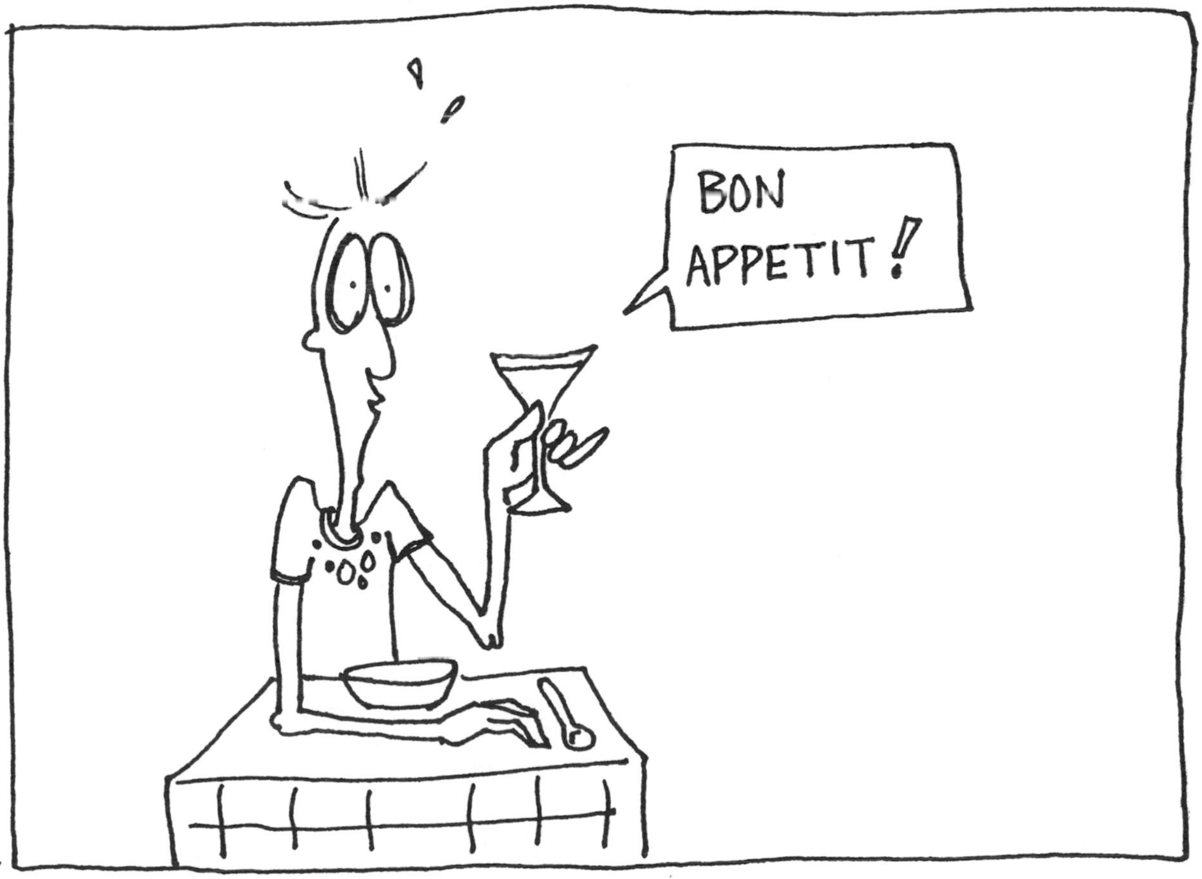
BON APPETIT!

44.

45.

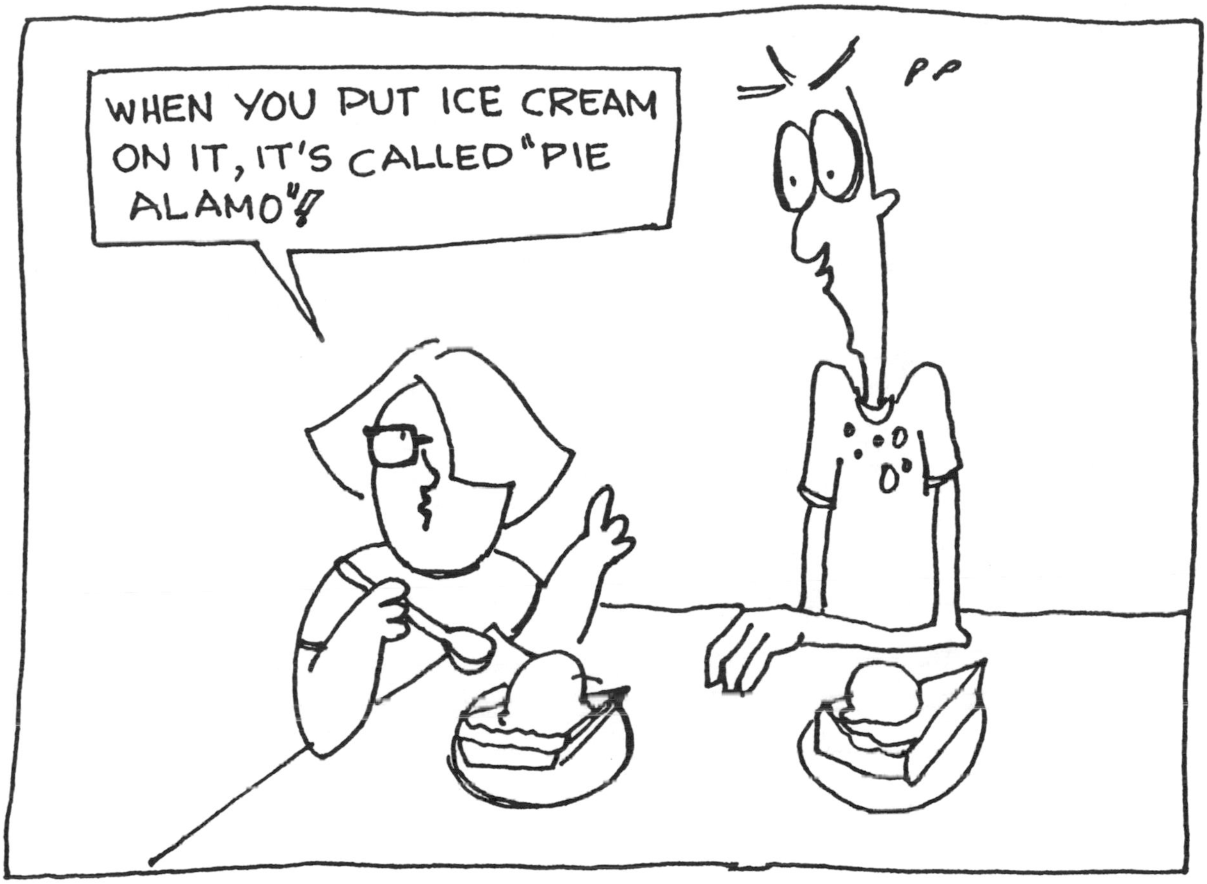

WHEN YOU PUT ICE CREAM ON IT, IT'S CALLED "PIE ALAMO"!

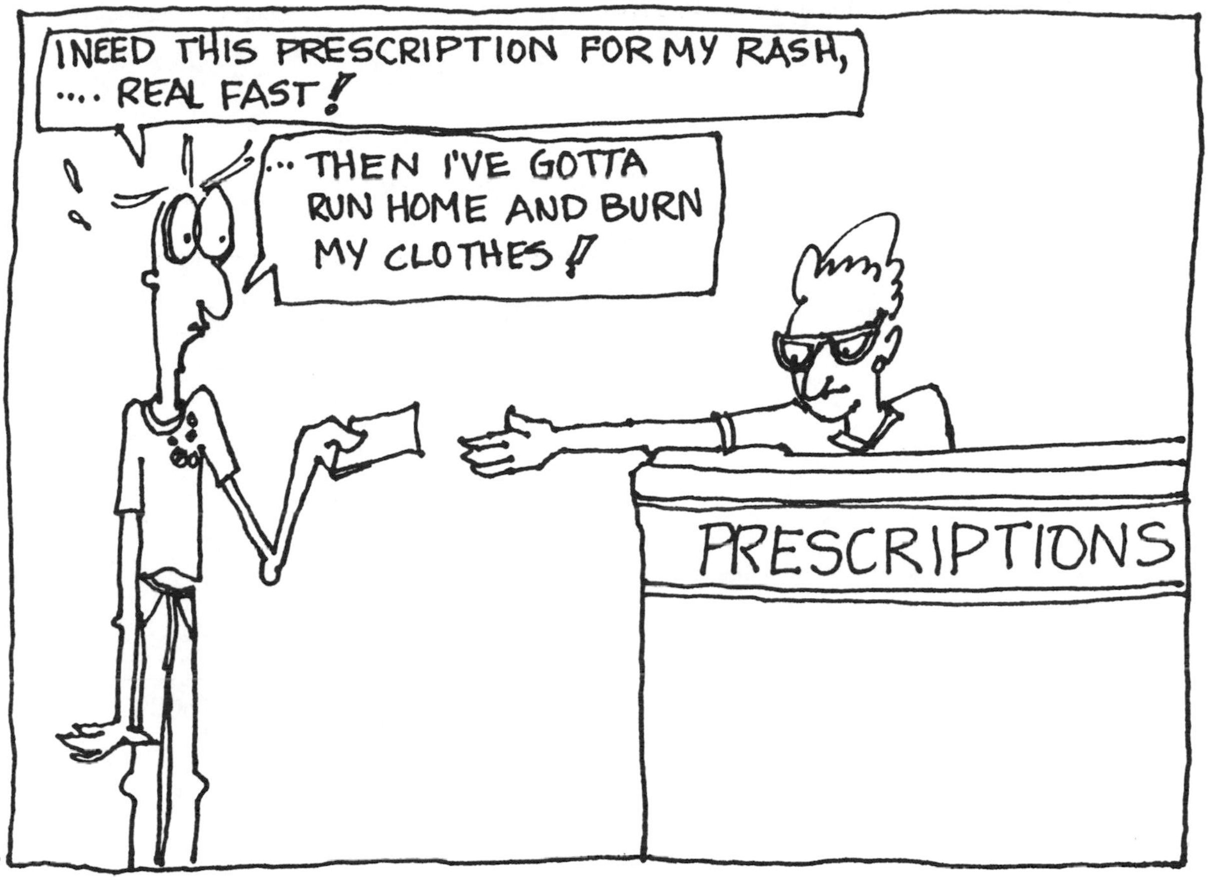
I NEED THIS PRESCRIPTION FOR MY RASH, ... REAL FAST!
... THEN I'VE GOTTA RUN HOME AND BURN MY CLOTHES!!
PRESCRIPTIONS

46.

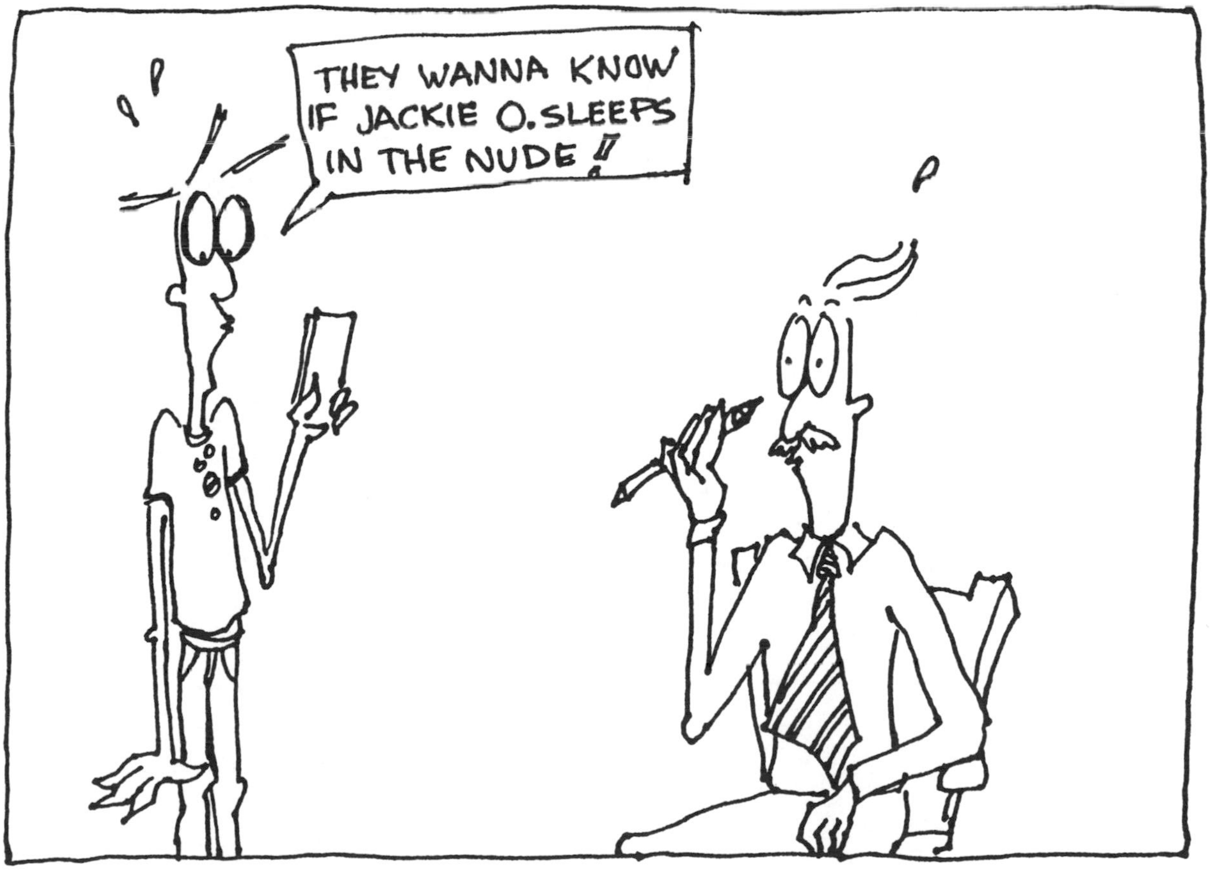
THEY WANNA KNOW IF JACKIE O. SLEEPS IN THE NUDE!!

47.

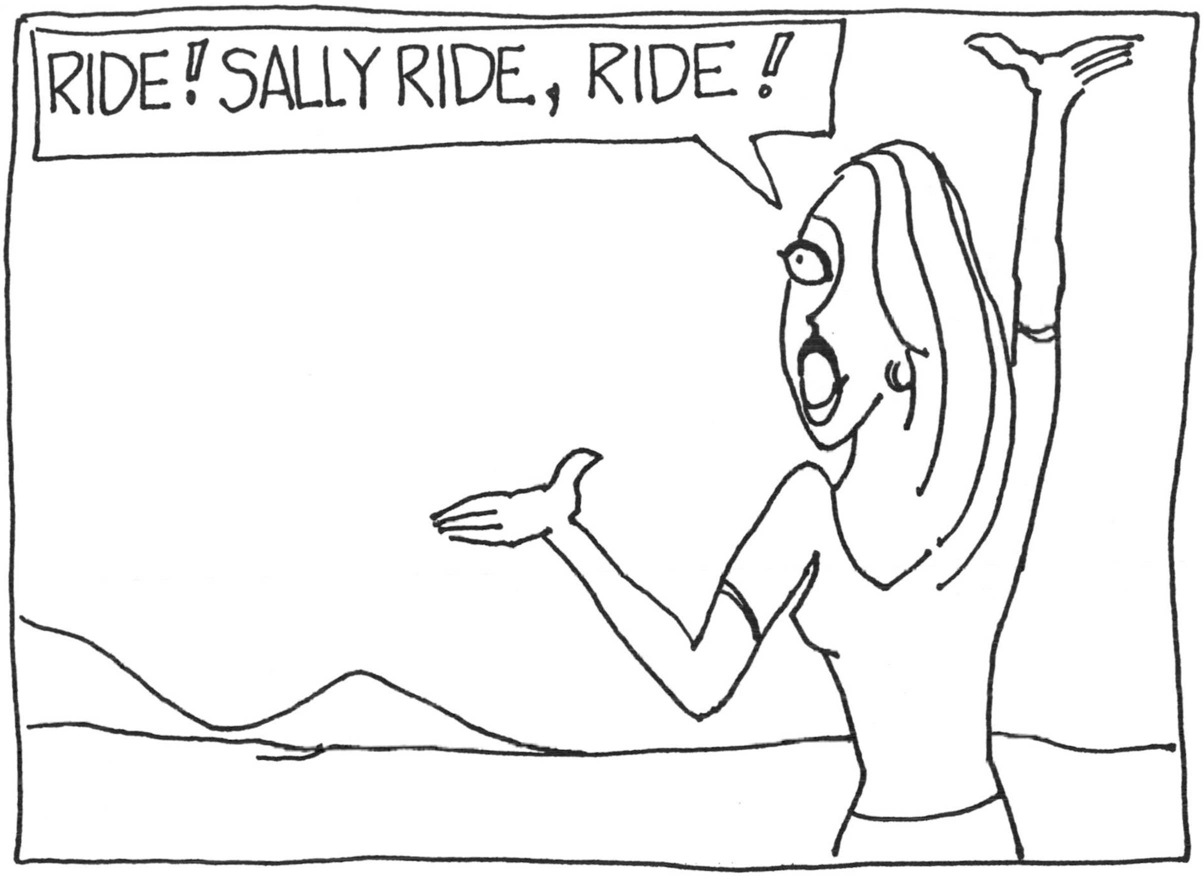
RIDE! SALLY RIDE, RIDE!

48.

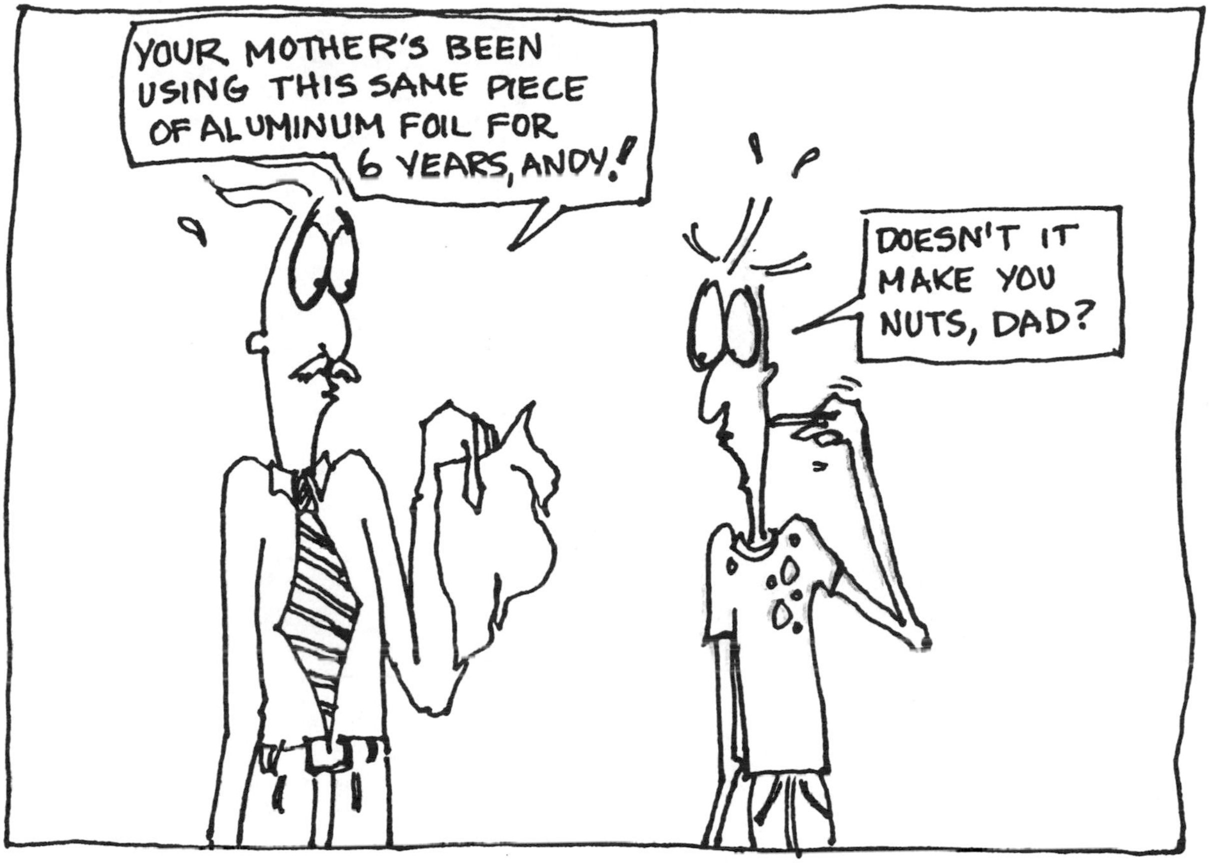
YOUR MOTHER'S BEEN USING THIS SAME PIECE OF ALUMINUM FOIL FOR 6 YEARS, ANDY!
DOESN'T IT MAKE YOU NUTS, DAD?

49.

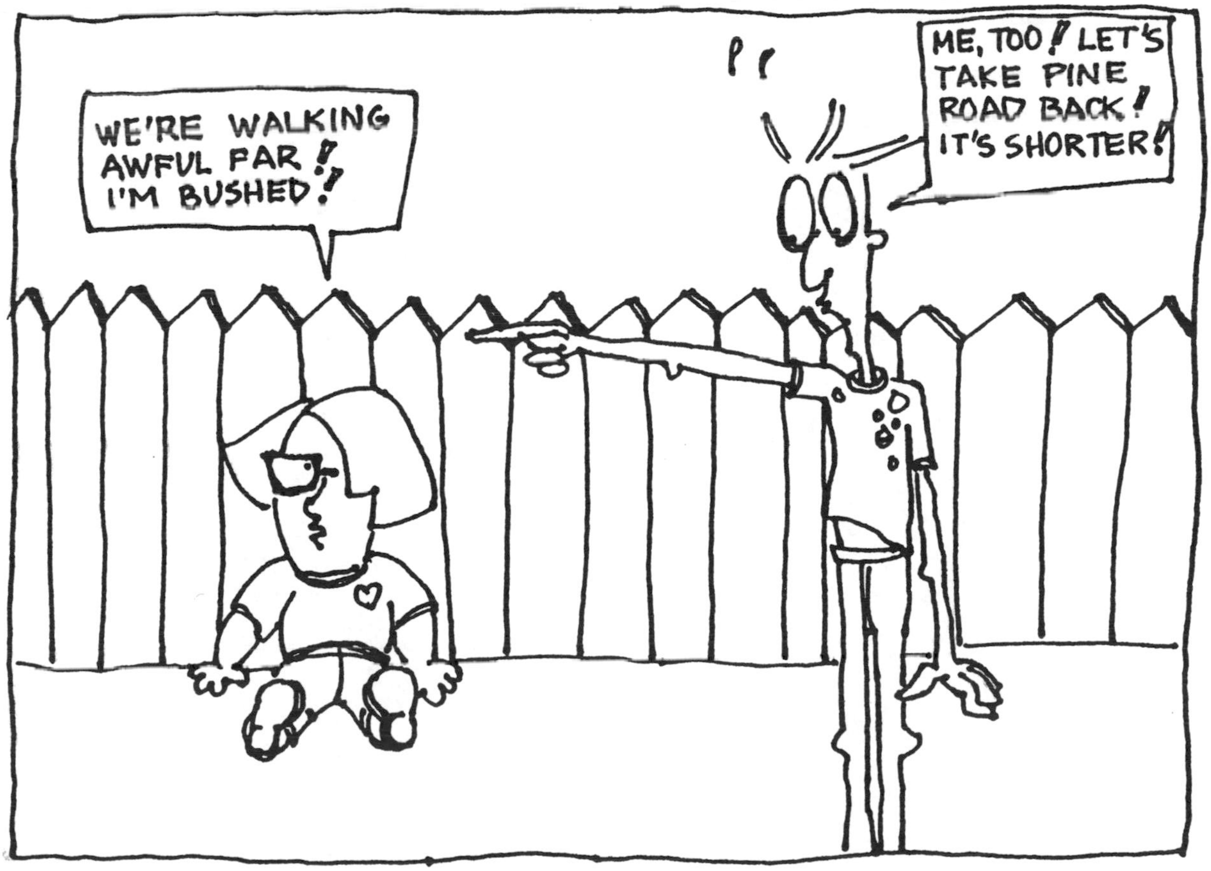
WE'RE WALKING AWFUL FAR! I'M BUSHED!
ME, TOO! LET'S TAKE PINE ROAD BACK! IT'S SHORTER!

50.

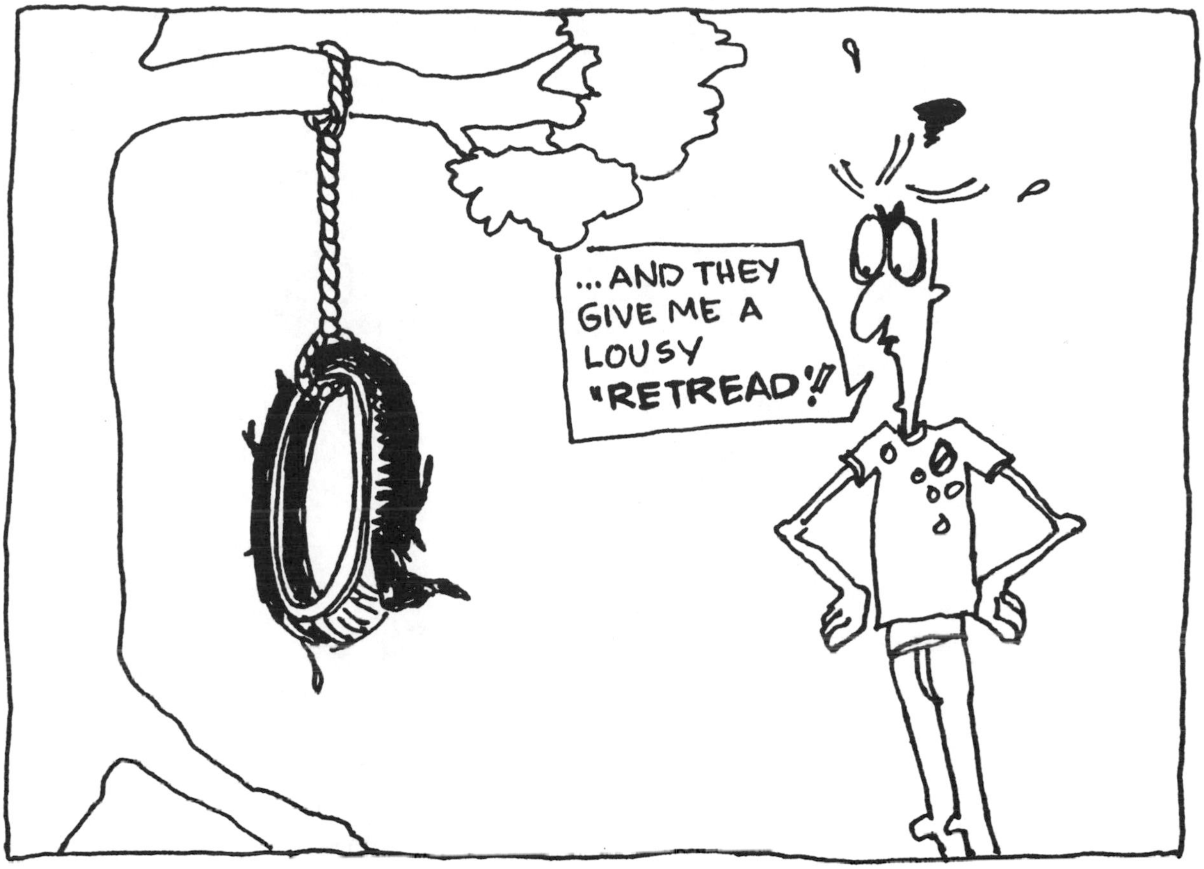
...AND THEY GIVE ME A LOUSY "RETREAD!!

51.

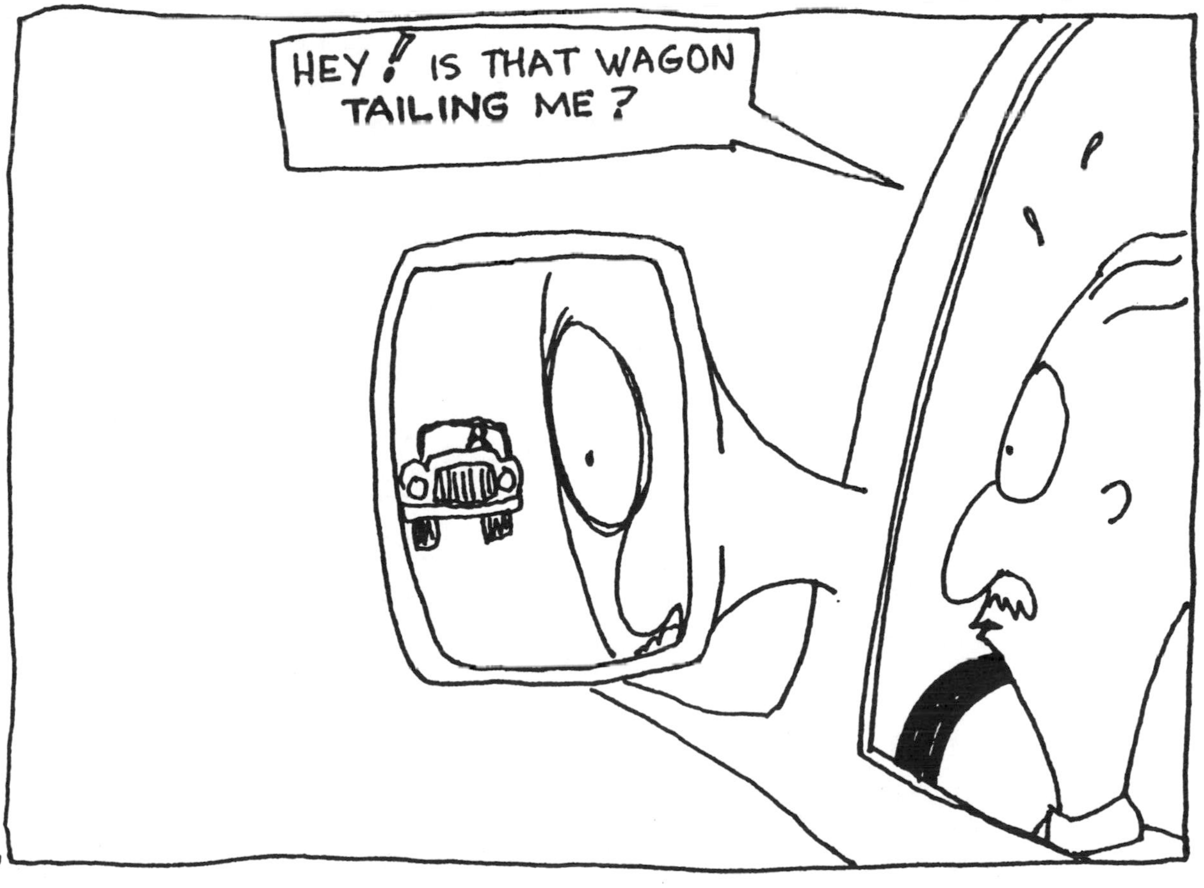
HEY! IS THAT WAGON TAILING ME?

52.

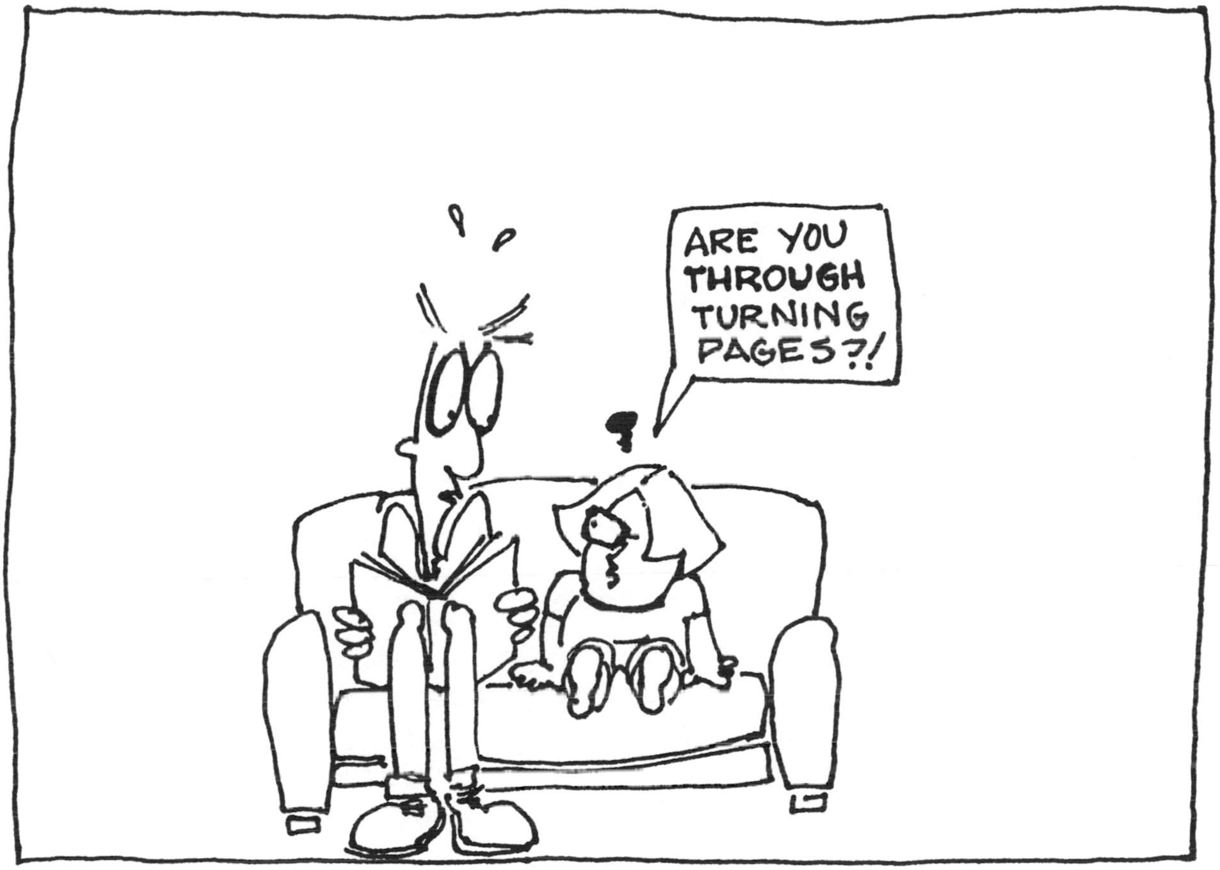
ARE YOU THROUGH TURNING PAGES?!

53.

54.

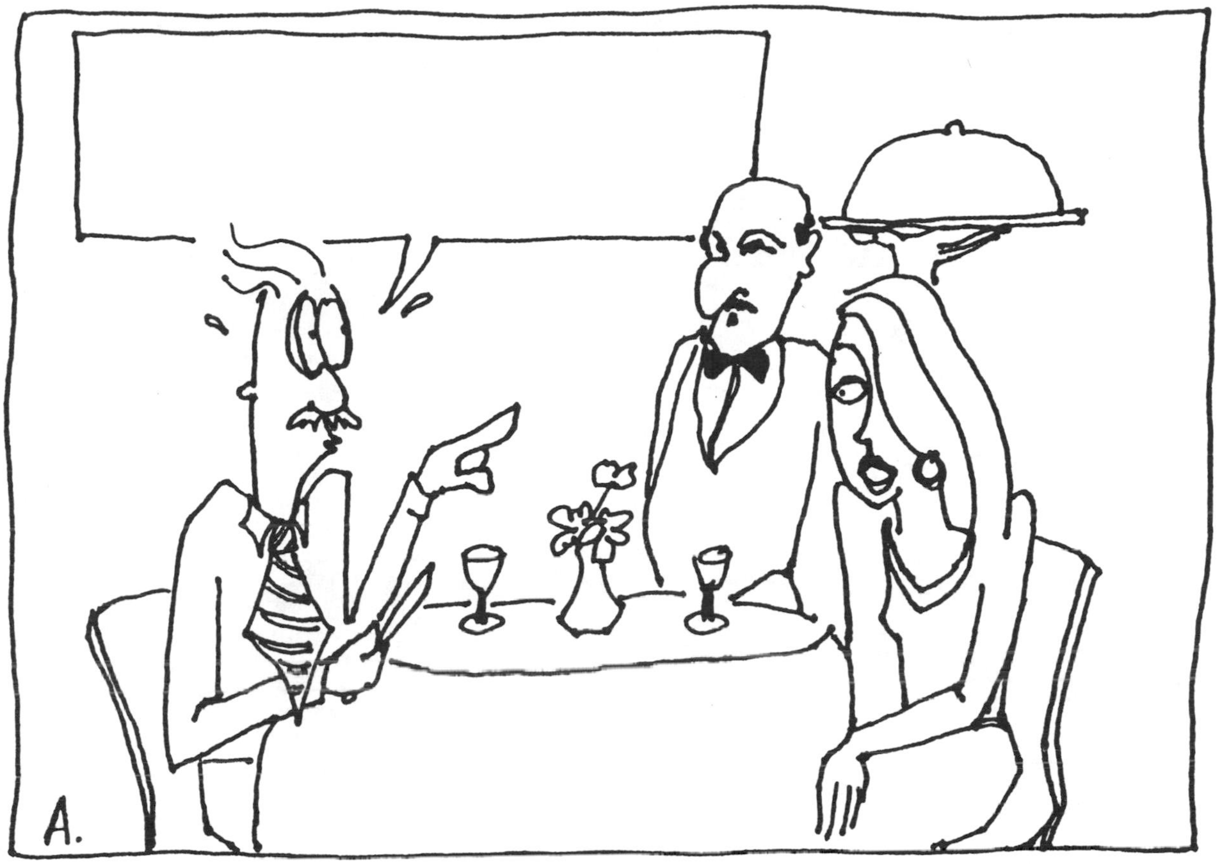
A.

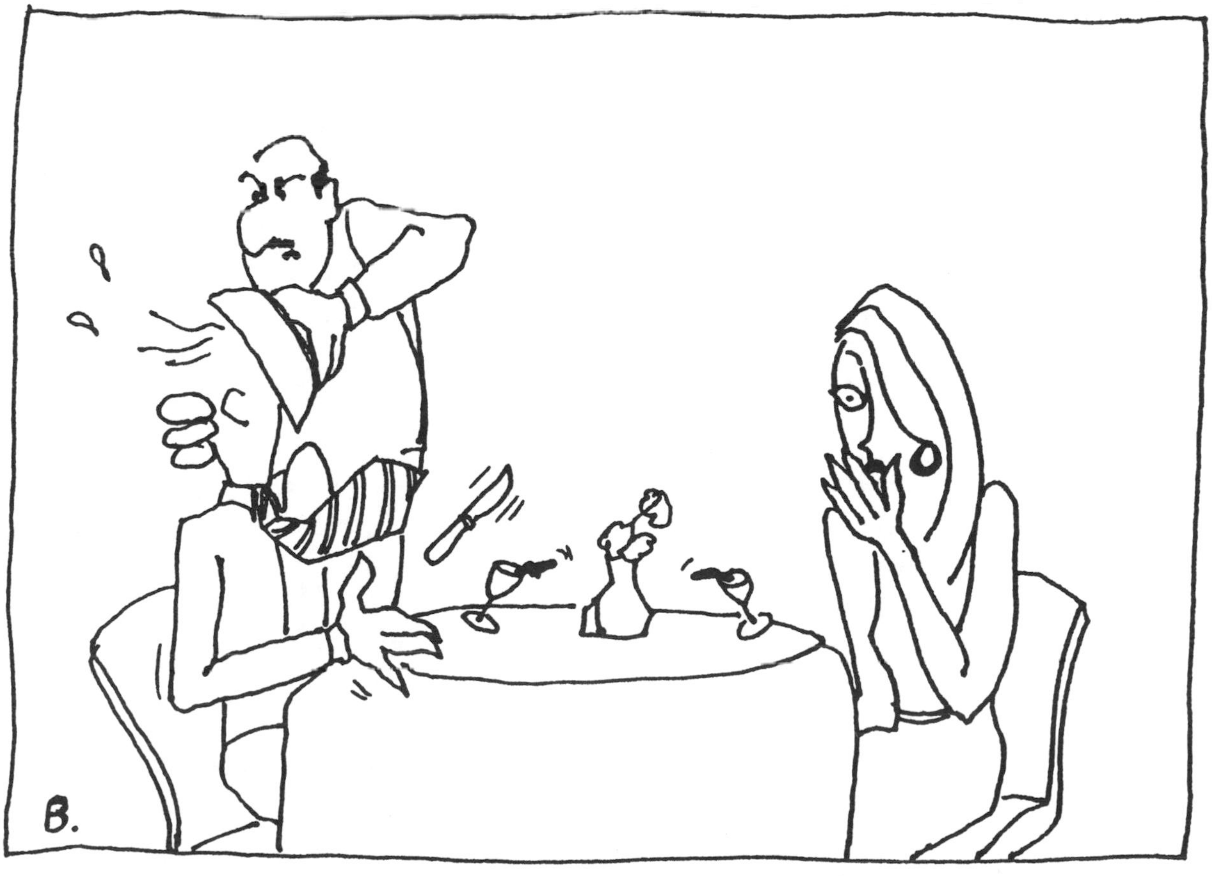
B.

54. C.

55.

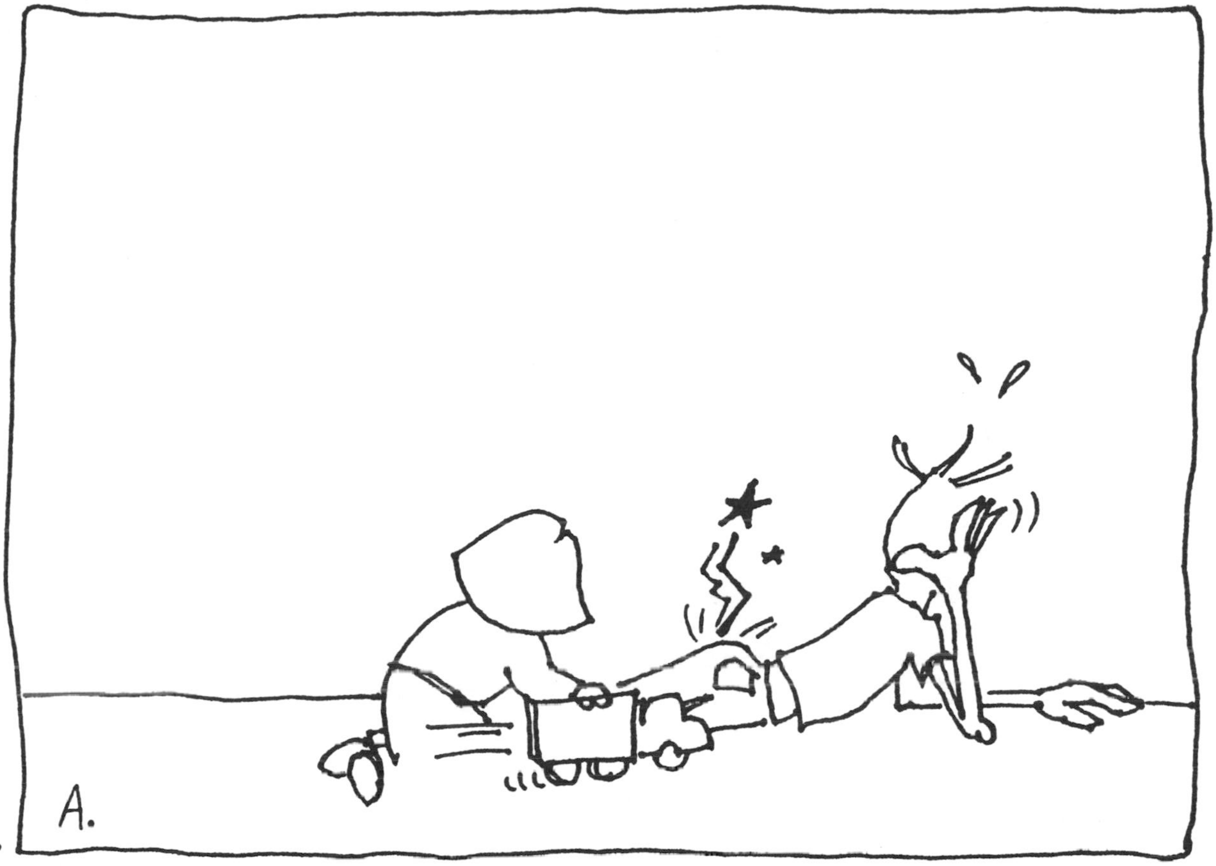
A.

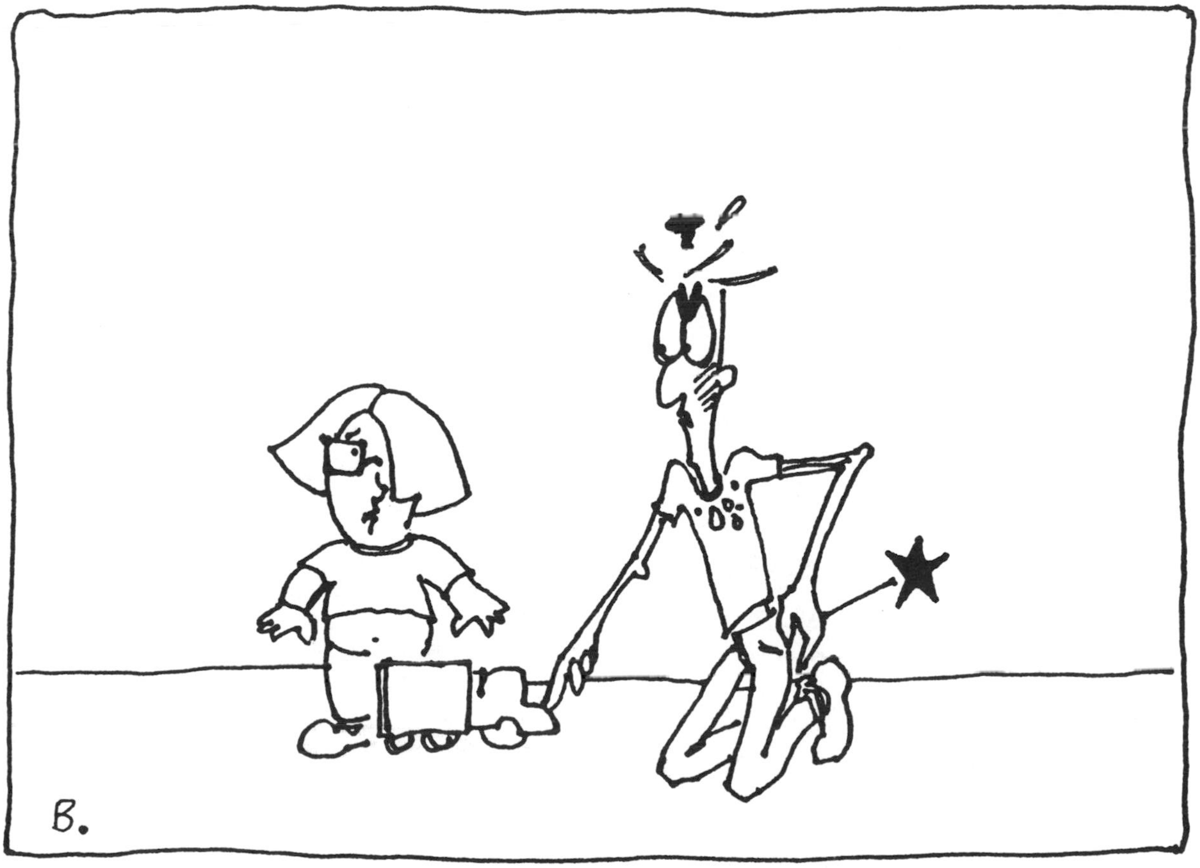
B.

55.

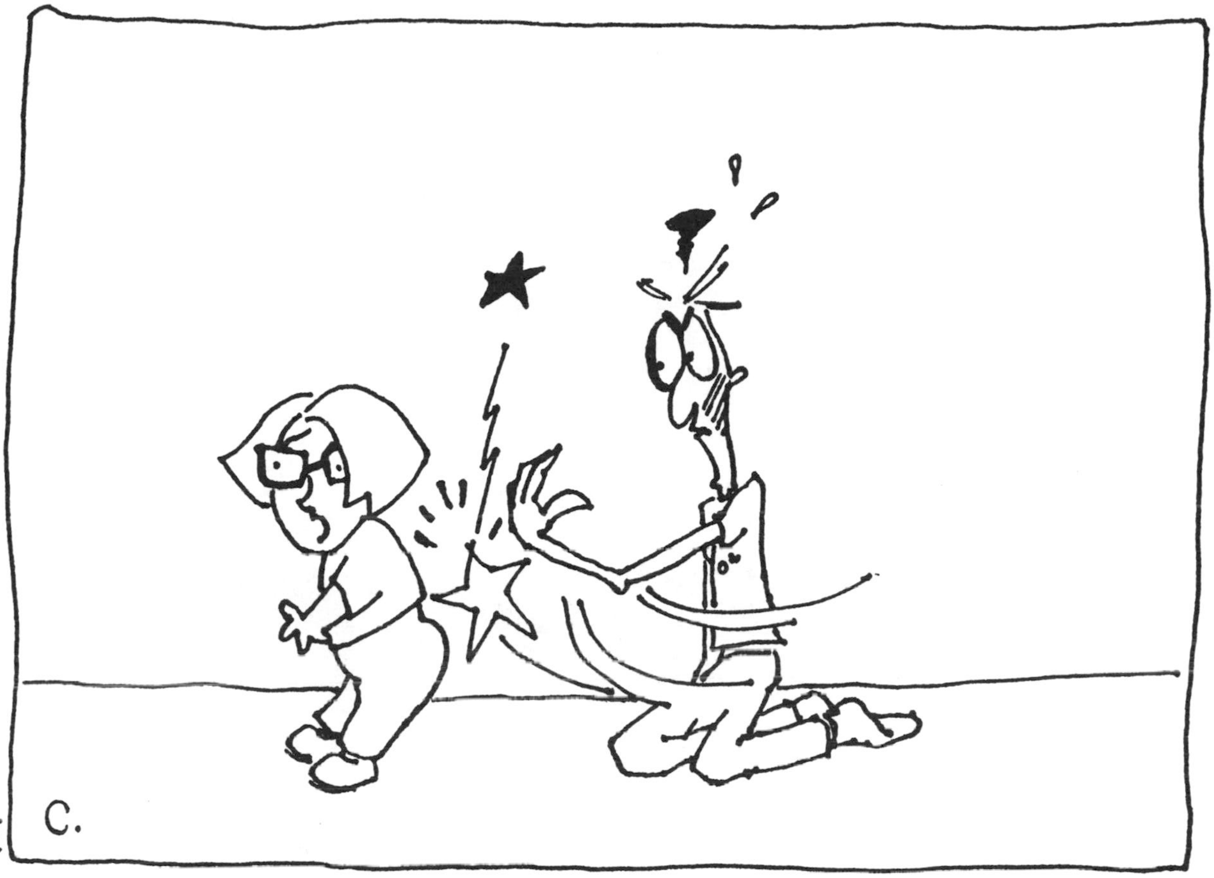
C.

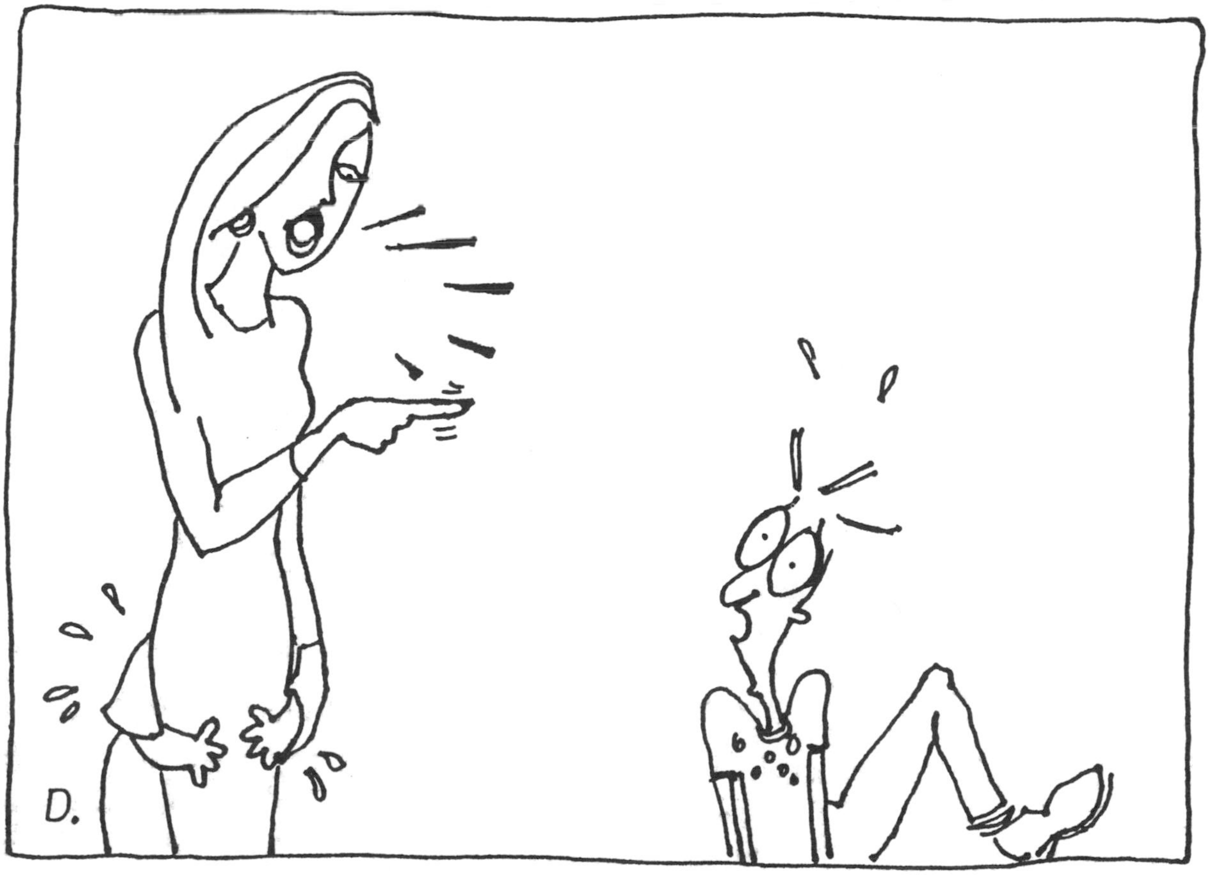
D.

56. A.

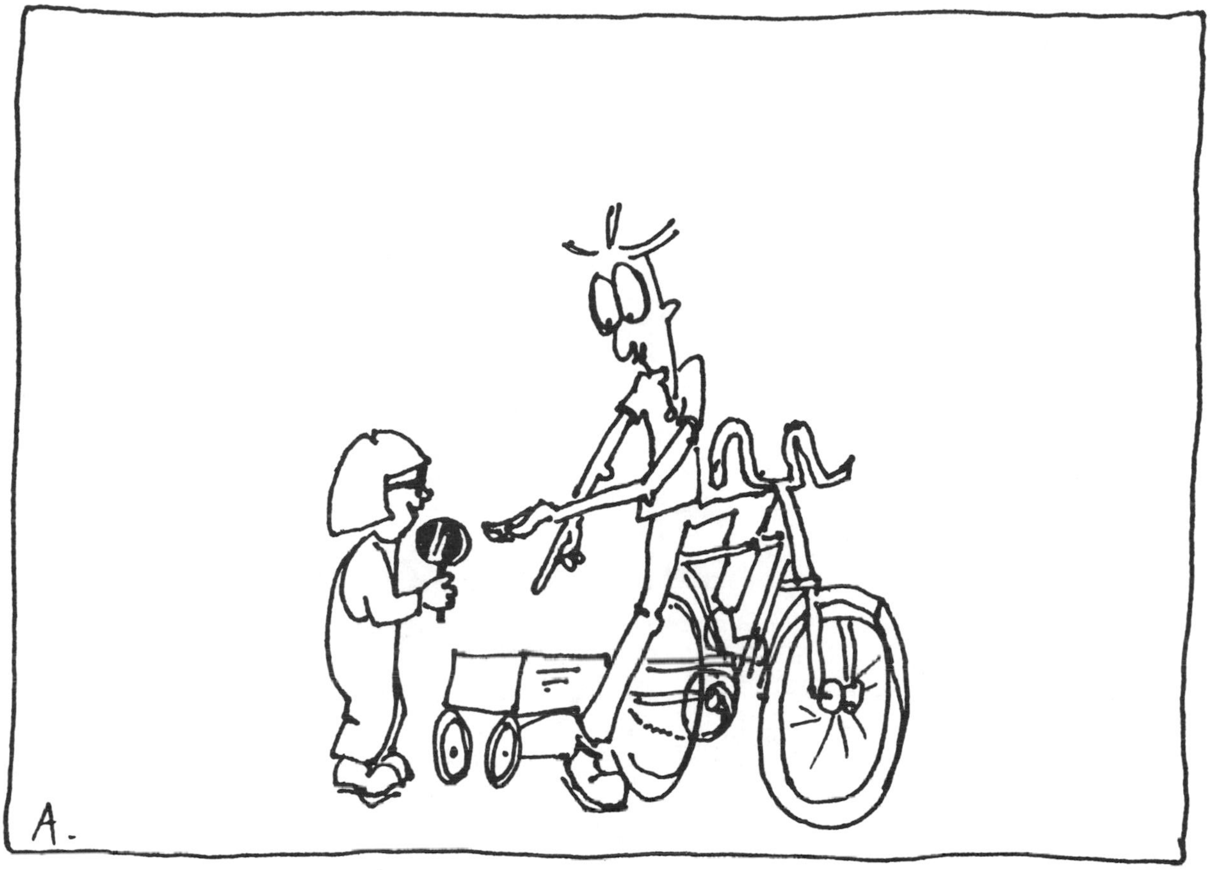

B.

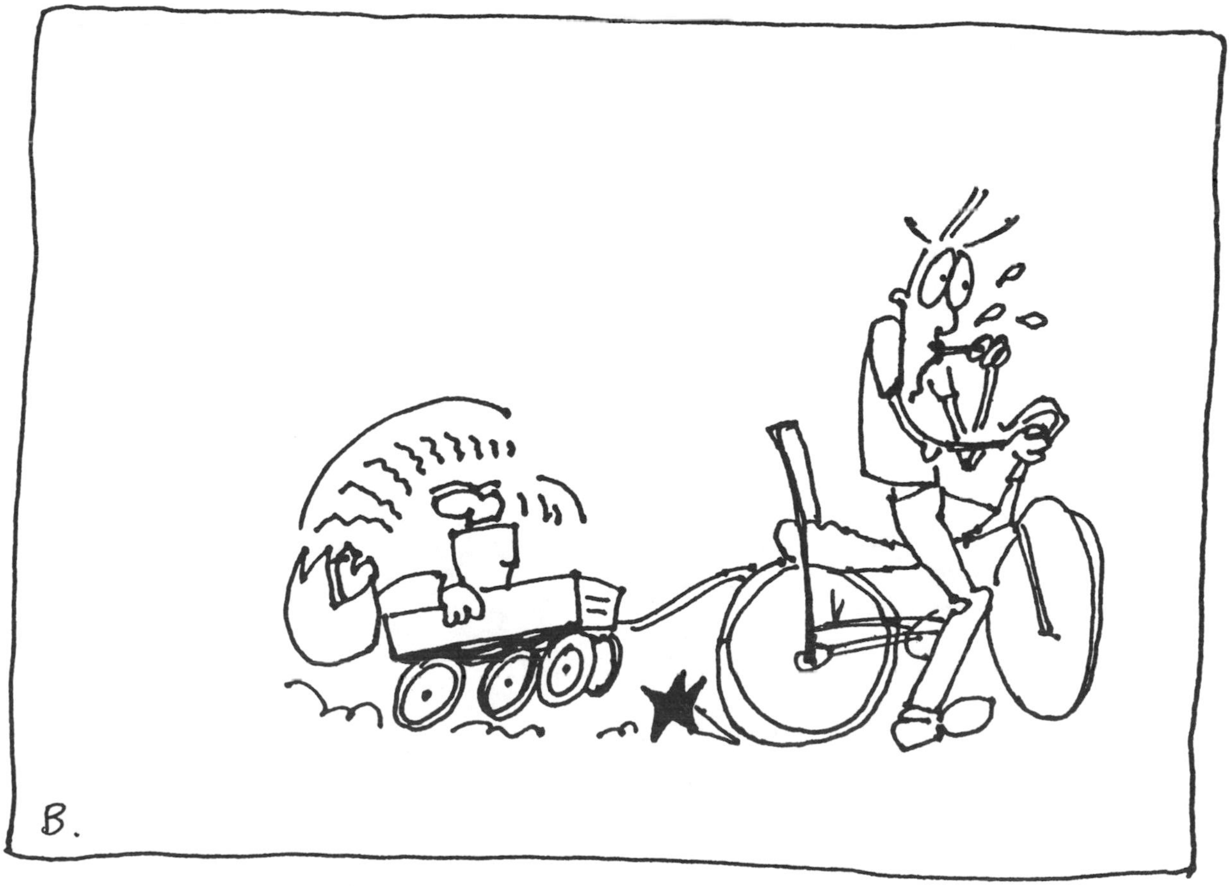

56.

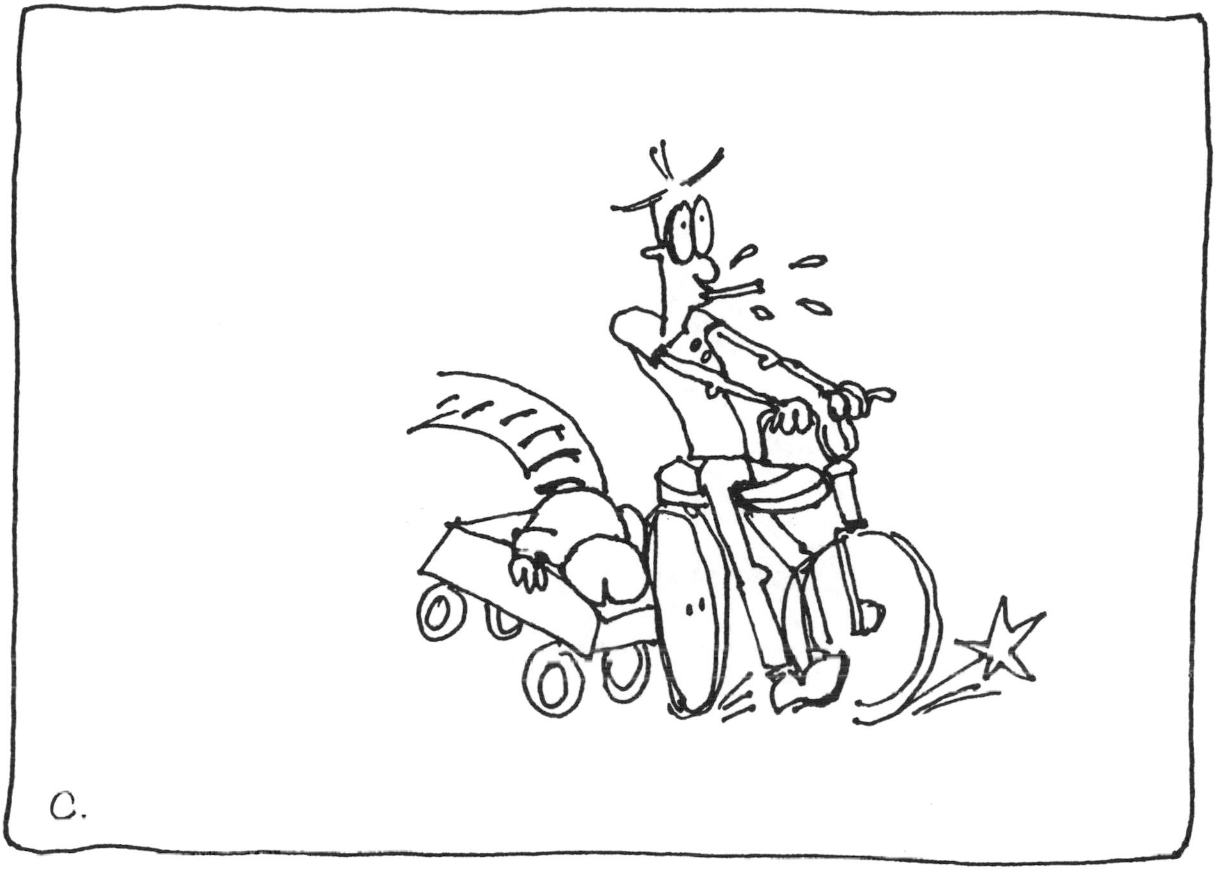

C.

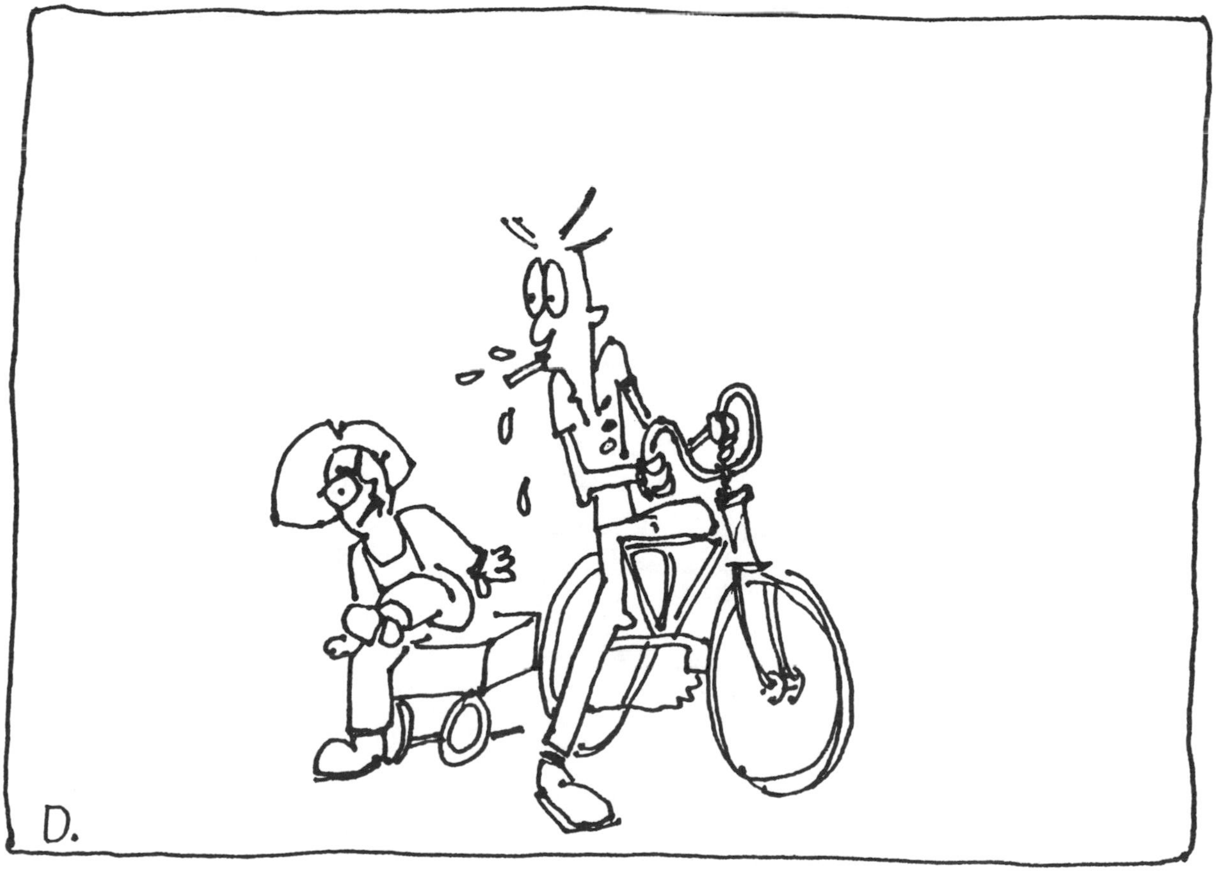

D.

56. E.

57.

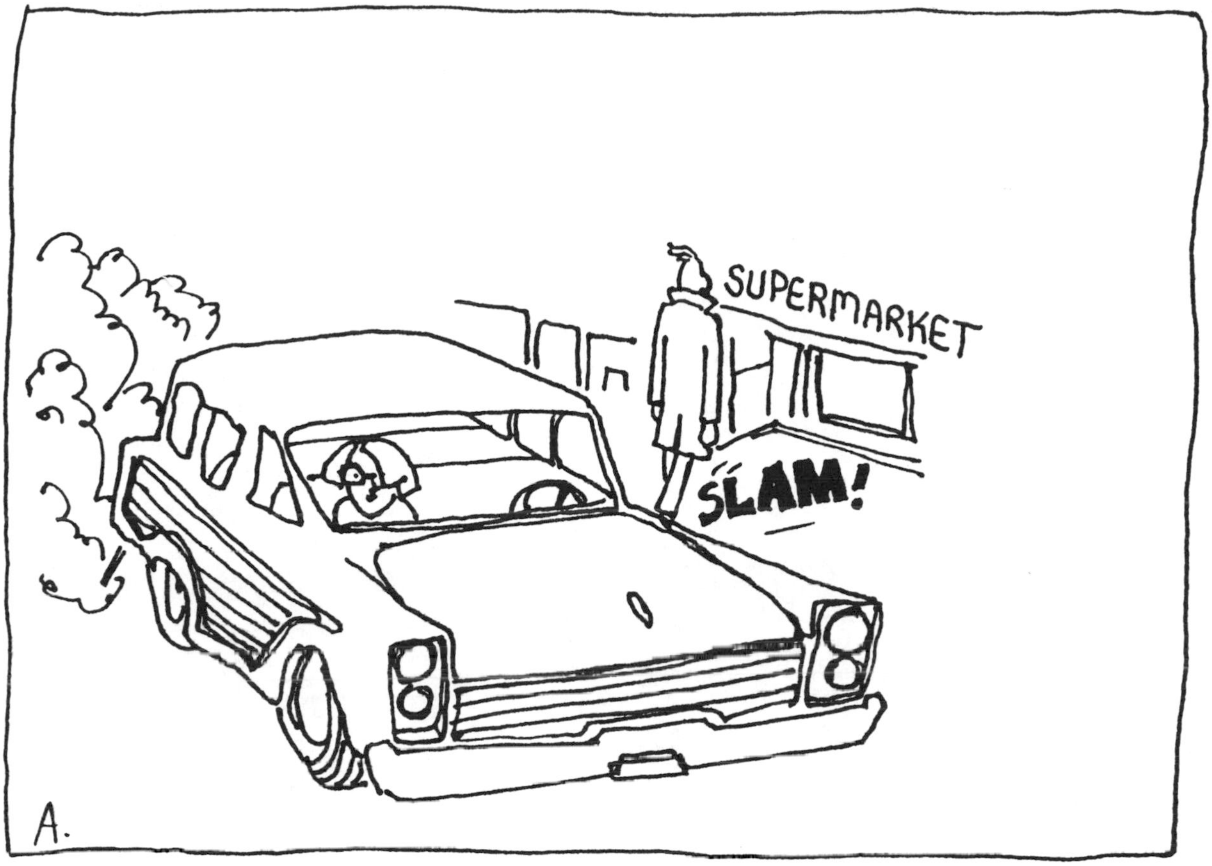
SUPERMARKET
SLAM!
A.

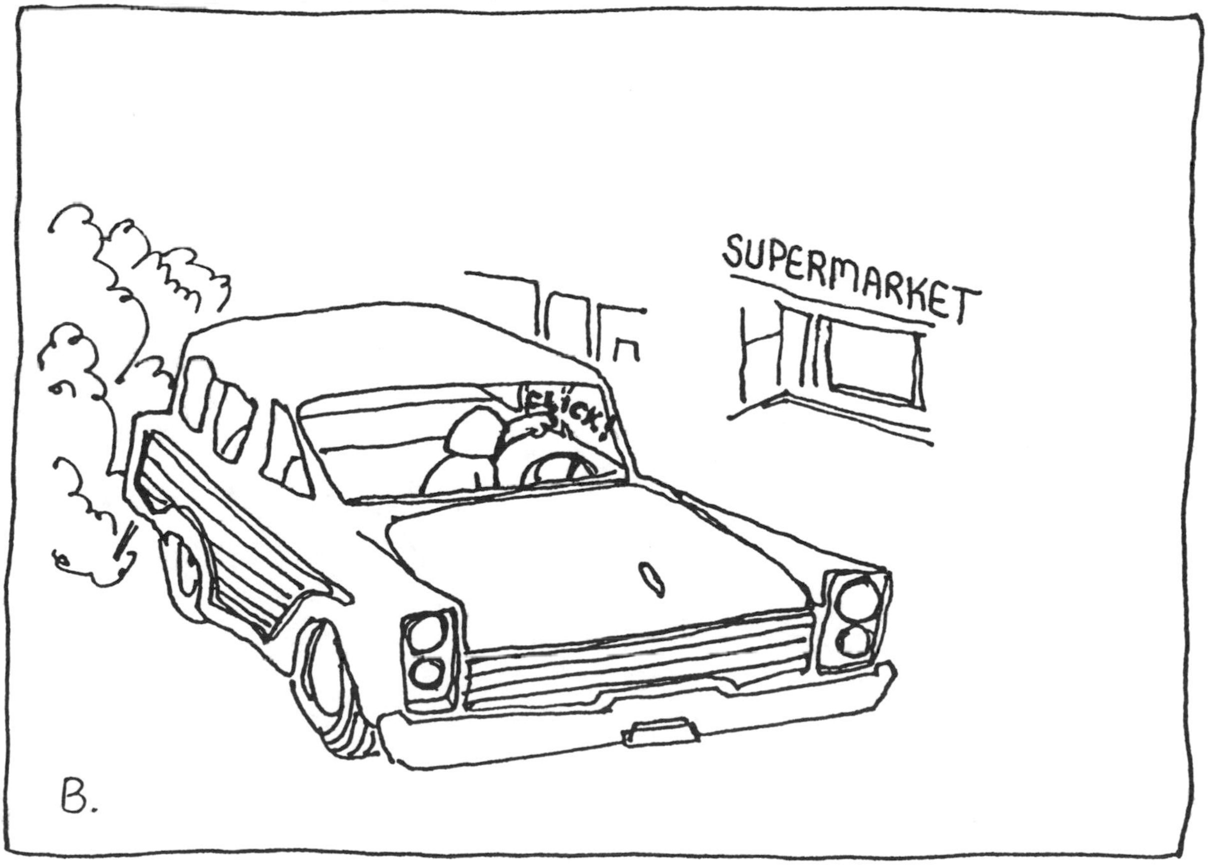
SUPERMARKET
CLICK!
B.

57.

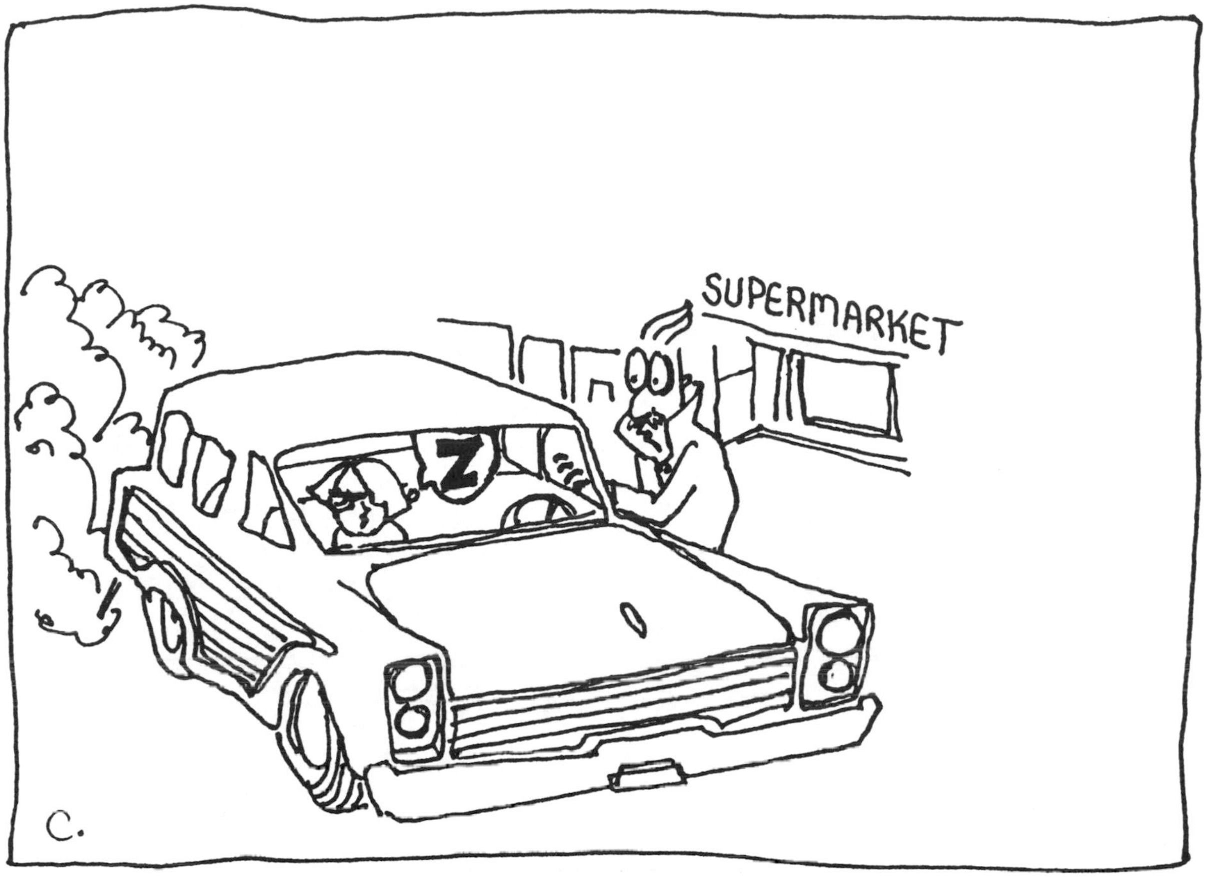
SUPERMARKET
Z
C.

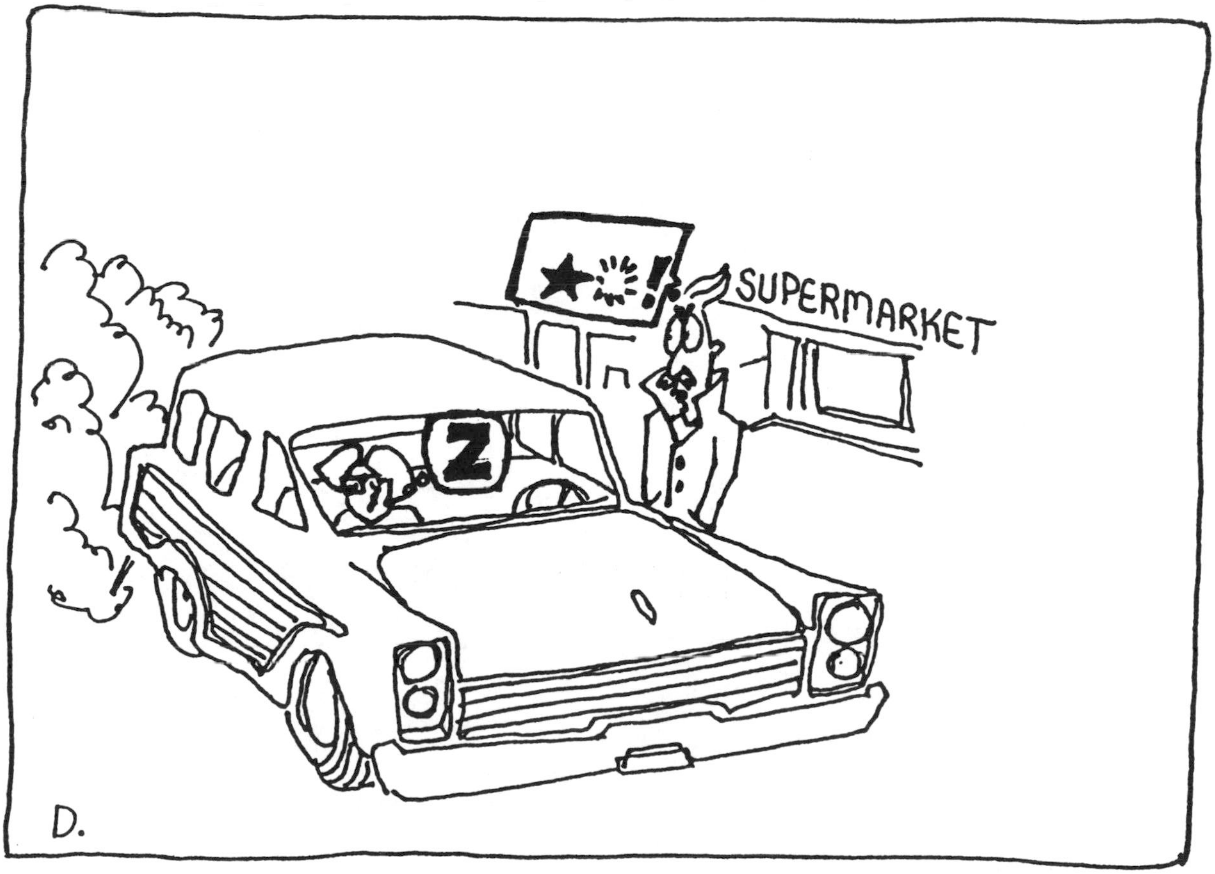
SUPERMARKET
Z
D.

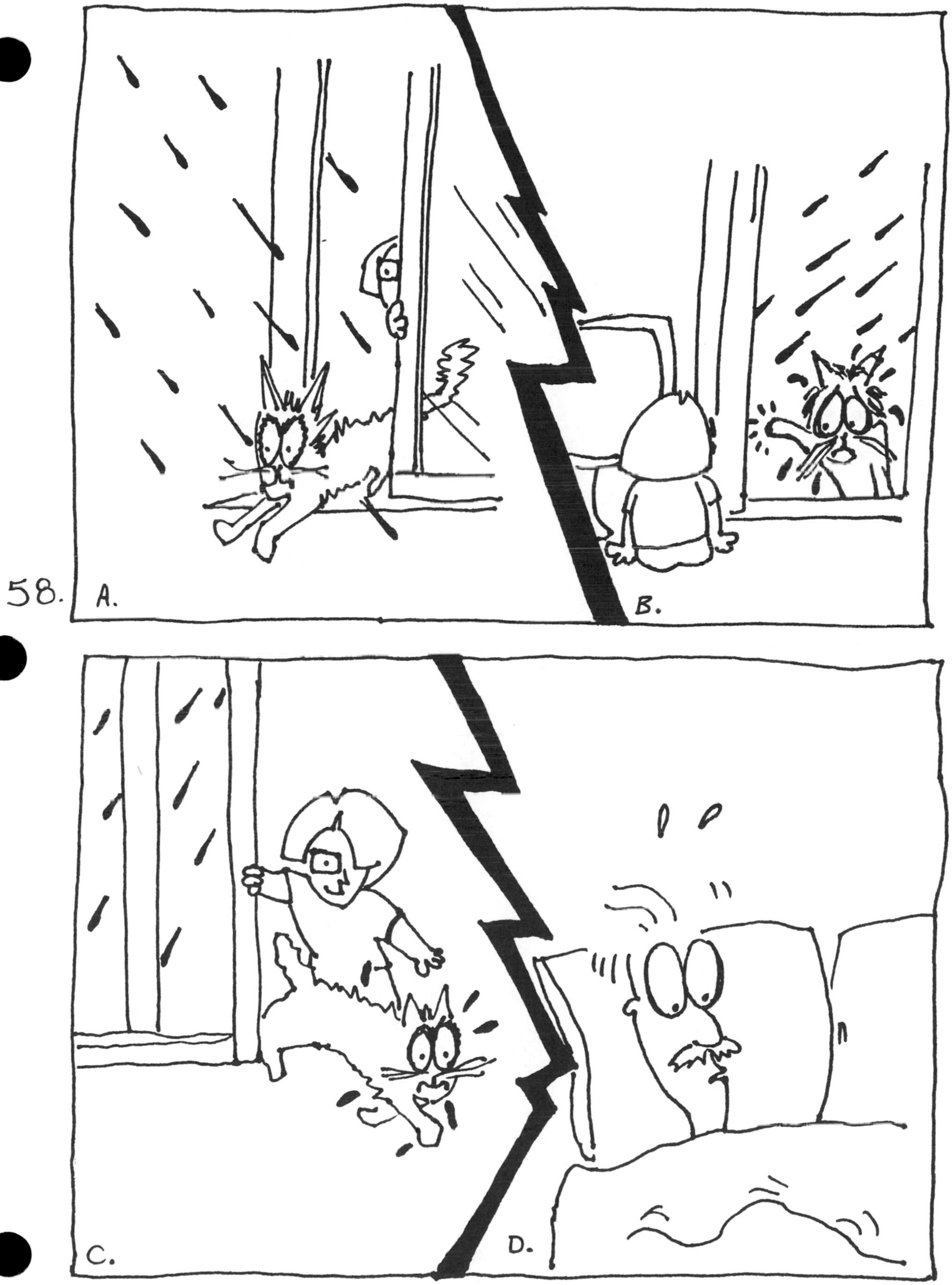
58.
A.
B.
C.
D.

58. E.

59.

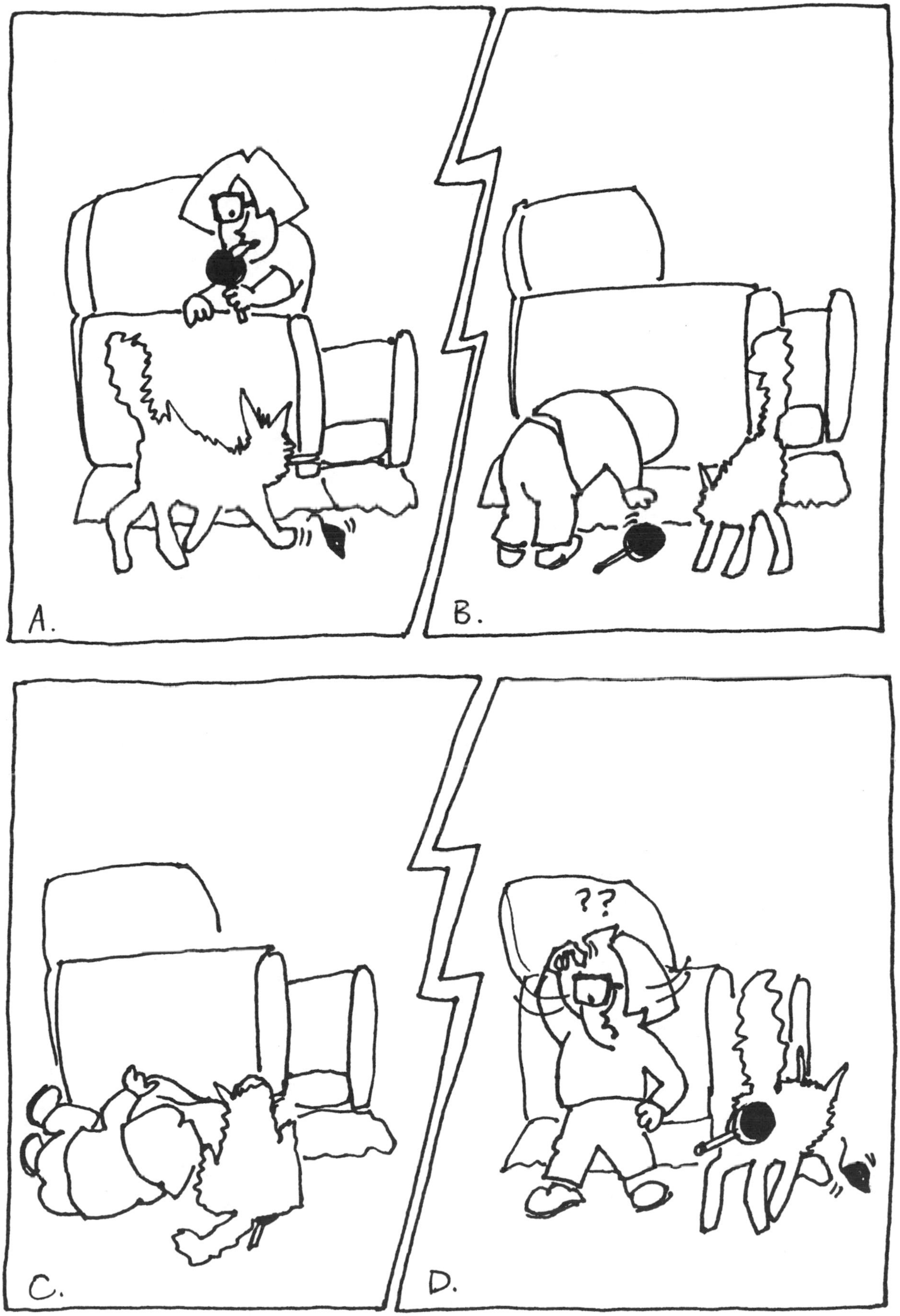

A.
B.
C.
??
D.

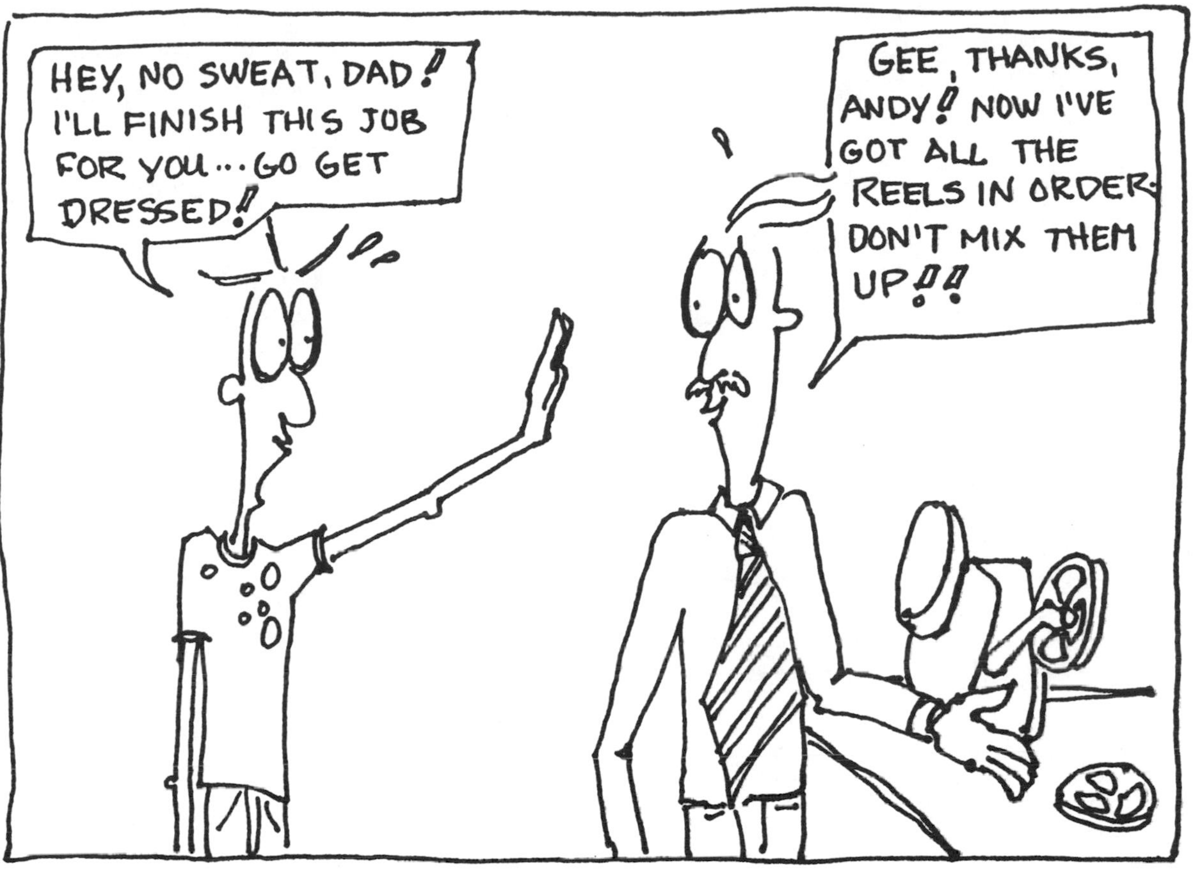
HEY, NO SWEAT, DAD! I'LL FINISH THIS JOB FOR YOU... GO GET DRESSED!
GEE, THANKS, ANDY! NOW I'VE GOT ALL THE REELS IN ORDER- DON'T MIX THEM UP!!

60.

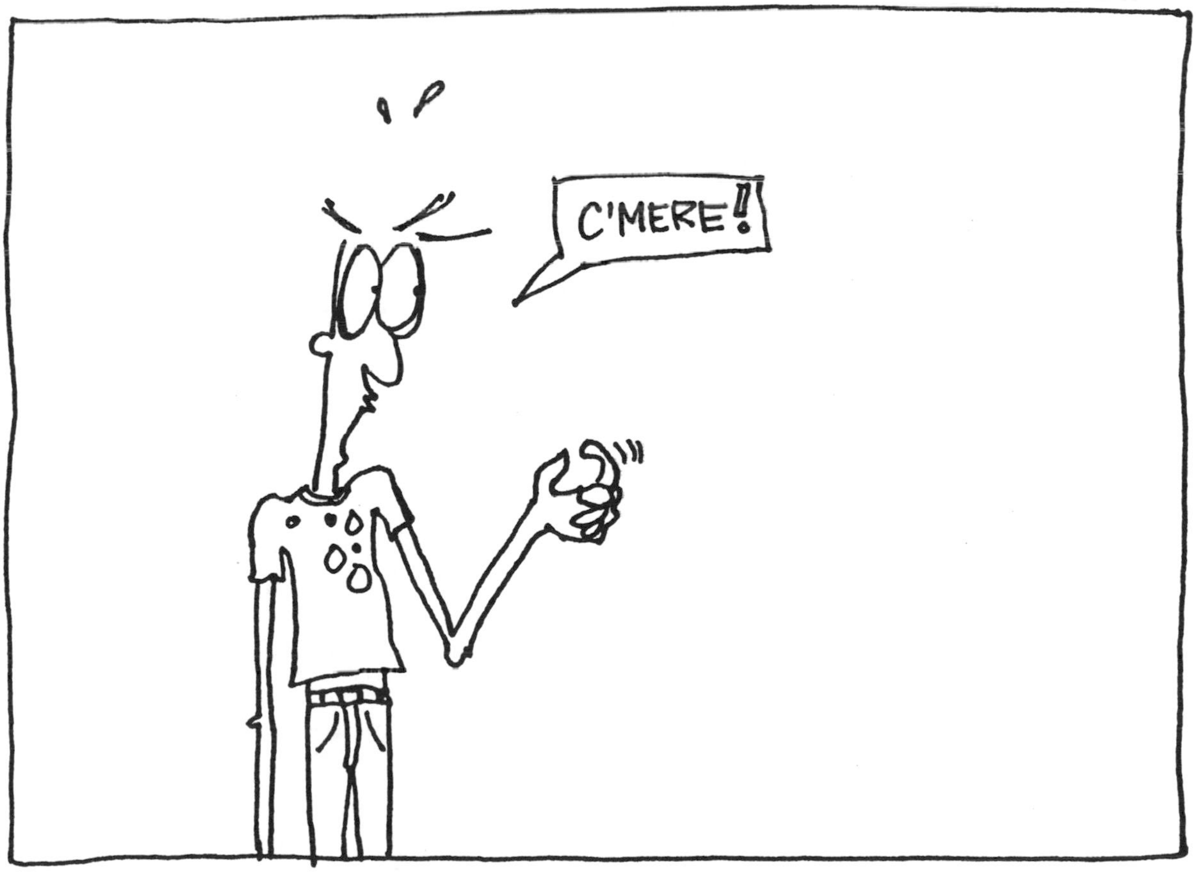
C'MERE!

61.

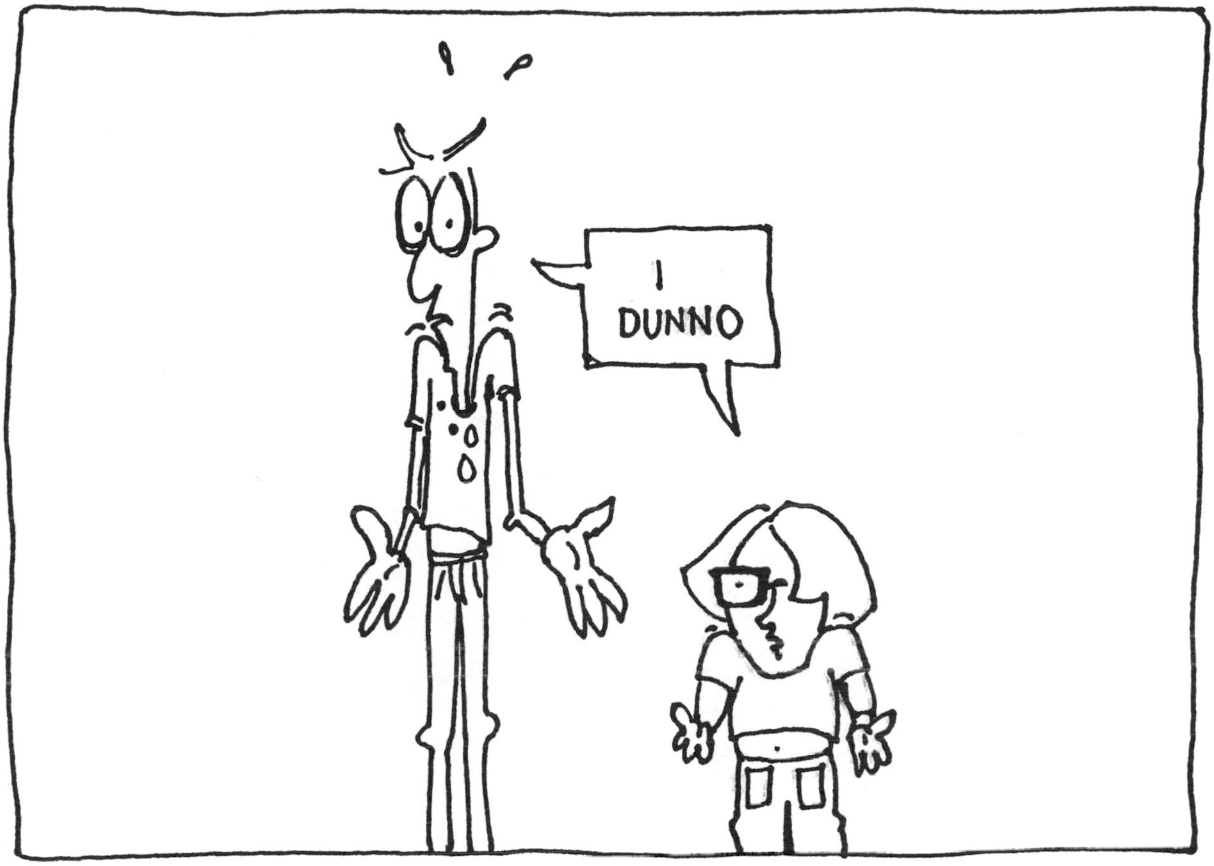
I DUNNO

62.

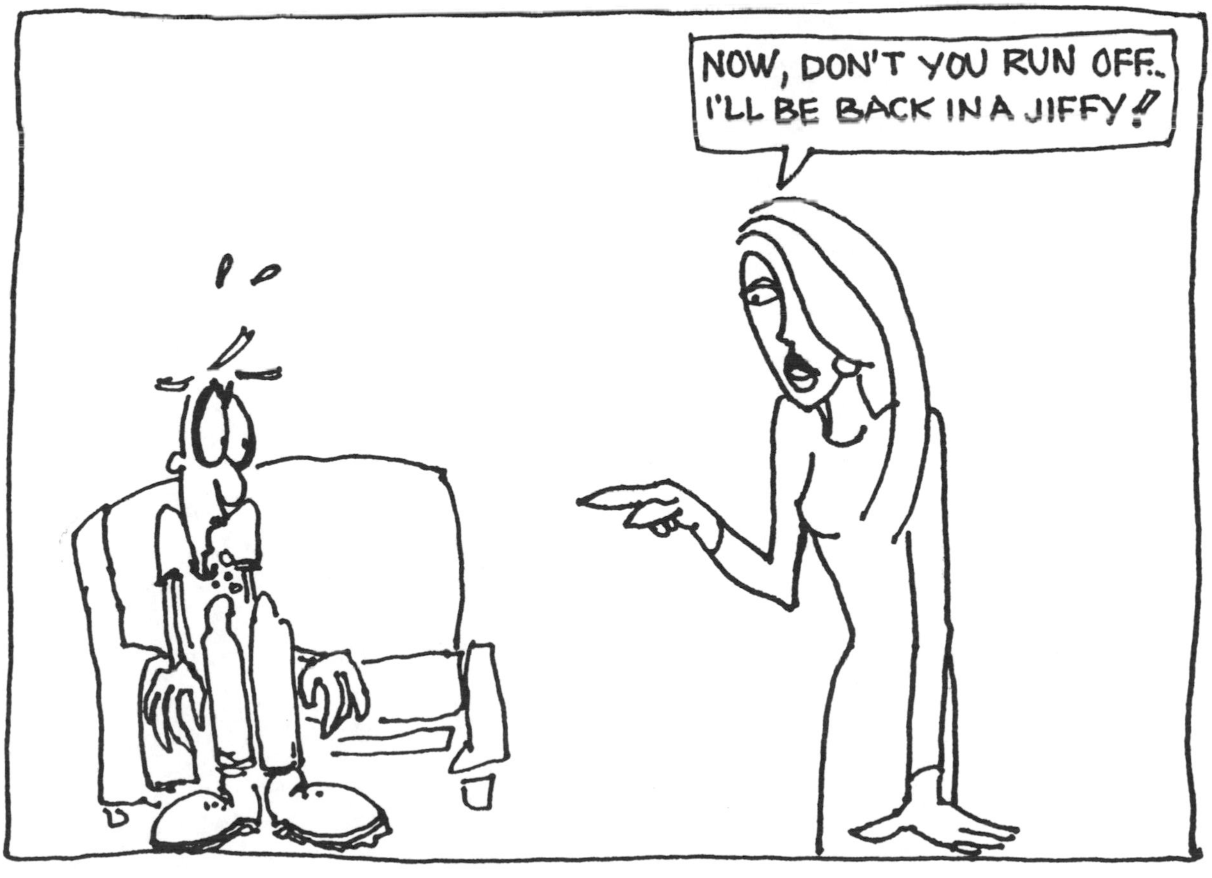
NOW, DON'T YOU RUN OFF.. I'LL BE BACK IN A JIFFY!

63.

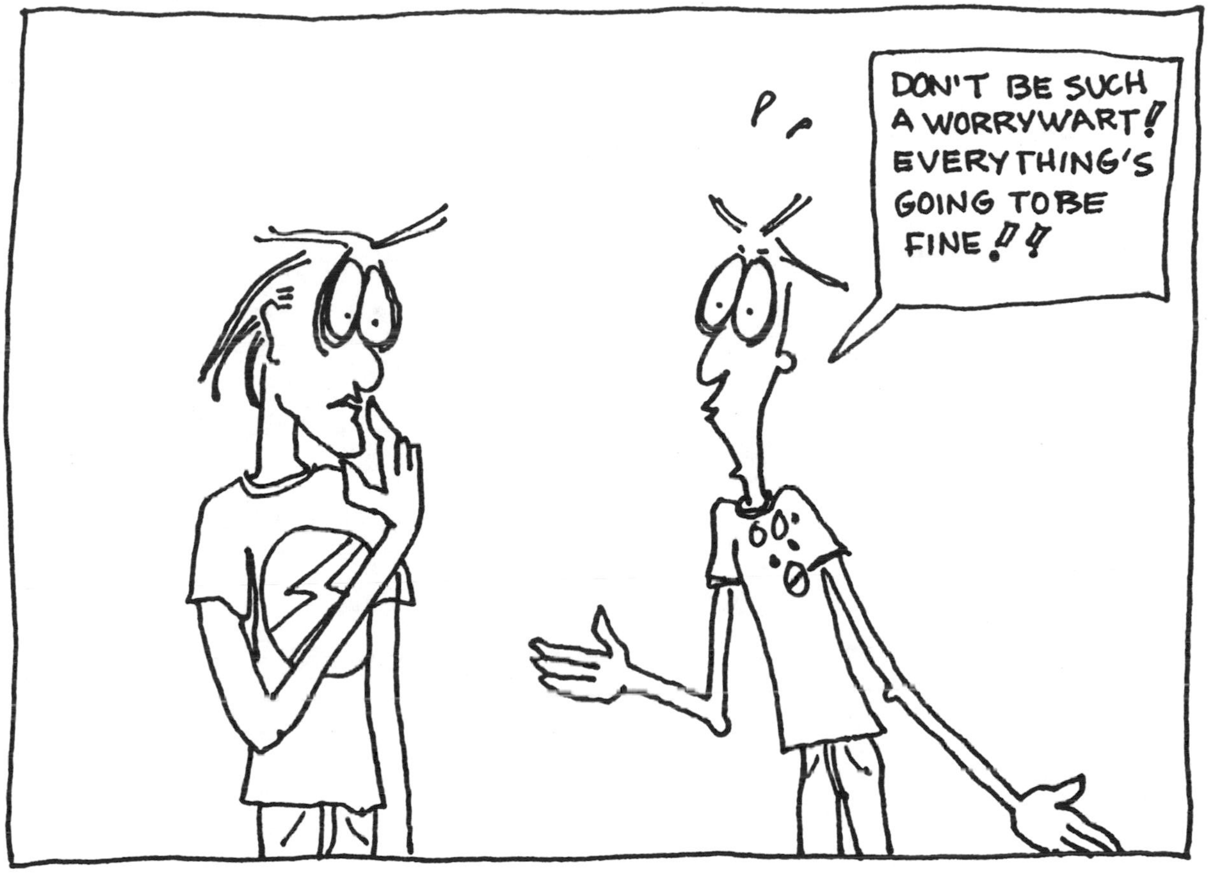
DON'T BE SUCH A WORRYWART! EVERYTHING'S GOING TO BE FINE!!

64.

65.

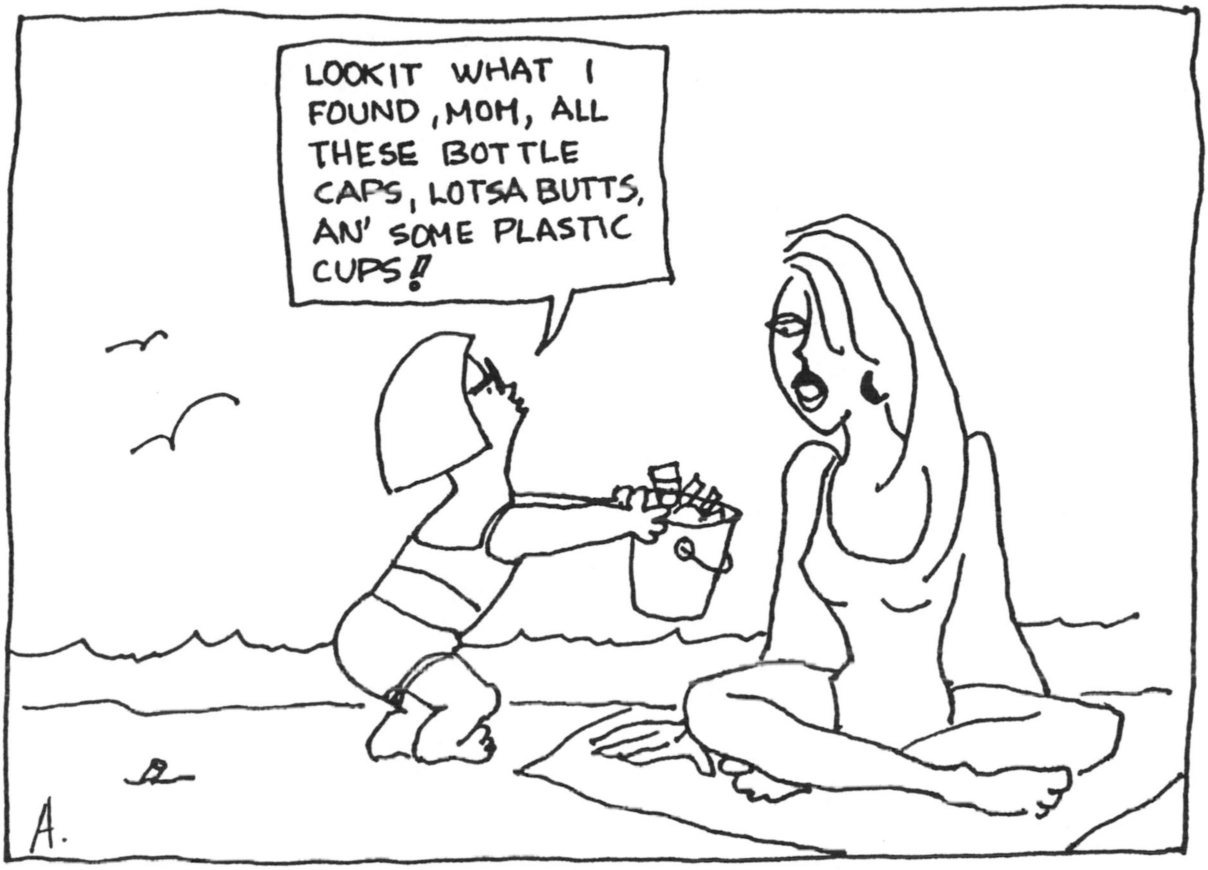
LOOKIT WHAT I FOUND, MOM, ALL THESE BOTTLE CAPS, LOTSA BUTTS, AN' SOME PLASTIC CUPS!
A.

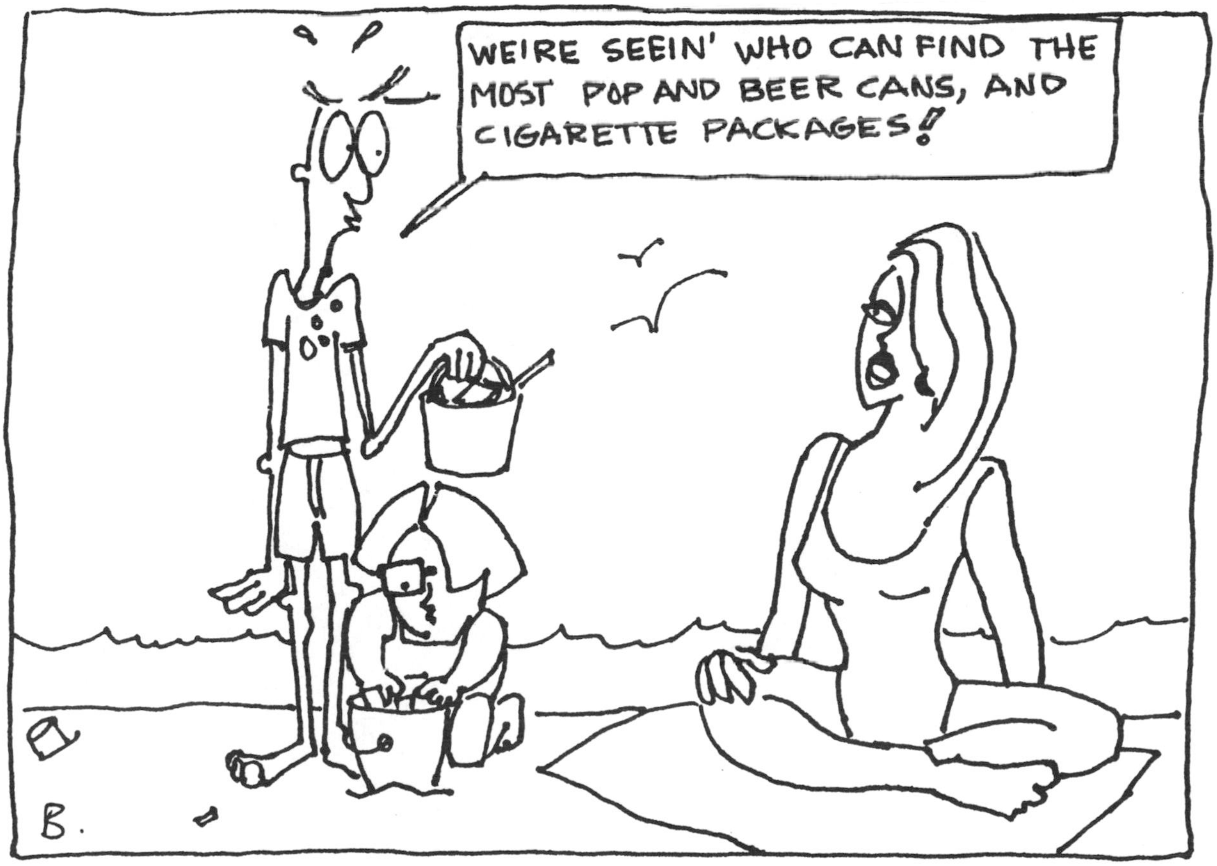
WE'RE SEEIN' WHO CAN FIND THE MOST POP AND BEER CANS, AND CIGARETTE PACKAGES!
B.

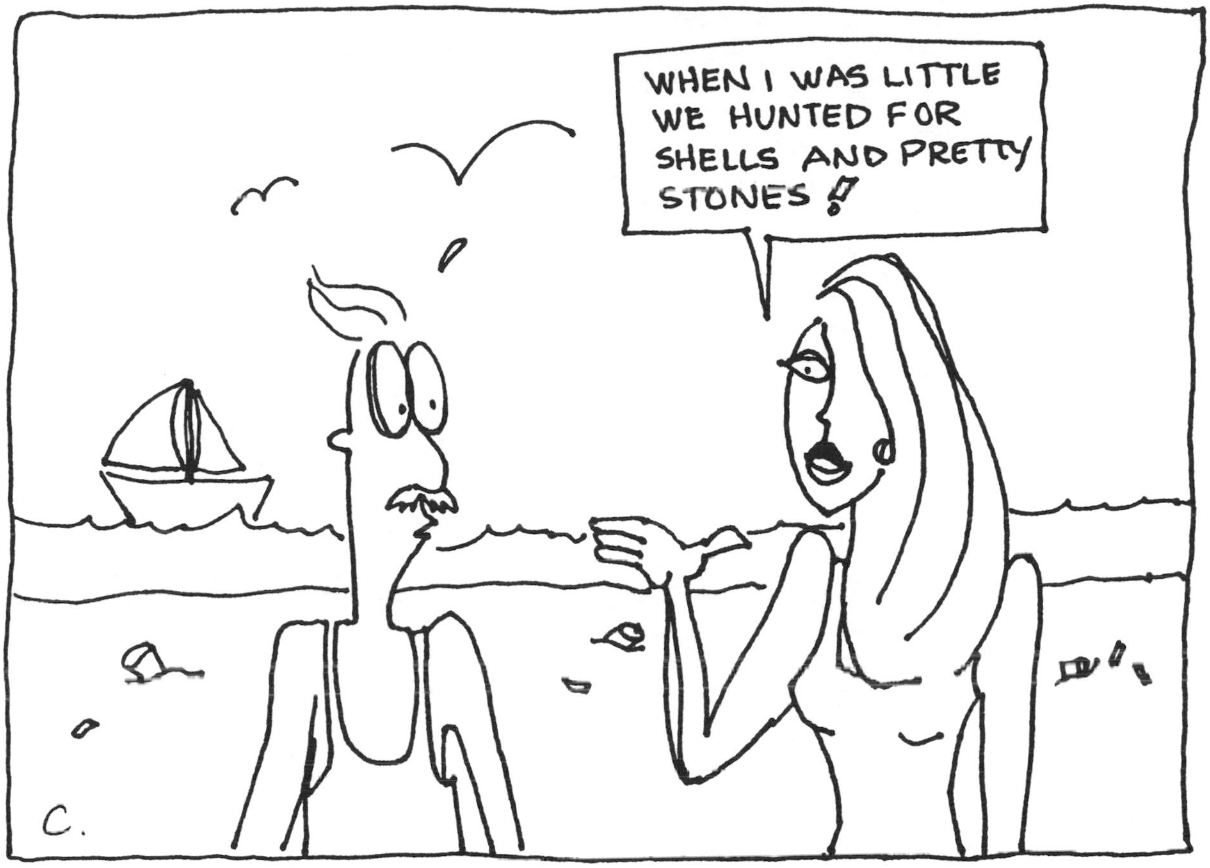
WHEN I WAS LITTLE WE HUNTED FOR SHELLS AND PRETTY STONES!

65. C.

66.

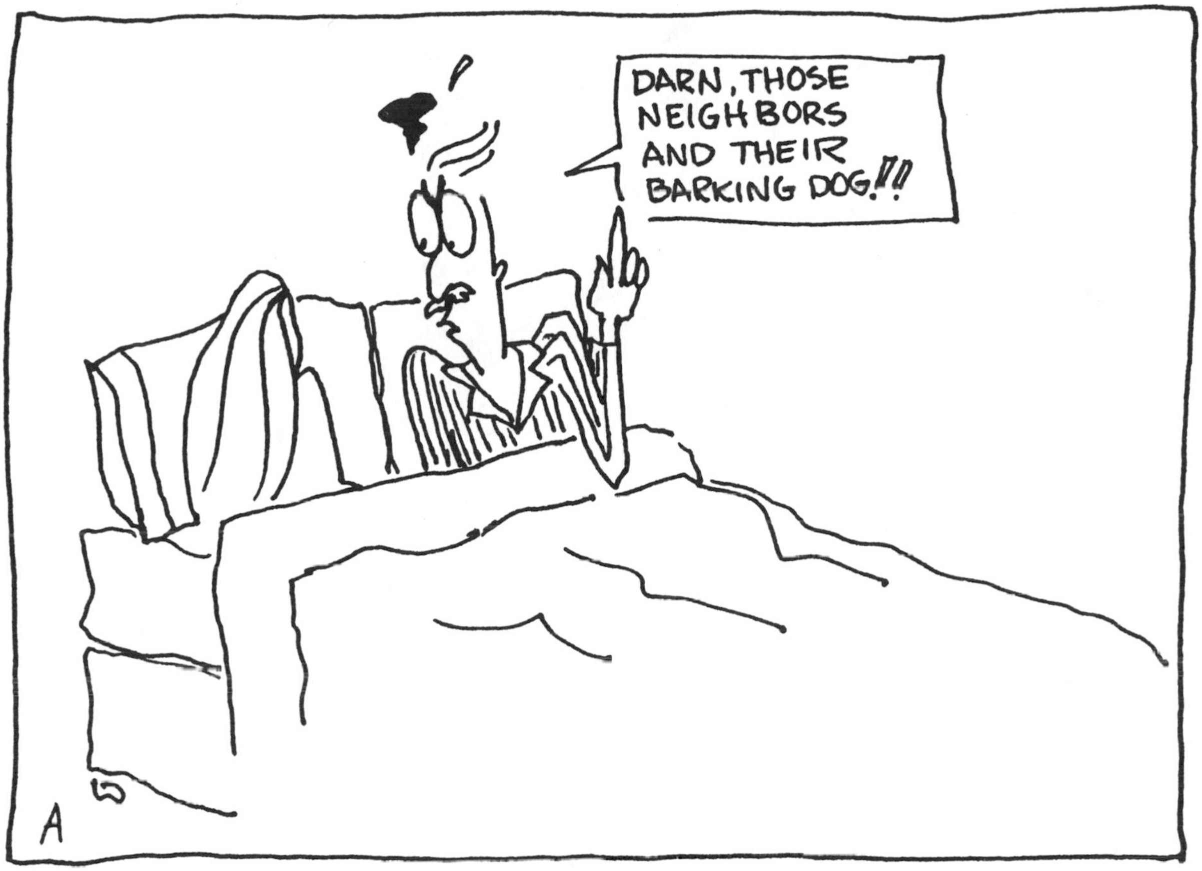
DARN, THOSE NEIGHBORS AND THEIR BARKING DOG!!!

A

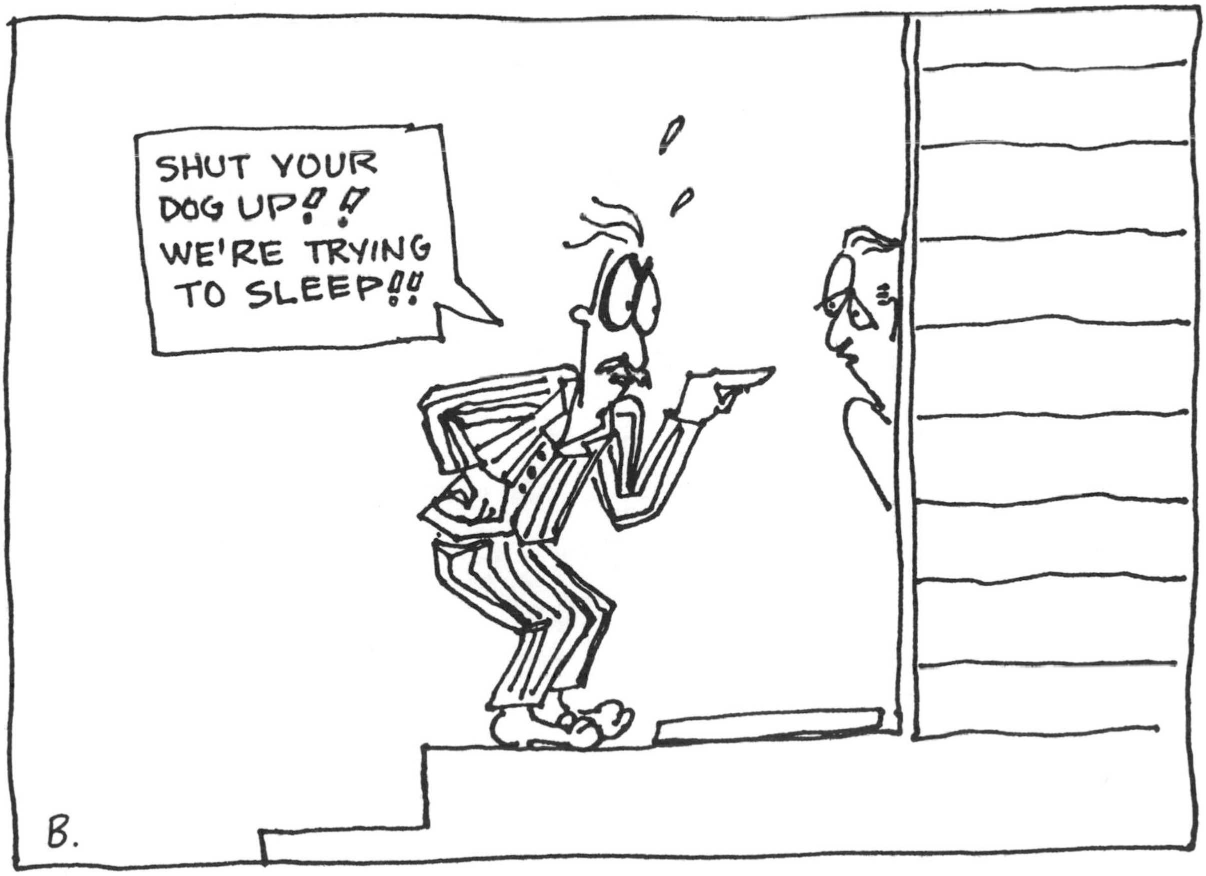
SHUT YOUR DOG UP!! WE'RE TRYING TO SLEEP!!

B.

66.

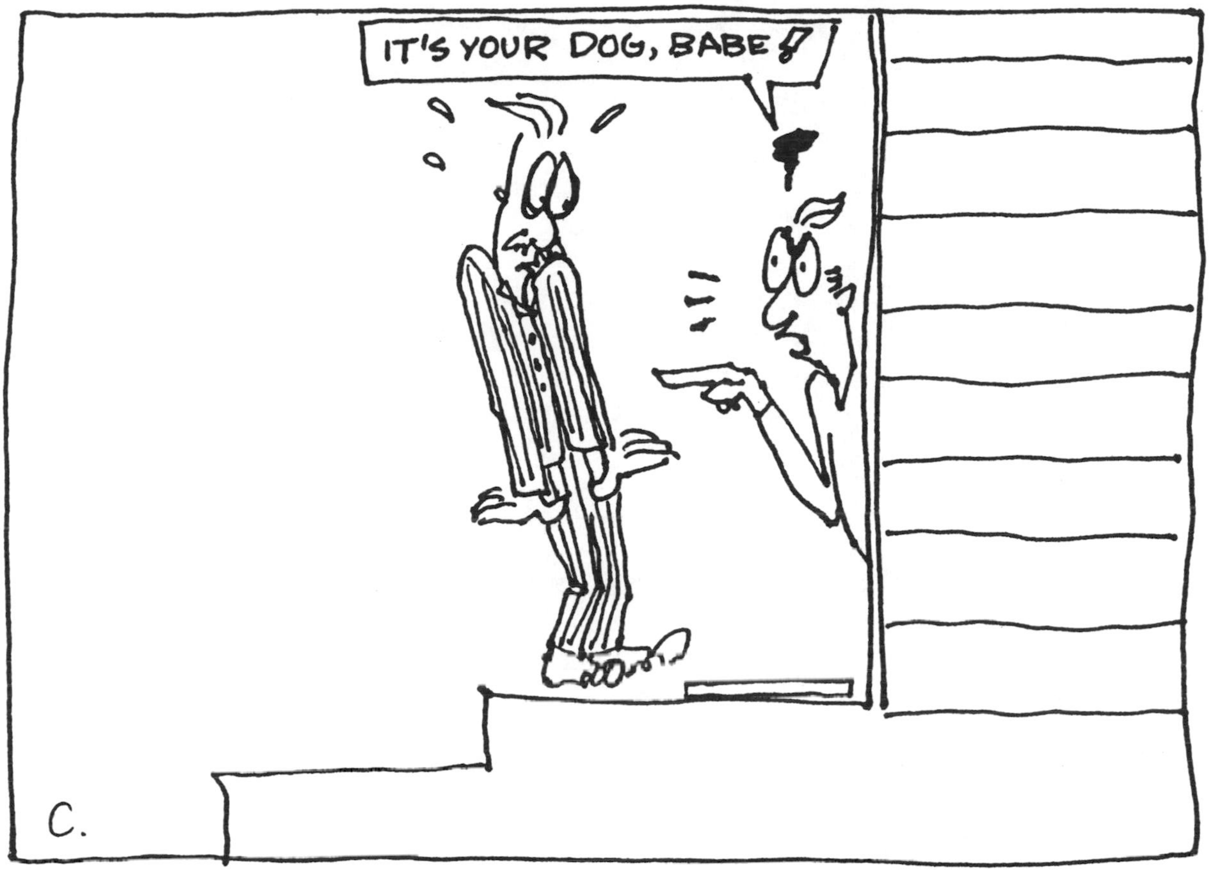
IT'S YOUR DOG, BABE!
C.

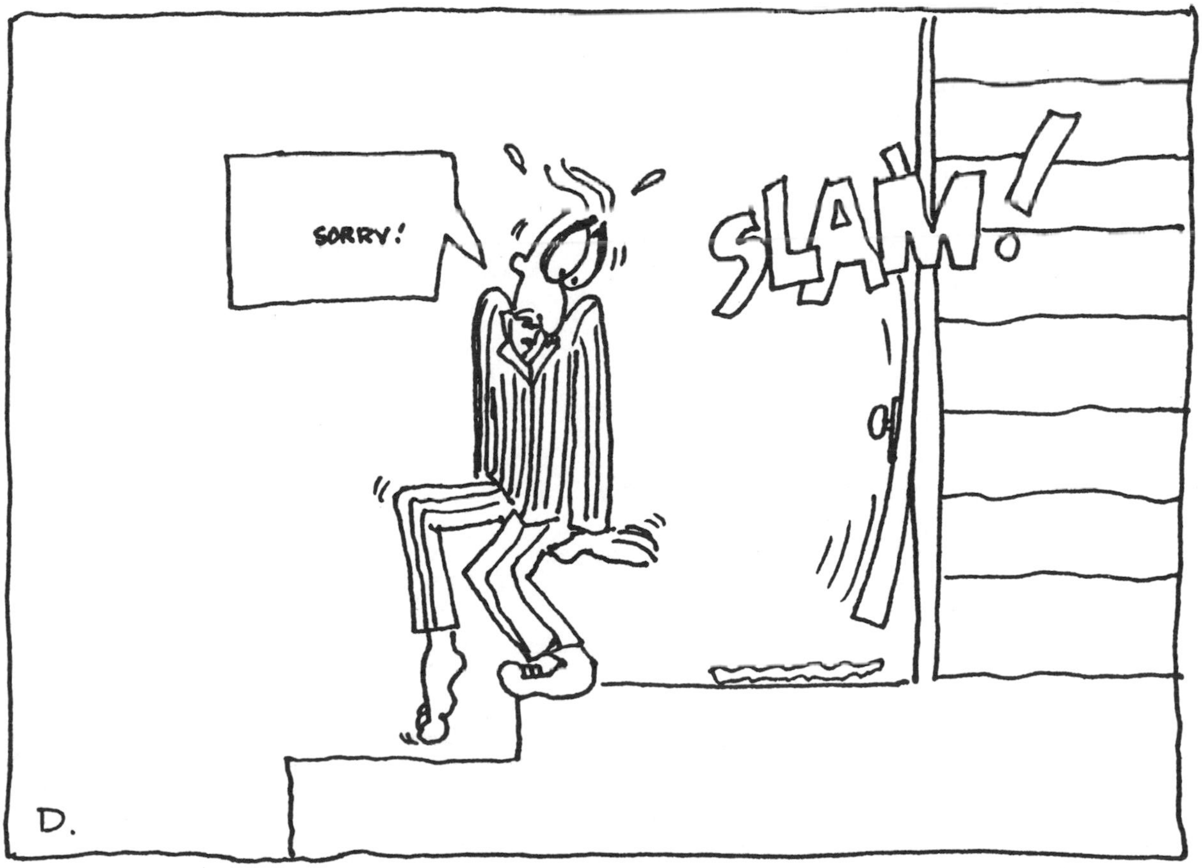
SORRY!
SLAM!
D.

67.

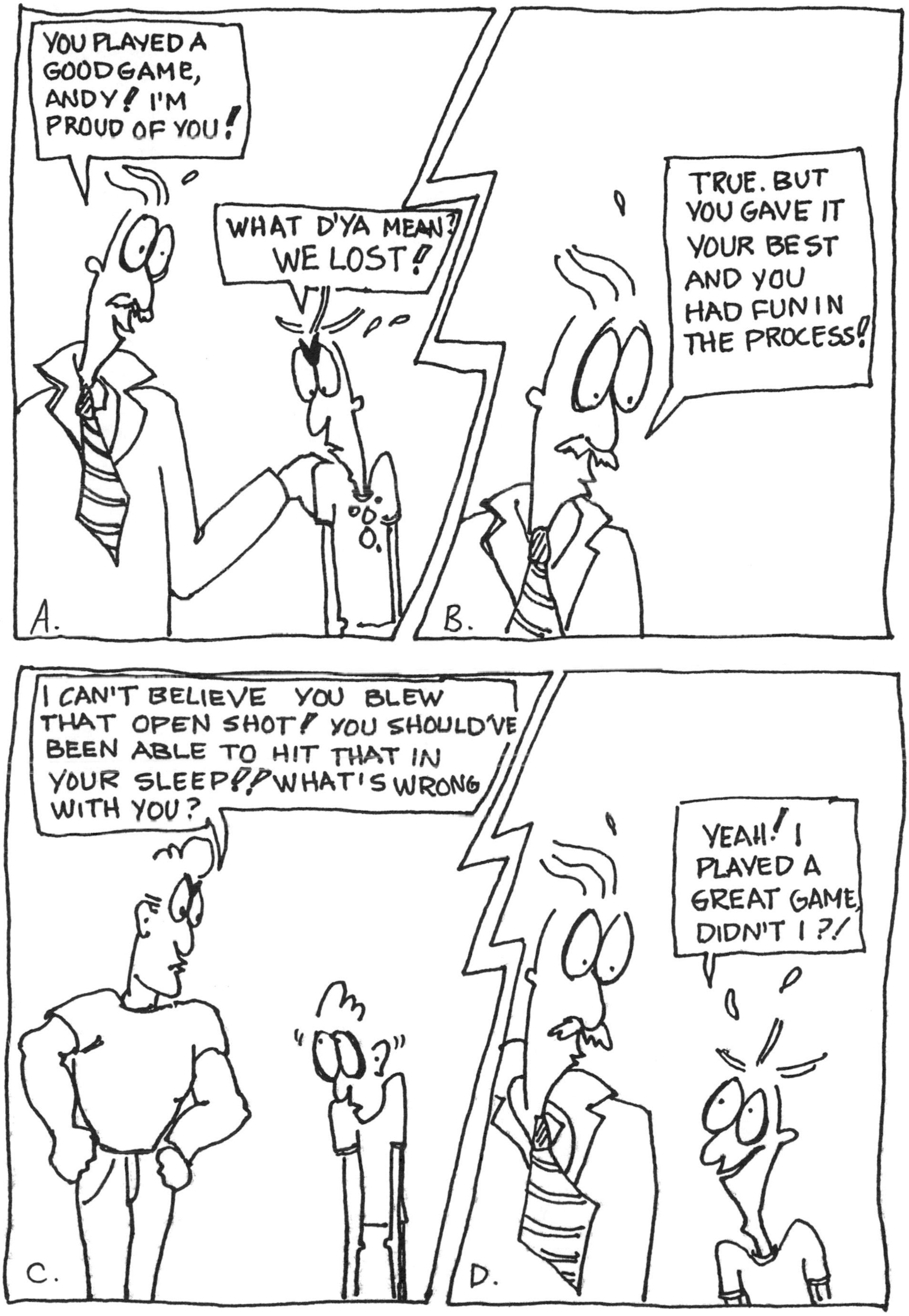
YOU PLAYED A GOOD GAME, ANDY! I'M PROUD OF YOU!
WHAT D'YA MEAN? WE LOST!
A.
TRUE. BUT YOU GAVE IT YOUR BEST AND YOU HAD FUN IN THE PROCESS!
B.
I CAN'T BELIEVE YOU BLEW THAT OPEN SHOT! YOU SHOULD'VE BEEN ABLE TO HIT THAT IN YOUR SLEEP!! WHAT'S WRONG WITH YOU?
C.
YEAH! I PLAYED A GREAT GAME, DIDN'T I?!
D.

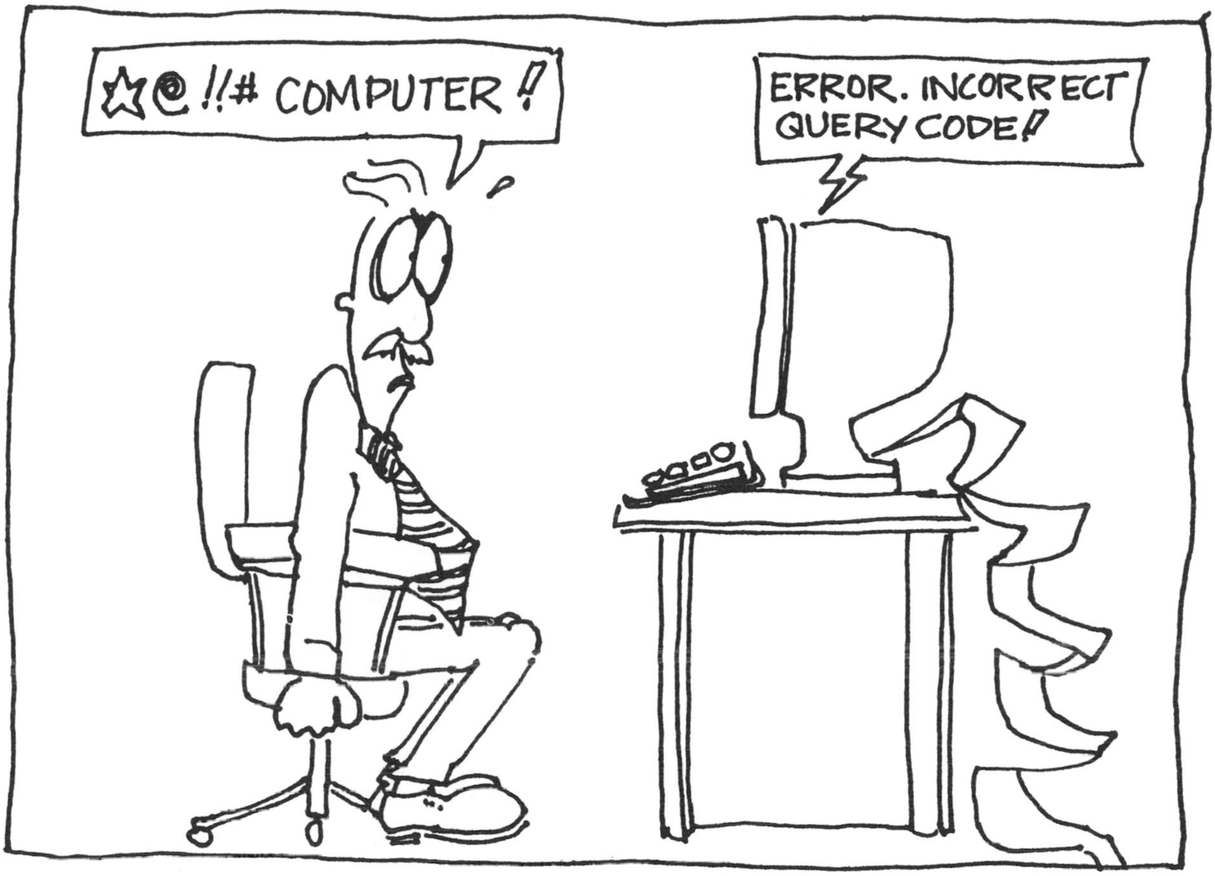
☆@!!# COMPUTER!
ERROR. INCORRECT QUERY CODE!

68.

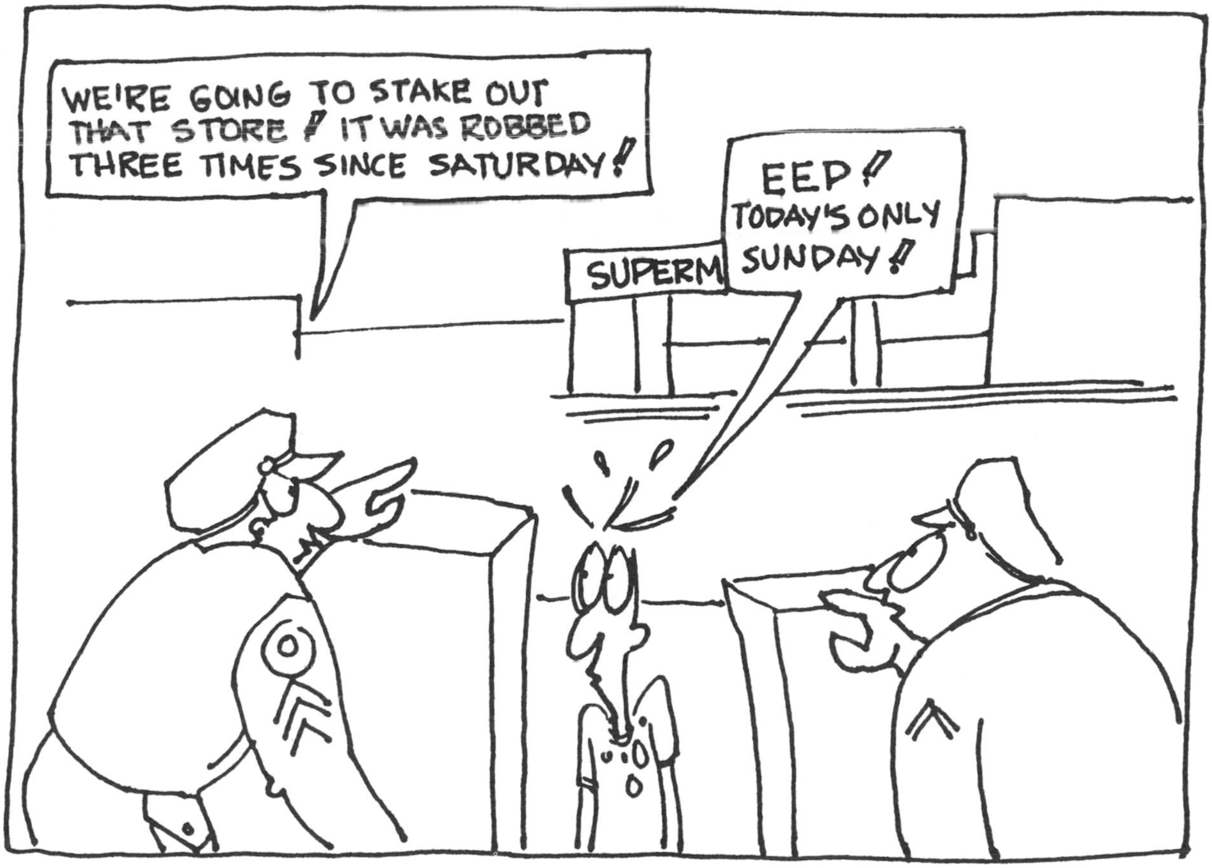
WE'RE GOING TO STAKE OUT THAT STORE! IT WAS ROBBED THREE TIMES SINCE SATURDAY!
SUPERM
EEP! TODAY'S ONLY SUNDAY!

69.

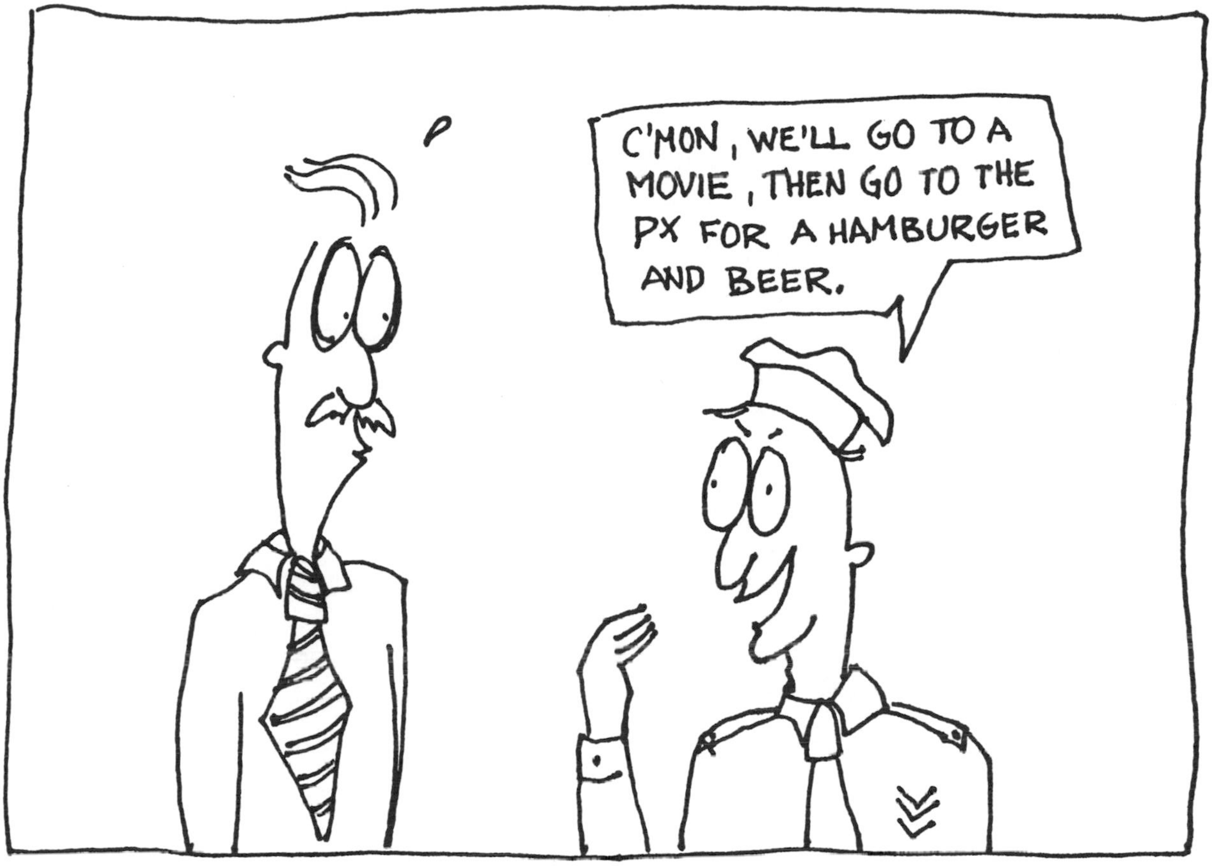
C'MON, WE'LL GO TO A MOVIE, THEN GO TO THE PX FOR A HAMBURGER AND BEER.

70.

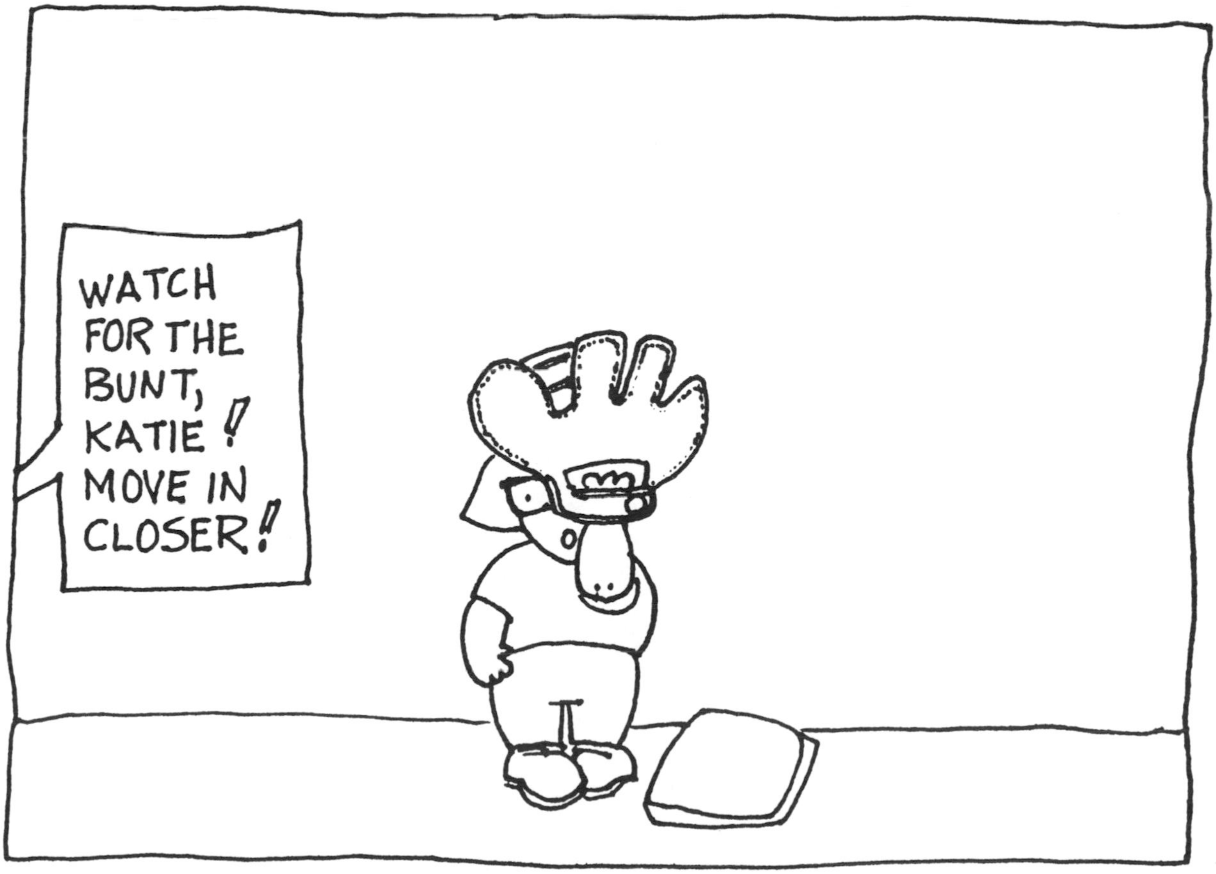
WATCH FOR THE BUNT, KATIE! MOVE IN CLOSER!

71.

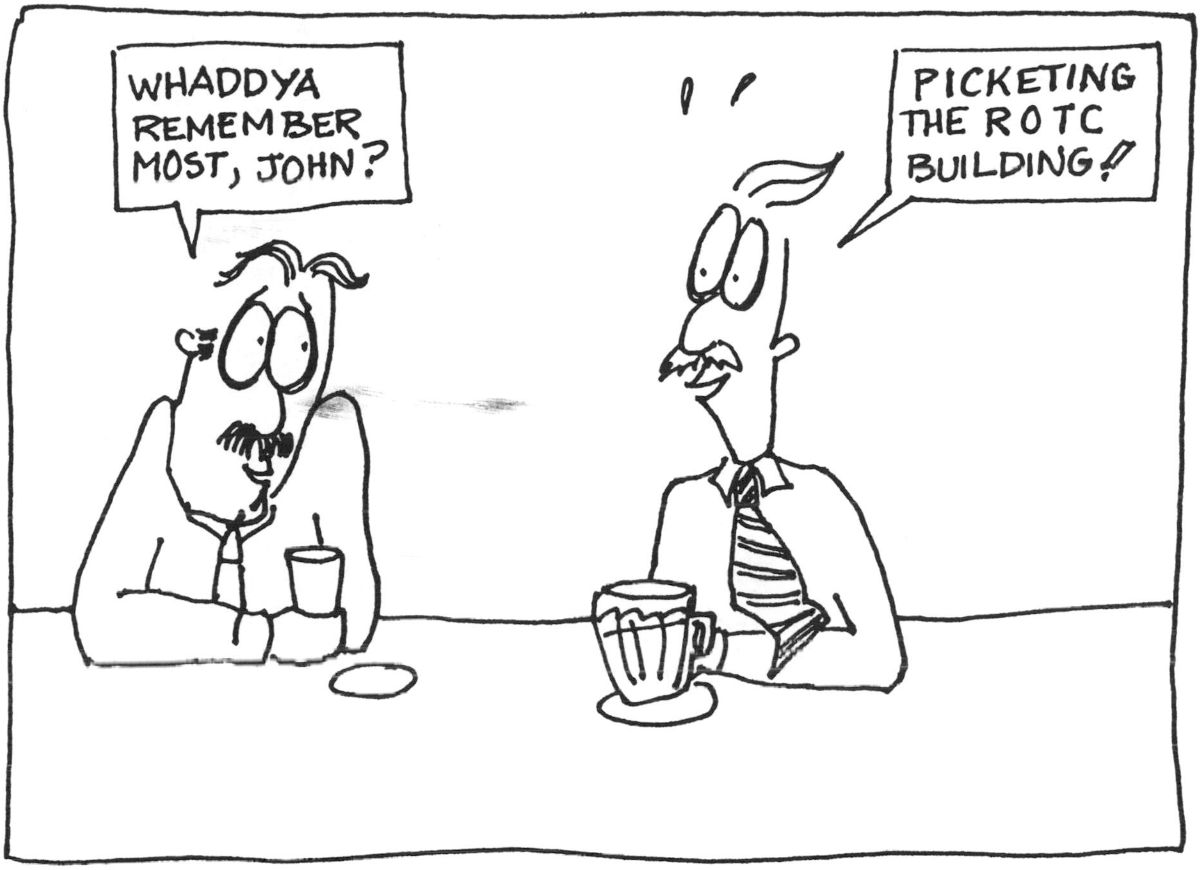
WHADDYA REMEMBER MOST, JOHN?
PICKETING THE ROTC BUILDING!!

72.

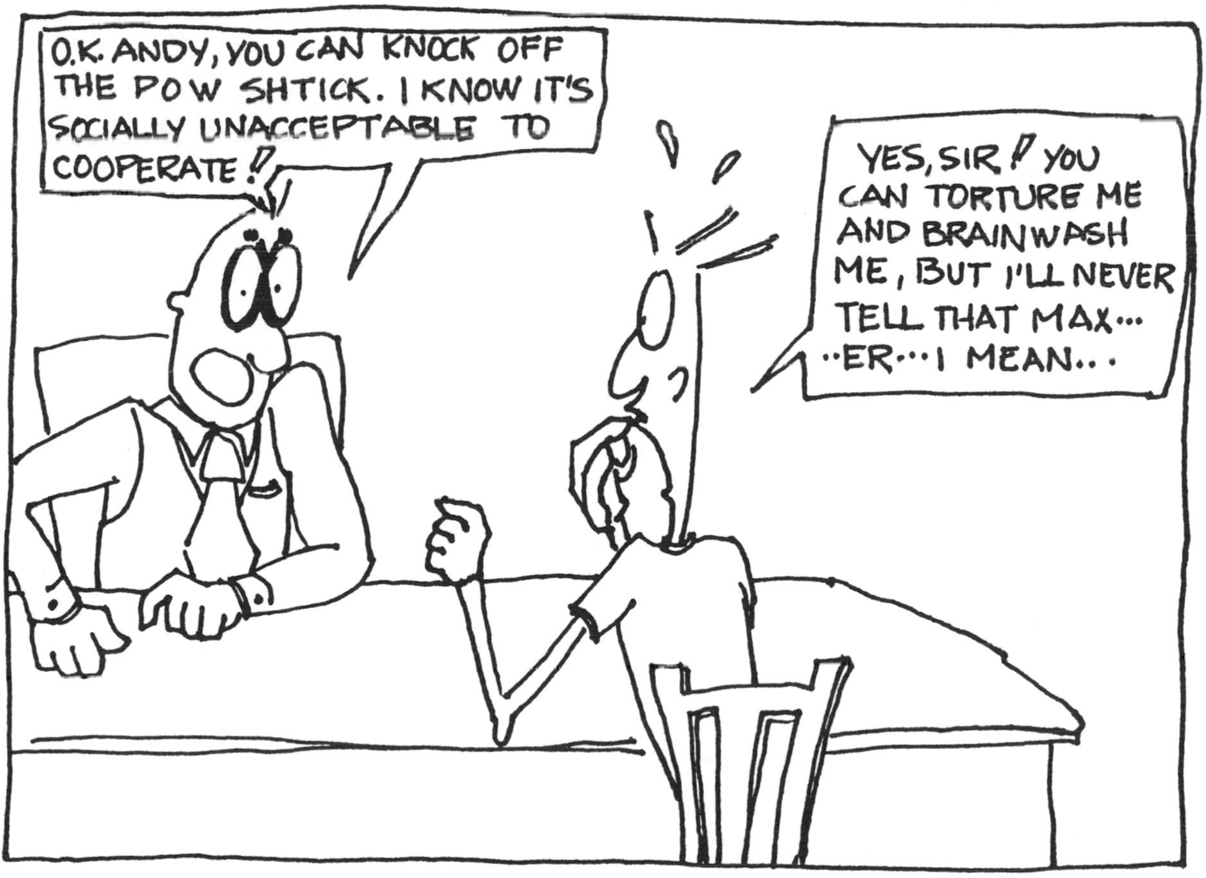
O.K. ANDY, YOU CAN KNOCK OFF THE POW SHTICK. I KNOW IT'S SOCIALLY UNACCEPTABLE TO COOPERATE!!
YES, SIR!! YOU CAN TORTURE ME AND BRAINWASH ME, BUT I'LL NEVER TELL THAT MAX... ..ER...I MEAN...

73.

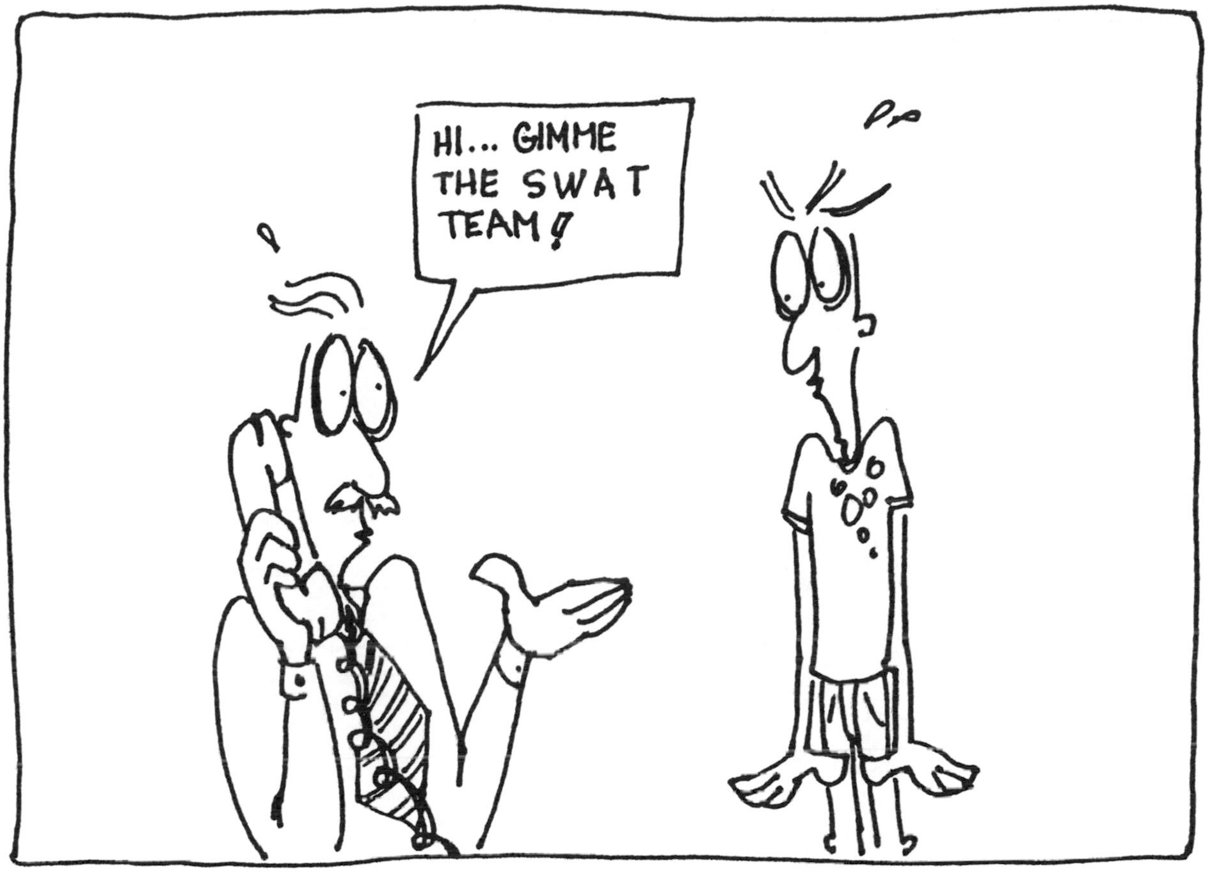
HI... GIMME THE SWAT TEAM!

74.

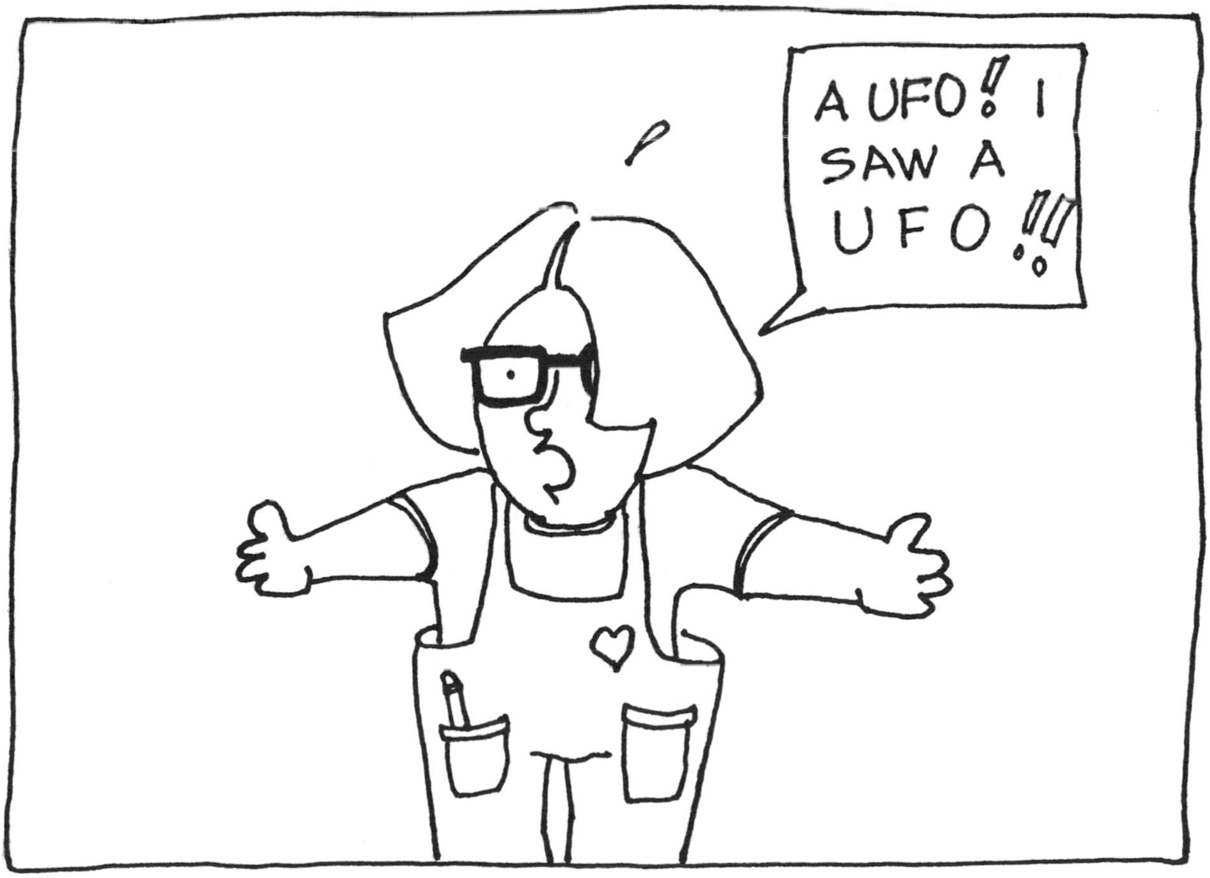
A UFO! I SAW A UFO!!!

75.

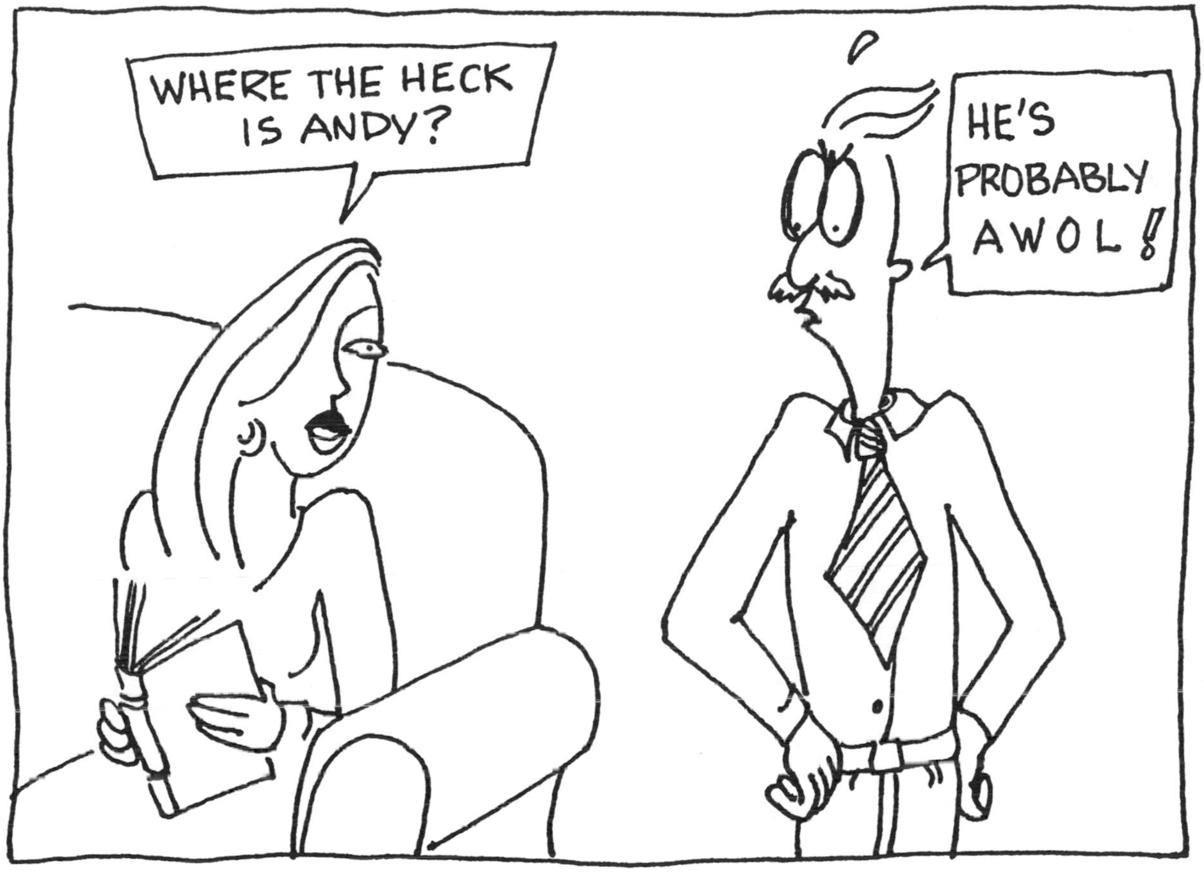
WHERE THE HECK IS ANDY?
HE'S PROBABLY AWOL!

76.

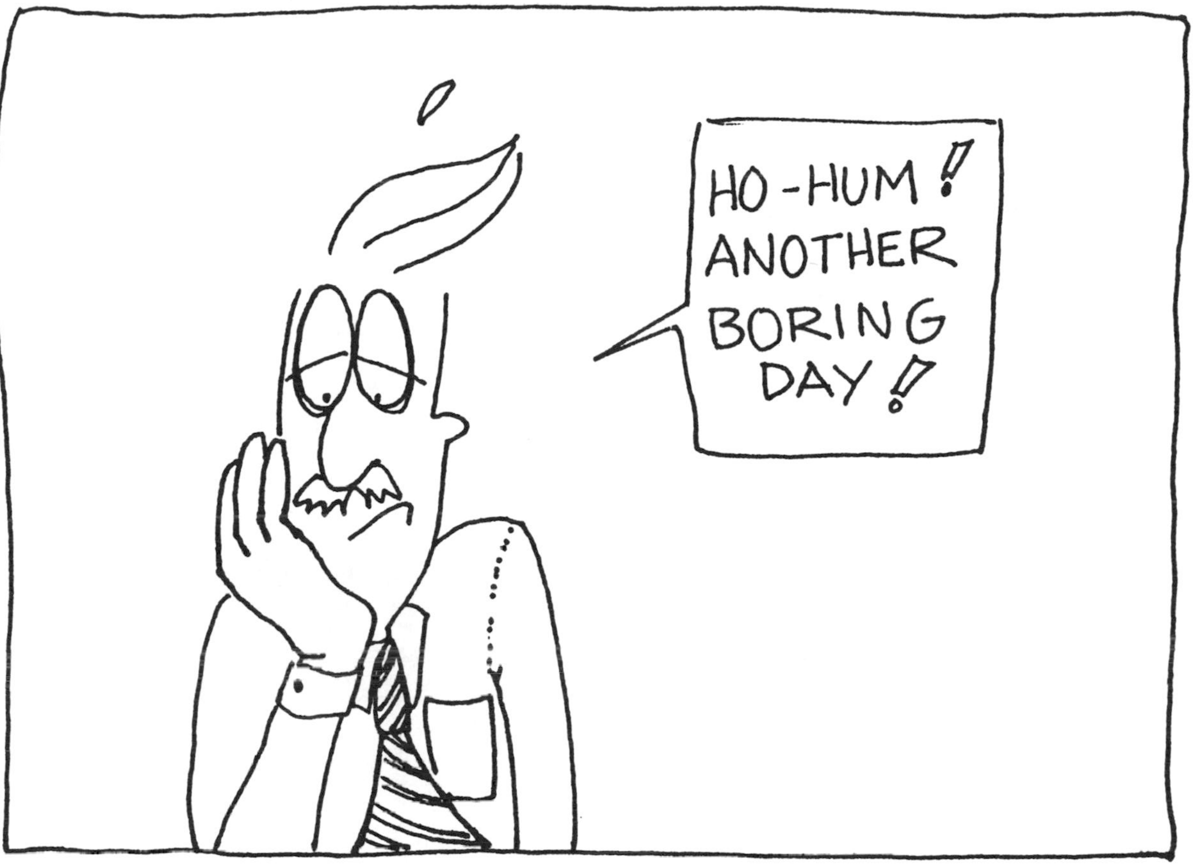
HO-HUM! ANOTHER BORING DAY!

77.

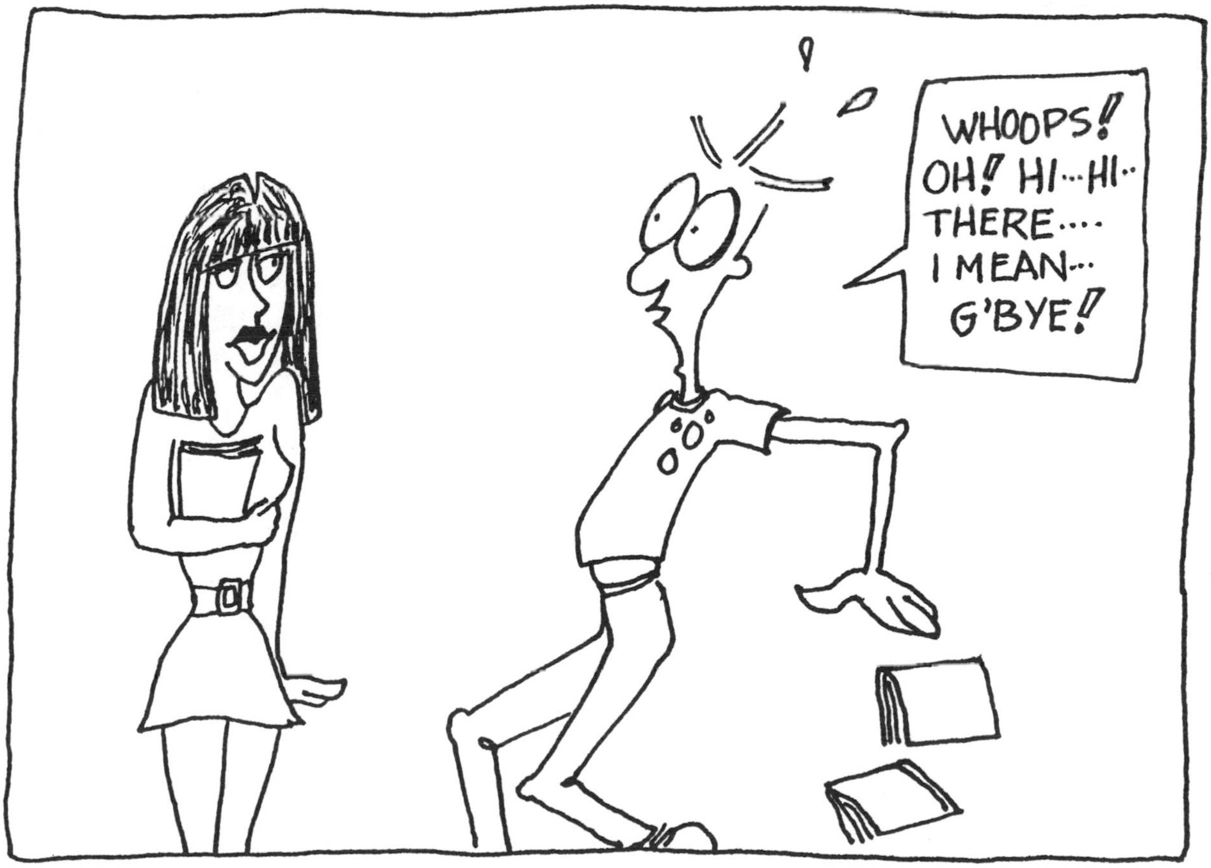
WHOOPS! OH! HI…HI… THERE…. I MEAN… G'BYE!

8.

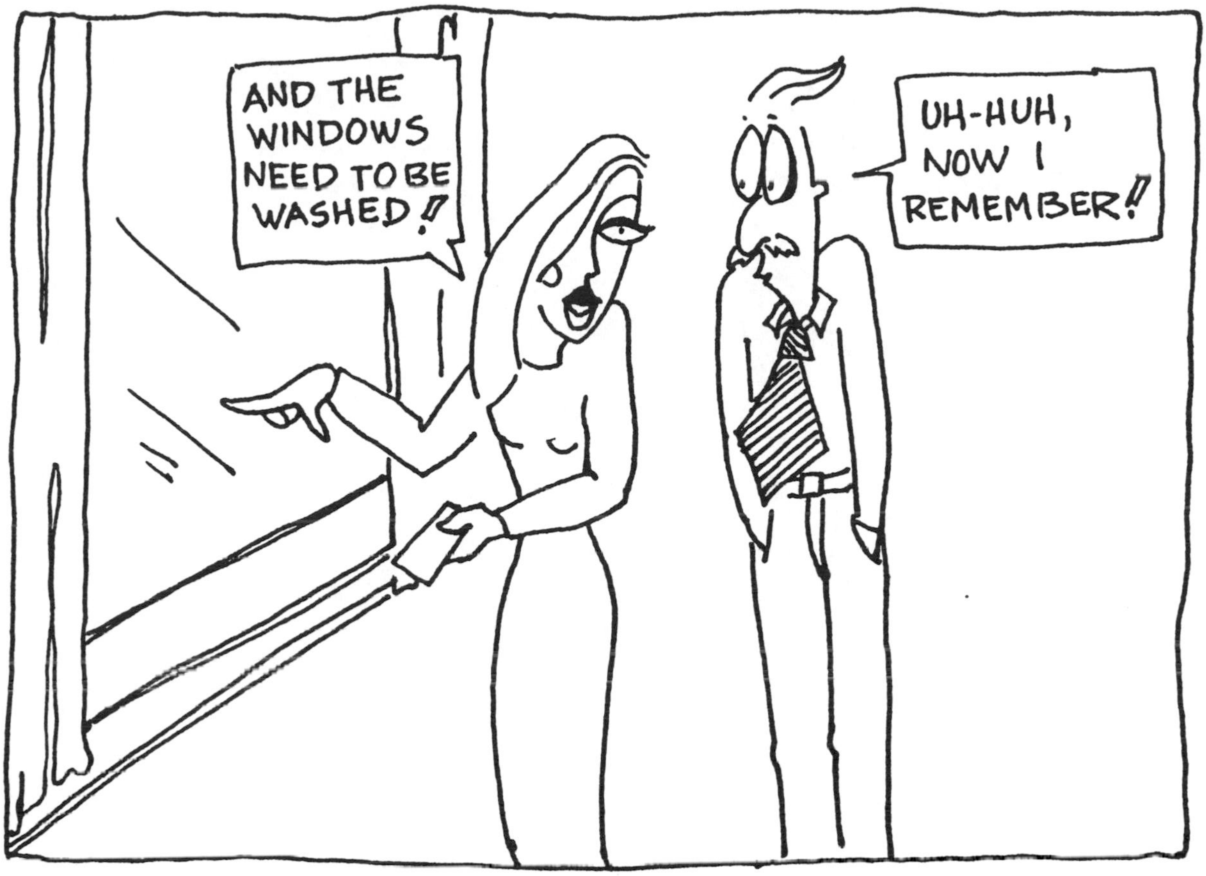
AND THE WINDOWS NEED TO BE WASHED!!
UH-HUH, NOW I REMEMBER!!

79.

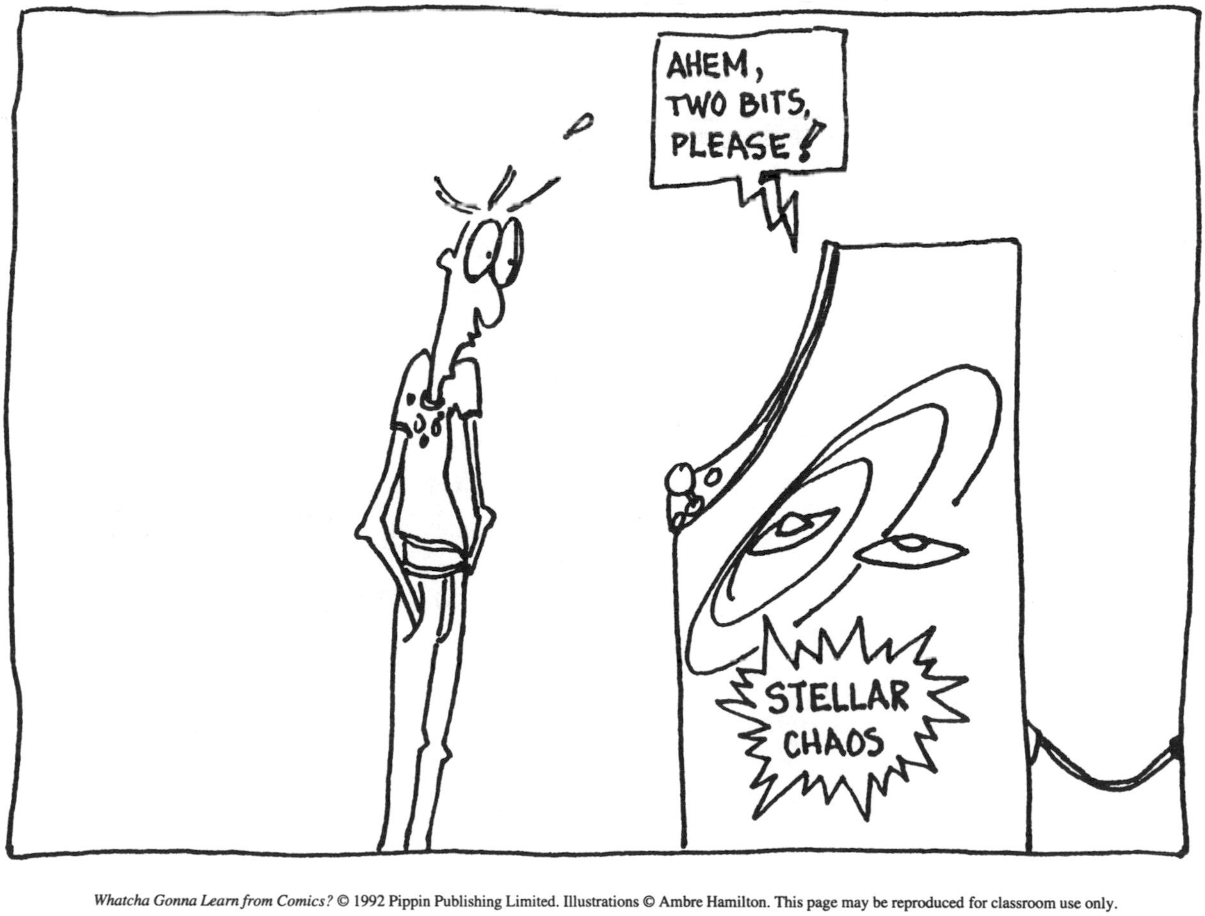
AHEM, TWO BITS, PLEASE!
STELLAR CHAOS

0.

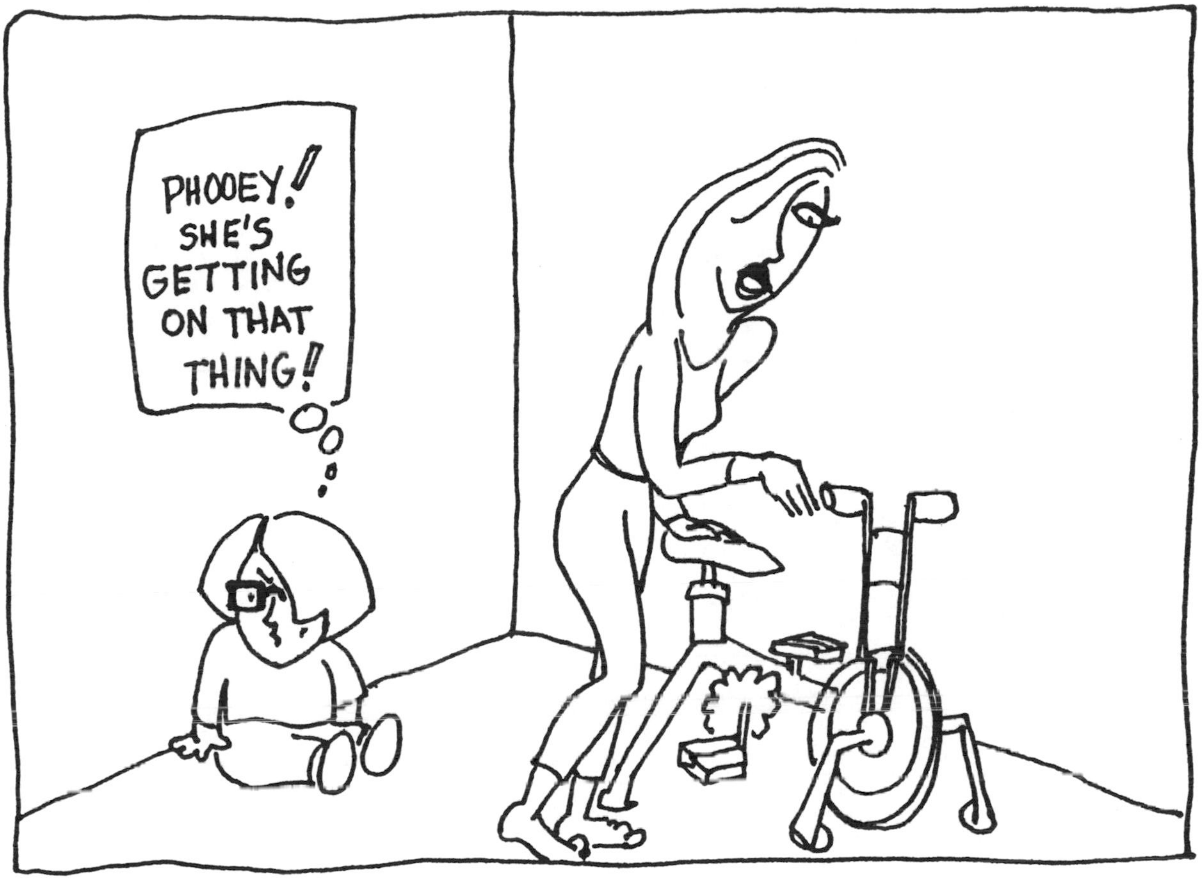
PHOOEY! SHE'S GETTING ON THAT THING!

81.

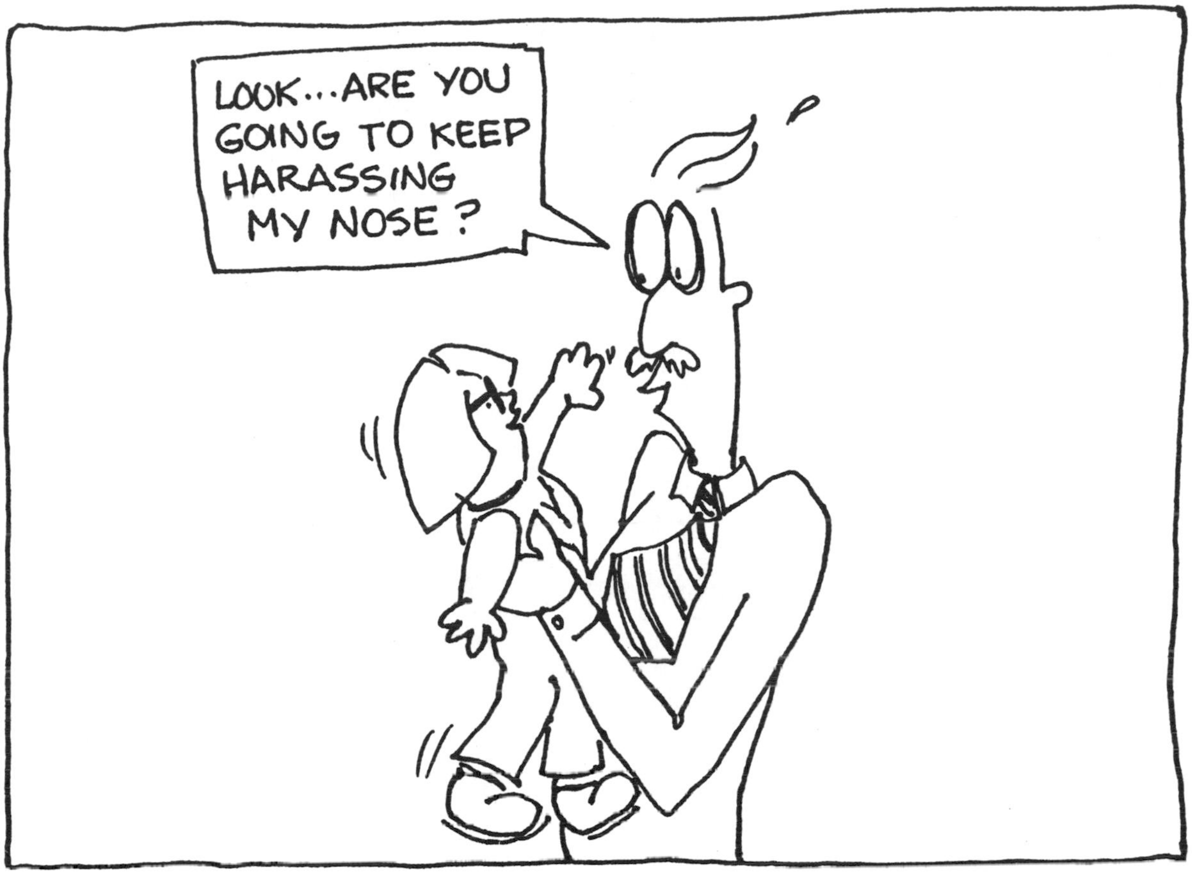
LOOK...ARE YOU GOING TO KEEP HARASSING MY NOSE?

82.

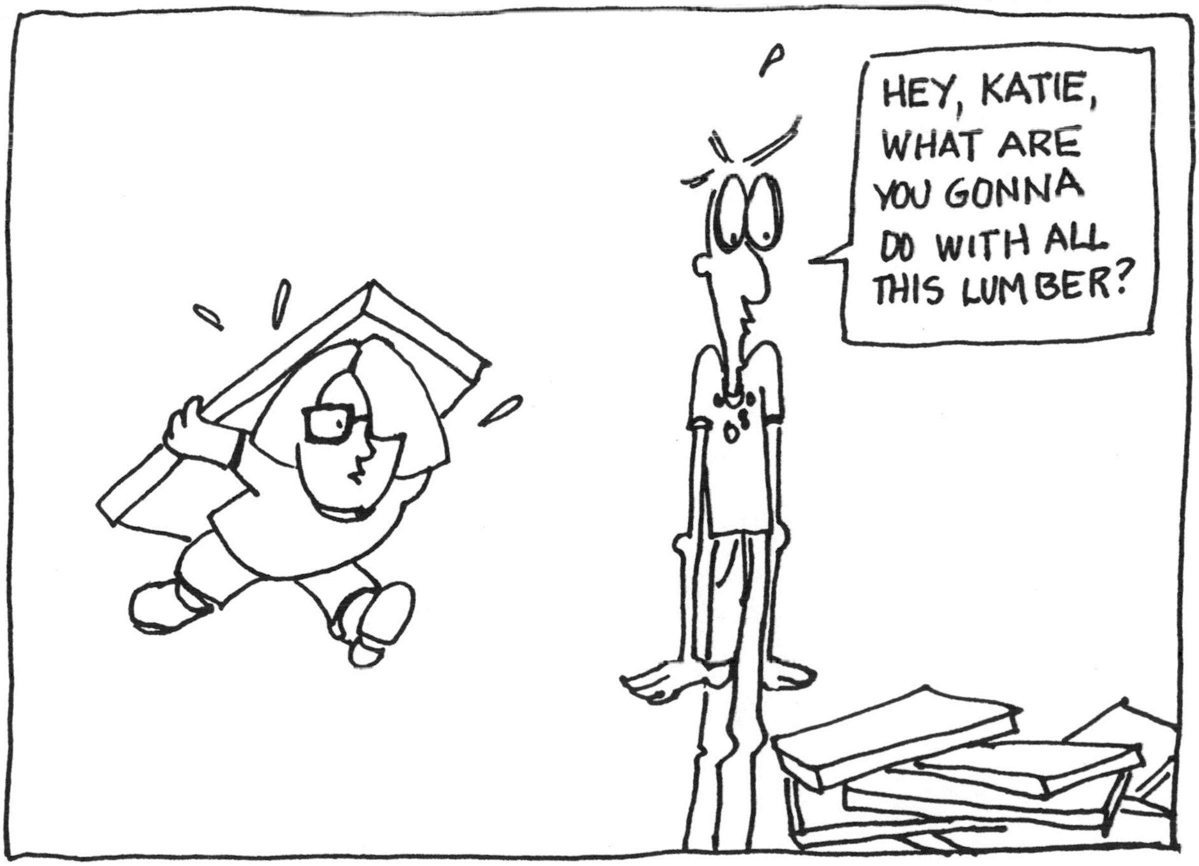
HEY, KATIE, WHAT ARE YOU GONNA DO WITH ALL THIS LUMBER?

83.

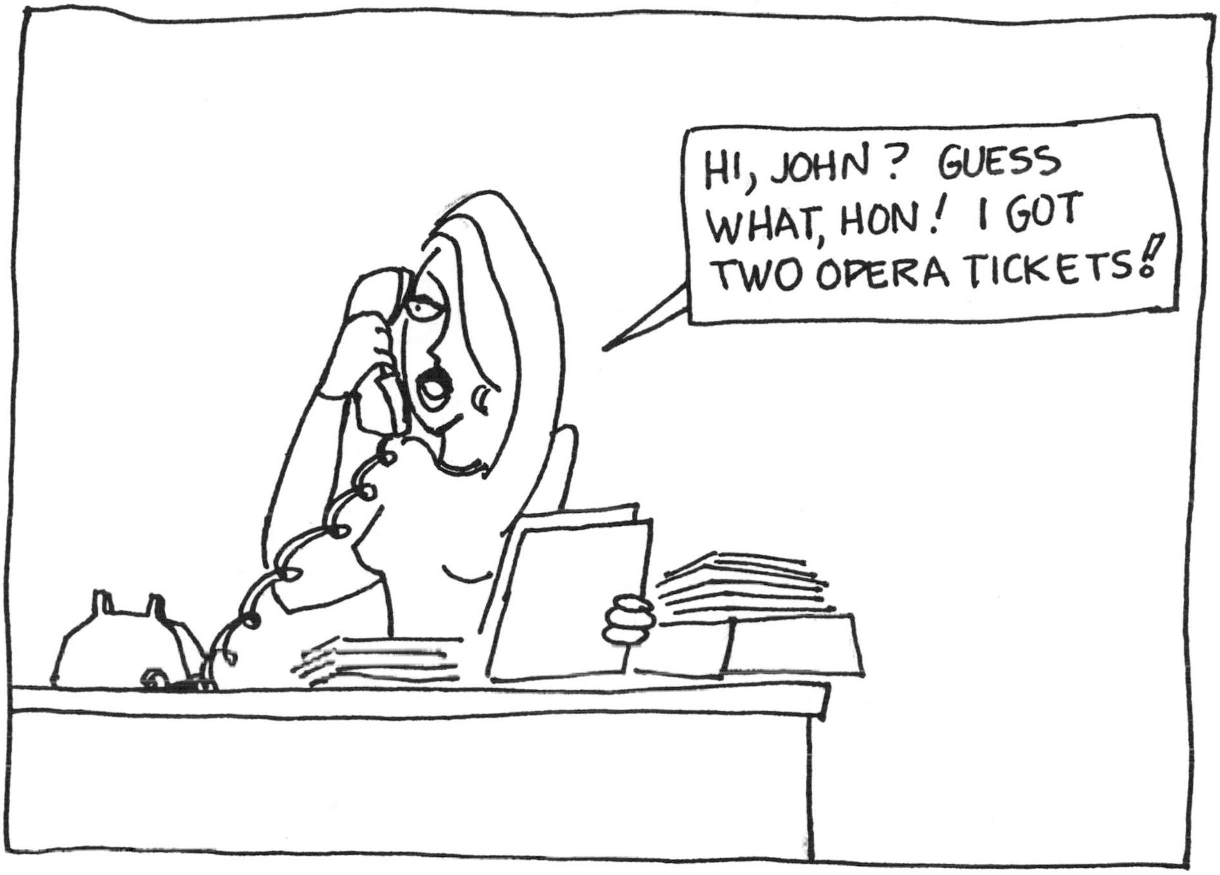
HI, JOHN? GUESS WHAT, HON! I GOT TWO OPERA TICKETS!

84.

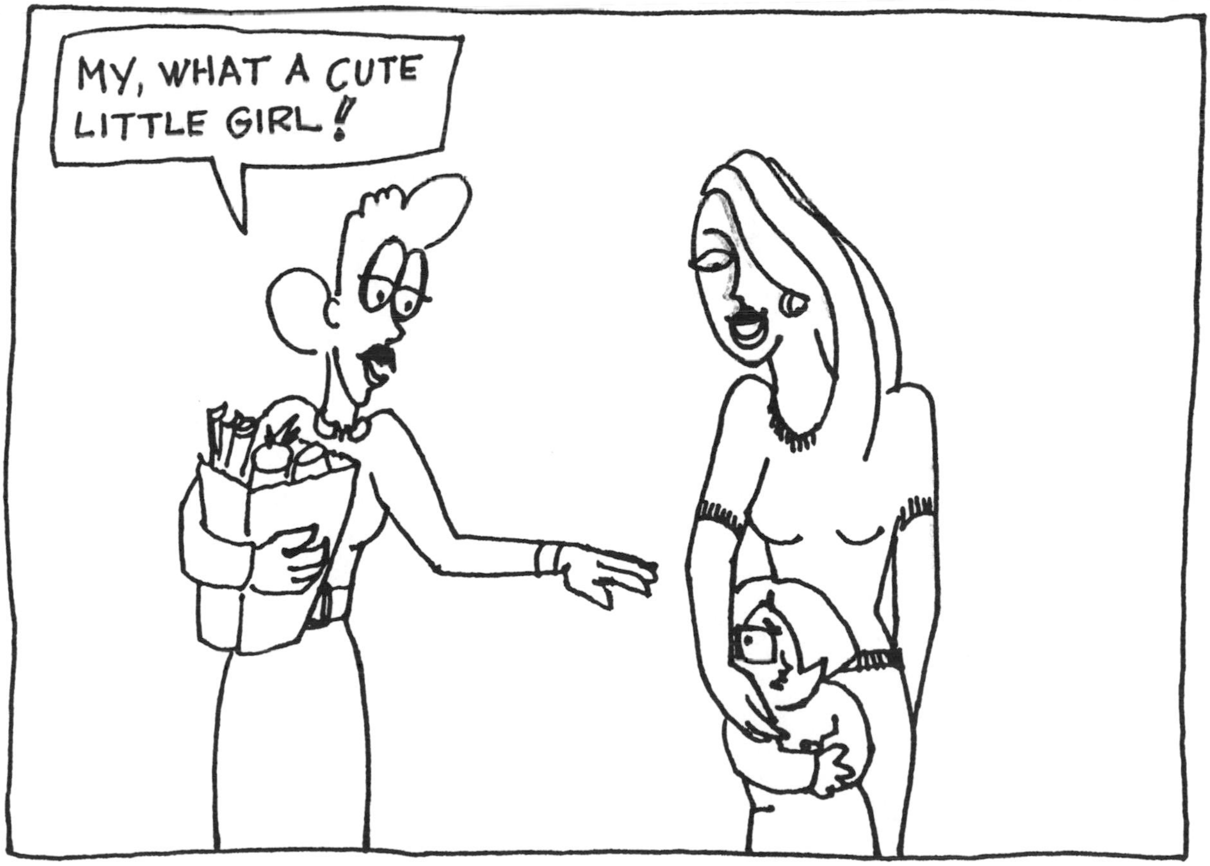
MY, WHAT A CUTE LITTLE GIRL!

5.

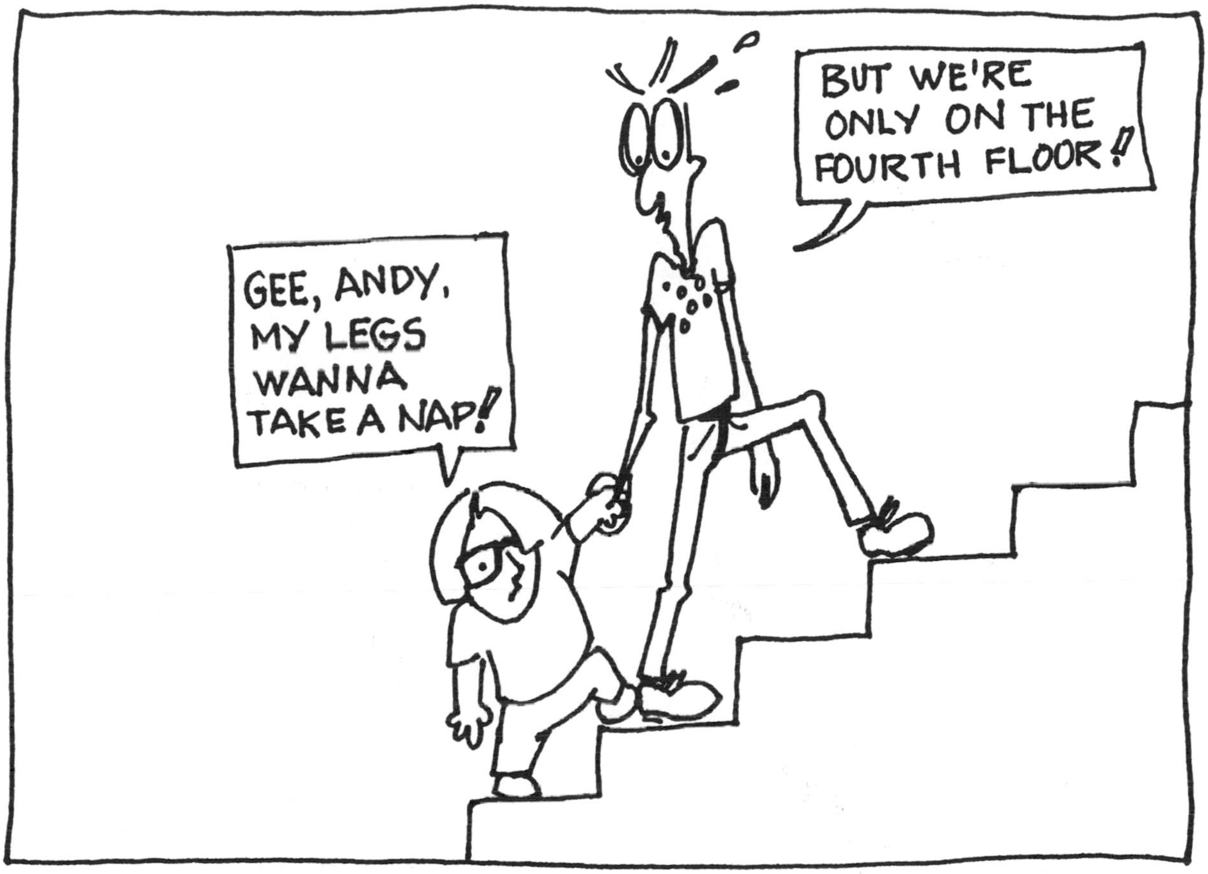
GEE, ANDY, MY LEGS WANNA TAKE A NAP!
BUT WE'RE ONLY ON THE FOURTH FLOOR!

86.

87.

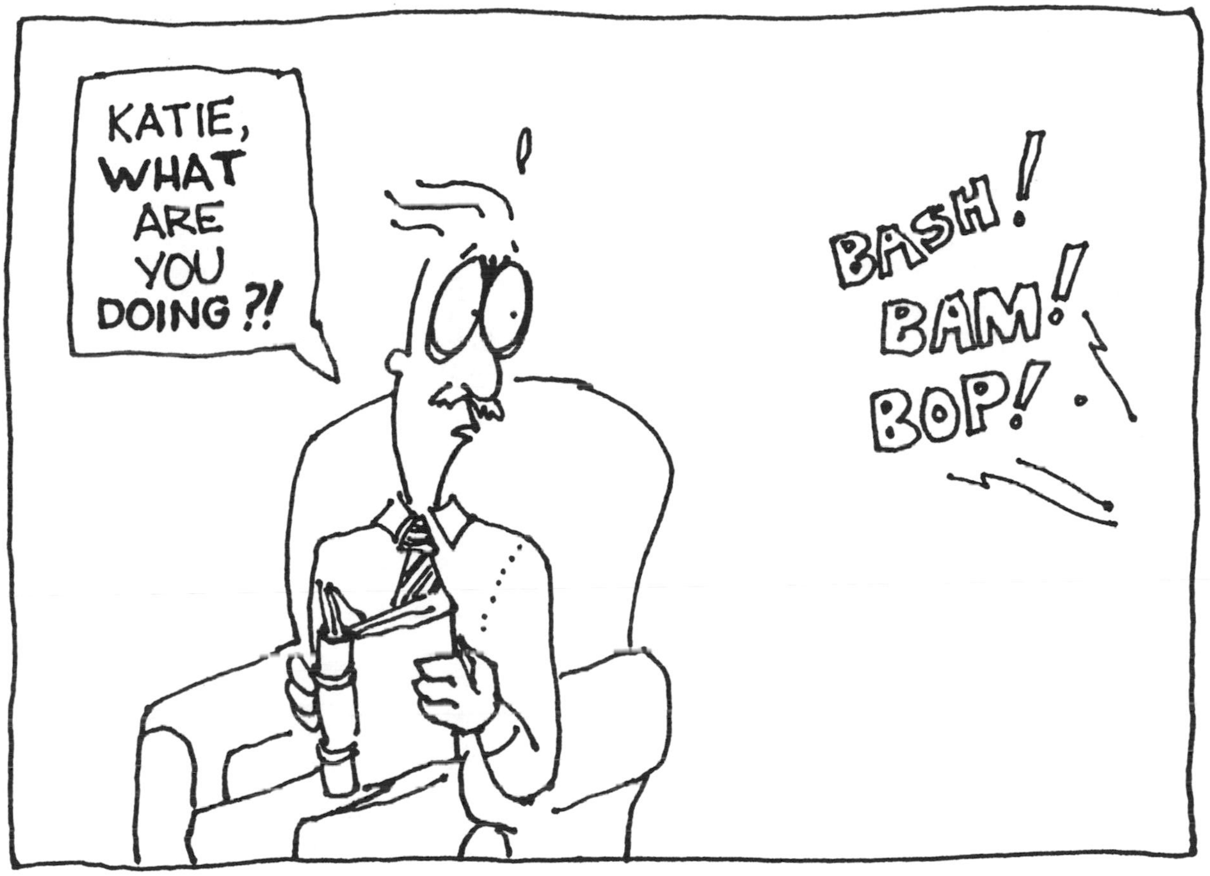
KATIE, WHAT ARE YOU DOING?!
BASH! BAM! BOP!

88.

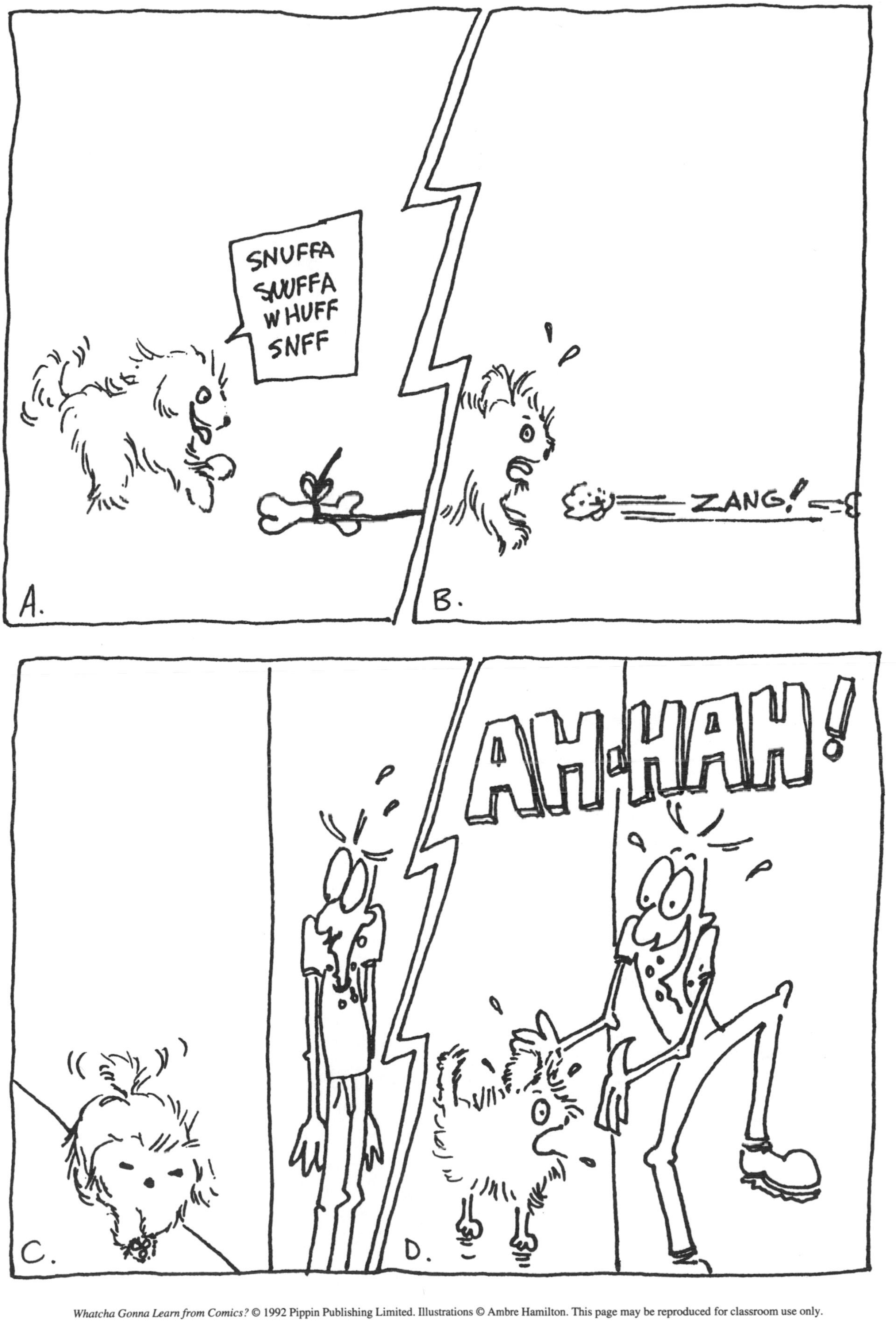
SNUFFA
SNUFFA
WHUFF
SNFF
A.
ZANG!
B.
C.
AH-HAH!
D.

88.

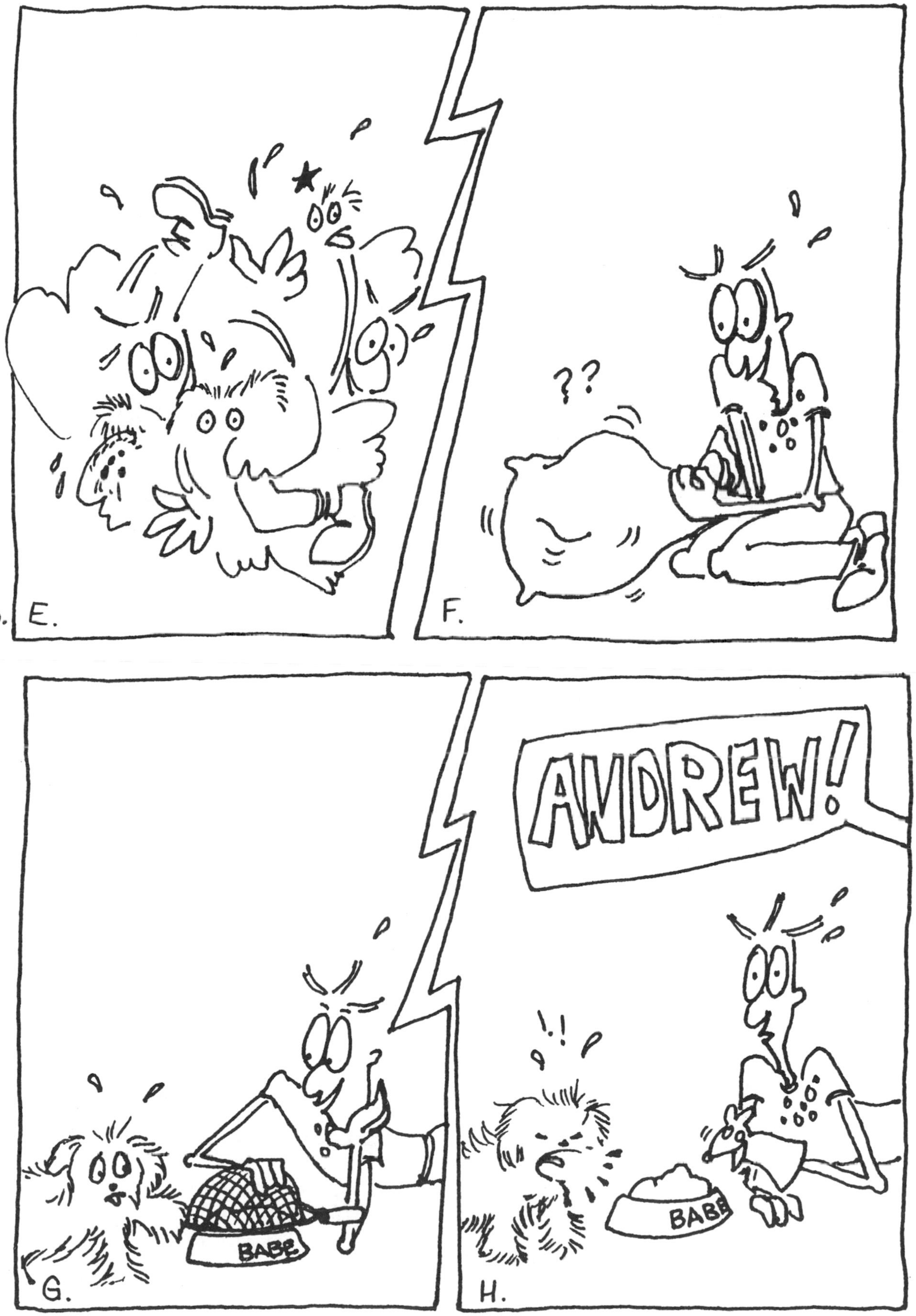
E.
??
F.
G.
BABE
ANDREW!
!!
BABE
H.

88.

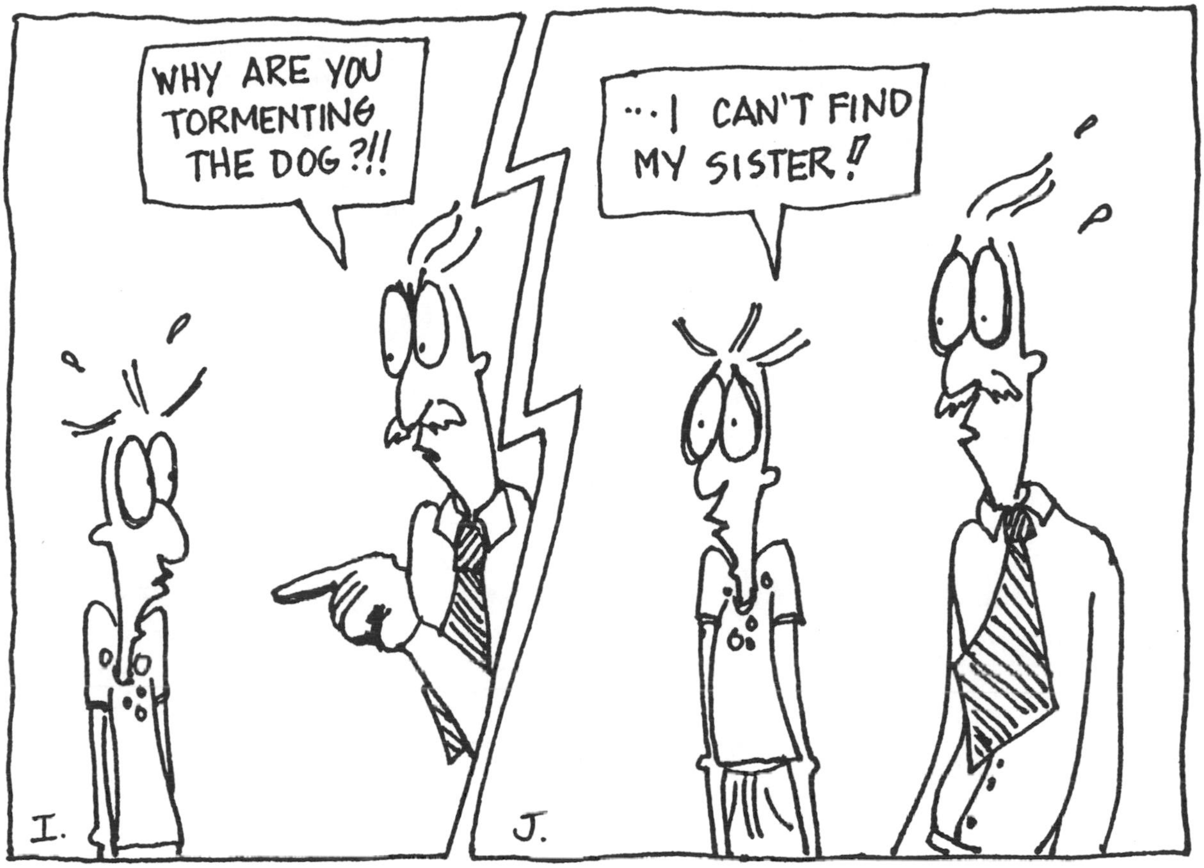
I.
WHY ARE YOU TORMENTING THE DOG?!!
J.
...I CAN'T FIND MY SISTER!!